Praise for *Slow Dance*

"An intellectual journey into disability... full of the drama of halting progress and dashed hopes.... What sets *Slow Dance* apart is its innovative style.... This is a book that pulses with life.... Klein's joie de vivre, her earthy humour... all make it seem like a privilege to accompany her on the struggle.... This is a brave book — on the part of the entire Klein family, given its intimacy — that offers both heroism and enlightenment." *NOW*

"More engrossing than most 'survivor' literature, *Slow Dance*... is a gritty and passionate account of the devastating illness that left Klein permanently disabled.... Earthy, profane and funny, it also offers some astute patient's insights into the health care system." *Maclean's*

"A book everyone should read." *The Toronto Sun*

"... disturbing and exhilarating... a vivid account of Sherr Klein's experience of being in a 'locked-in' state..." *The Vancouver Sun*

"*Slow Dance* is a book about stroke and disability; it's also a gripping page turner and a love story. Indeed, it is many things, some jarring, some uplifting and inspirational. But most of all, it is provocative, forcing us to think, to confront our assumptions, prejudices and fears." *The Ottawa Citizen*

"... compulsively readable, the work of a skilled documentarian."
The Globe and Mail

"*Slow Dance* is a collaborative effort that speaks to the transforming power of community... an intensive and multifaceted view of how catastrophic illness may shatter lives but can also cause us to recombine the fragments in new and wholly unexpected ways." *Quill & Quire*

"... poignant and illuminating." *The Montreal Gazette*

MRI reveals a circumscribed, solitary, intra-axial, vascular, expansive lesion — typical of a cavernous angioma. The pt's neurological condition and the location of the lesion would make a direct, open operation extremely hazardous.

Enjoy!
Bonnie Klein
Roberts Creek

SLOW DANCE

A Story of Stroke, Love and Disability

BONNIE SHERR KLEIN

in collaboration with

Persimmon Blackbridge

VINTAGE CANADA

A Division of Random House of Canada

FIRST VINTAGE CANADA EDITION, 1997

Copyright © 1997 by Bonnie Sherr Klein

Canadian Cataloguing in Publication Data

Klein, Bonnie
Slow dance: a story of stroke, love and disability
ISBN 0-676-97030-3

I. Klein, Bonnie — Health. 2. Cerebrovascular disease — Patients — Canada —
Biography. 3. Cerebrovascular disease — Patients — Rehabilitations — Canada.
4. Physically handicapped — Canada — Biography. I. Title.

RC388.5.K54   1997a   362.1'9681'0092   C96-930998-8

The quotation on page 277 is from "Ton Numéro," a poem by
Gérald Godin in his *Ils ne demandaient qu'à brûler*. Copyright © 1987,
L'Hexagon. Translated by Bonnie Klein.

Printed and bound in Canada

FOR MICHAEL,

AND FOR ALL THE FAMILY
AND FRIENDS WHO PULLED
US THROUGH.

"All of us who write out of calamity know this before all else: there is nothing exceptional about our lives, however these may differ in their particulars. What we can offer you, when the time comes, is companionship in a common venture. It's not a lot, I know, but it may come in handy."

NANCY MAIRS
Voice Lessons

≈

"Yes, quads wish they were paras, paras wish they were able-bodied, and the able-bodied wish they were Jane Fonda."

JOHN CALLAHAN
Don't Worry, He Won't Get Far On Foot!

≈

"This is the only dance we dance."

MARLENE GORRIS
writer-director, *Antonia's Line*

CONTENTS

≈

PREFACE

Ten years ago, if I were setting out to make a film about catastrophic illness and subsequent disability, I would not have
cast myself in the lead role. In my pre-stroke ignorance, I probably would have looked for someone stronger and braver than
I — not yet knowing that we are all capable of much more
bravery than we think.

I would have written a "heroine" who did not have the
financial advantages that I have. She would have been younger
— in her twenties or thirties — which is more typical with congenital strokes like mine, before she had had a chance to build
a life and family of her own. I certainly would not have chosen that she be married to a physician, as I am, who could
challenge and when necessary manipulate the medical system
to take care of his wife. People might rightly say: What would
have happened if her husband had not been a doctor, had not
known what and whom to ask? We can't deny the access and
resources we had as a medical family. On the other hand,
through our story people can see that medicine, even when
well-meaning, is not infallible or always humane or even wise.

But Life gets in the way of Art; the role was cast upon me,
and I've played it the best I can.

Surviving the stroke has been the most challenging and creative project of my life. There were no guides or maps. I had never known anybody as sick as I was. For the first three years I was isolated with no role models. It was both scary and exhilarating. I was inventing every moment, as in the best of documentaries, with no script.

After my first, relatively mild, stroke, and even after the devastating second stroke which totally transformed my life, friends would say, "Someday, when all this is over, you will make a film or write a book about it." This message, meant to be reassuring, instead made me upset and angry. Somehow, their words seemed to trivialize what I was living. My life is not just raw material for my work — or is it?

Despite my resistance to that idea, I did start keeping a journal as soon as I could manipulate a pencil, several months after the stroke. The journal became a tool for my survival; I used it to mark my progress, to ask the questions and articulate the fears I shared with no one else. My journal helped ground me in this strange new life where everything I had taken for granted — my body, my thoughts, the earth under my feet — had become shifting, unpredictable territory. The African-American writer Alice Walker once said that she writes the books she needs to read. Well, I was writing myself into understanding, into recovery of my self.

So initially I was not writing with a book in mind; in fact, I wanted to finish with this stroke thing and resume my life, which to me meant doing meaningful work in the world outside myself and my body. I was suspicious of what I considered to be people's morbid curiosity about the details of my stroke. But when I spoke about it publicly at the première of *Mile Zero* — the film I had begun before the stroke but did not complete until fourteen months after — the response changed my opinion. People were more than just curious or sympathetic; they were hungry for information and talk about disability, loss, death. Strangers and friends told me stories about their father, their friend, their self, about disabilities they had never admitted to anyone, let alone discussed. A book could be useful.

I continued my daily handwritten journals. Soon there were volumes of flowered notebooks and miles of taped interviews with my husband Michael and our family, friends and various health workers who played a role in our story. These conversations helped me retrieve memories of a time I was barely present. They also gave me a chance to tell each person what they had meant to me; in turn people told me how my illness had affected their lives.

Three years after my stroke, when I accompanied Michael on sabbatical in Boston, I sat down to write the book. But, again, life interfered with art: I found it too lonely to immerse myself in the painful past at the very moment when I felt ready to re-enter the world. I shelved the book project, and even my journals became less regular as I started to figure out how to live as my new self. This meant getting to know other people with disabilities, and becoming part of the growing movement for disability rights.

When Michael and I finally settled in Vancouver, five and a half years after my stroke, I unpacked my journals and started work on what was to become the CBC radio series, "Bonnie and Gladys." Through the journals I re-traced my odyssey and discovered connections and meanings that had been invisible to me while I was living it. Enough time had passed and I was finally ready to dive into the book.

Still, I knew I didn't want to be alone with all the memories and nightmares; I wanted company and the joy of creative collaboration that I had often experienced in my years as a documentary filmmaker with Canada's National Film Board. This seemed to be unusual in mainstream literary circles, where the writer works alone and hands the editor the resulting manuscript. Instead, I searched until I found the perfect collaborator, Persimmon Blackbridge.

Persimmon and I have much in common: We are both "crossovers" from other genres — I as a former filmmaker and Persimmon as a sculptor, video-maker and performance artist, as well as a writer of books. We are both feminists — though many would perceive us as polar opposites. As a member of the art collective Kiss & Tell, denounced as "that abhorrent lesbian show" in the Alberta legislature, Persimmon's work has been seized and banned by Canada Customs, while my anti-pornography film, *Not a Love Story*, got me labeled "Ms. Anti-Sex." But false dichotomies never got in the way of our respecting each other's work.

We are also both "disabled," though only my disabilities are visible. Persimmon has learning disabilities, which have given her a lifetime of practice in finding creative ways around unusual problems. She and I recognize each other's need for rest, time to search for the right word or finish a thought.

Confident that I could trust Persimmon to help me tell my story, we sorted through the journals and tapes that I'd had transcribed onto computer disks. Persimmon then went home to her computer and organized this raw material — the film equivalent is "rushes" — a tedious and, to me, mind-boggling job.

While Persimmon was busy assembling and editing the material we had selected into a rough draft, I would be left with an "assignment" sheet full of her questions. They were designed to flesh out the details of the stories; weird questions like "What did the sheets feel like?"; "What did the physio smell like?" Smell?! I laughed at these questions, but as I sat

outdoors with my notebook trying to answer them, the memories trickled, then flooded out. The physio smelled of coffee,
and that reminded me of — well, you'll soon see.

When I thought I could remember no more, or procrasti-
nated over a section, Persimmon suggested we "just talk about
it" while I rested on my bed. Her listening skills made me feel
safe enough to recover the worst horrors at last. We taped hours
of additional memories, which Persimmon edited and cut into
the narrative.

We got together regularly to trade goodies. I would give
Persimmon new writing, and she would present me with an
assembled morsel. The manuscript moved back and forth between us until we stopped knowing whose idea was whose. I
would praise her for an apt phrase and Persimmon would say
"Yes, it's from your journal." Our only arguments were to
insist the other accept due credit. To say I "wrote" the book
and Persimmon "edited" it would not acknowledge the reality
of our collaborative process, or credit Persimmon's enormous
sensitivity in drawing the story out of me, making elegant tran-
sitions between fragmented ideas, and devising literary solutions to ideological problems — not to mention walking my
dog Lucy when I was too tired out, or the many hugs and
laughs we shared.

As this book leaves our hands and goes out into the world, I
am left with unresolved questions. The issue of language for
describing disability nags at me. I choose the word "disabled"
as the best of a bad lot. I dislike its negation of ability but I dislike even more those awkward euphemisms like "differently
abled" that negate the daily physical struggle with which some
of us live, as well as the discrimination we often face. Like the
writer Nancy Mairs, I sometimes call myself a cripple, though

that doesn't adequately describe my particular constellation of disabilities. Obviously, I cannot presume to label other people with such culturally-charged epithets.

I greatly prefer to name — and thereby reclaim — the truth, and believe the important thing is for each of us to name ourselves and tell our own stories. I'm more than a little pleased that, having been cast, I'm able to tell this one.

BONNIE SHERR KLEIN

Author's Note
In some instances names have been changed to
protect privacy and reputations.
In the vast majority of cases, the names are real.

STROKE ONE

≈

PRELUDE

Journal: July 9, 1994

The wind has ripped through my notebook, losing my place
and interrupting the flow of words. I'm outside on a favourite
park bench, the one Michael calls my "office," feet resting on
my paisley electric scooter, Gladys, with Lucy, our golden
retriever, sprawled next to me. Behind me is blue sky busy
with kites of all shapes and tails, including a Star of David.
And in their midst, a Canadian flag outside the Coast Guard
station. In front of me is Vancouver's English Bay, full of
pleasure boats, with sailboats and kayaks scampering among
them, and a few daring swimmers. This is where I do my best
writing. I still have trouble being stuck indoors, after all my
hospital incarcerations and the isolation of Montreal winters
where neither scooter nor canes are safe on the icy streets.

Working at my desk would certainly be easier. It's 11:30
by the time I exercise, swim, eat breakfast and pack Gladys
with my writing paraphernalia: sharp pencils, composition
book, Persimmon's many questions and my scribbled notes,
Lucy's doggy snacks and water bowl, my sunblock and sun
hat, and today a *lunch* so I won't have to go back when I'm
hungry. The only hitch is a bathroom for my frequent peeing,
but there's a semi-accessible one (what I call half-assed-
cessible) a short scoot away.

It strikes me that I needed these seven years to get to this place, this peace, where I feel safe to write. The memories are no longer a threat. Not only do I feel safe, but I'm excited. Each time I write I remember more. Even the painful memories are a strange pleasure, lost pieces of myself floating in on the tide.

≈

WHAT I DID ON MY SUMMER VACATION

Michael and I canoed the Missisquoi River, skinny-dipped in our home-made pond, and made love in the morning light. It was Monday, August 3, 1987. I think that was the day we pitched a tent — it was hot in the house, and to sleep outdoors is a romantic notion that takes me back to my hippie days at Big Sur.

It was our first and last vacation alone in the Vermont cabin where we'd spent weekends and holidays with our children for the last ten years — the cabin that we'd finally decided to sell. The nest was emptying. Seth, now nineteen, would leave for the University of Toronto in the fall. Naomi, seventeen, had just graduated from high school. They were both back home in Montreal, with summer jobs.

I knew this marked a new phase of life and I felt down-hearted. I wasn't ready for the child-raising days to be over.

Hard as it was to juggle the big F's of my life — family, film-making and feminism — I wasn't ready to let go; I was only just beginning to get the hang of it.

But no kids meant long, lazy mornings in bed with my husband, a luxury I was prepared to appreciate. At home there was no such thing: Michael was Chief of Family Medicine at the Jewish General Hospital. His life was crammed with patients and staff meetings and hospital politics and babies who insisted on being born in the middle of the night. Mine wasn't much different; if I wasn't off on a film shoot or buried in the editing room, I was at some emergency meeting to save Studio D, the feminist unit at the National Film Board where I was a staff film director.

Michael and I needed time to reconnect. On the surface, we were the Perfect Family, and I was the woman-who-had-it-all. I did, but not without a price, which was often my relationship with Michael. We had survived the tempestuous seventies when feminism rewrote the scripts of our lives. We had learned to balance very different and demanding and stressful professions, knowing we were there for each other to come home to. But a chronic source of conflict had to do with parenting Naomi. Michael responded to her painful and rebellious adolescence with anger. They rose to each other's bait, and I was neither a silent nor unbiased observer. Although Naomi and I fought our own battles, I flinched at Michael's impatience and sided with my female child, creating an impossible (and probably classic) familial knot. The last year had been one of the worst in our nearly twenty years of marriage.

It had been my worst year professionally as well. Studio D had turned down my most recent film proposal and I'd had to beg for private funding. I was furious at the rejection, but underneath the anger I was starting to doubt my worth as a filmmaker. Maybe at forty-six I was getting too old. Maybe documentary was passé. But filmmaking was all I knew — what on earth would I do with the rest of my life? Maybe on this vacation I would finally figure out what I wanted to be when I grew up.

Tuesday: the hottest day of the year. Michael and I set out early for a twenty-mile bicycle ride, all the way to Enosburg Falls. I loved riding, because or in spite of the fact that I only learned when Michael bought me a bicycle as a thirtieth birthday present. As an urban child my parents had forbidden me to learn to cycle. When Michael first tried to teach me, I promptly steered into a heavy chain blocking off a park road from automobile traffic. The chain caught me by the neck and threw me from the bike. Michael brought me home all bloody, sat me on our bathroom toilet and washed and stitched up my head. I continued to bicycle but it never became second nature to me, as it might have if I'd learned as a child.

On this hot day I was a worse rider than usual. I wavered over bumps and fell at a railroad crossing. My clothes clung to my sweaty body in uncomfortable places. My legs were two pieces of wood. I remember wondering, as I have frequently wondered while panting up the sides of various mountains: How much is too much? Where is the line between what's good for me and what's harmful? Will I know when to stop? Michael is a jock — he doesn't know the meaning of moderation; his idea of fun is to see how far he can push himself before he drops, and his attitude towards work is about the same. My attitude had always been more *laissez-faire*, to do what I enjoy, like dancing and tennis, not earnest aerobics classes or stationary bicycles. But I knew I could no longer take my body for granted as I had my first forty years.

We turned back sooner than we'd planned, but we'd brought our tennis rackets knowing the town courts were on our way home. They were empty except for George, the town tennis pro. Too tempting. Michael trotted next door to the supermarket for a giant-sized Gatorade and some bags of Doritos, vilely flavoured with fake onion. I'd never had Gatorade before. It made me feel like a real athlete, even in my then pitiful condition.

So there I was on that morbidly hot day, exhausted but determined to keep up my end as we played two on one with George. I played embarrassingly badly. My face was purple, Michael told me later. Finally I quit and sat in the shade while Michael fought it out.

Afterwards, we bicycled the few miles back to our cabin. I spent the rest of the day hanging out in our bedroom, which was on the basement level dug into a hill, and so relatively cool. I had no appetite, but drank carton after carton of Bulgarian fruit juice, the kind with bad pictures of berries on the outside and gold-foil lining. Clearly a case of heat prostration. Or maybe it was that disgusting bag of Doritos.

That night I spent stumbling between the bed and the bathroom. I couldn't walk without holding onto the walls. My legs were shaking and my guts were turning inside out. Michael slept soundly. I remember thinking, "This might be what dying feels like." But there was no reason for me to be dying, so I didn't wake him.

The next morning I called Muriel Duckworth and Kay Macpherson to say we would not be coming to float lanterns on Lake Memphramagog in memory of the bombing of Hiroshima.

I was disappointed. Muriel and Kay are long-time peace acti-
vists, whom I met while making the film *Speaking Our Peace*.
Muriel had become like a mother to me, a spiritual elder, her
warmth embracing our whole family. Kay's sharp-edged humour
brings my wilder flights of political idealism firmly down to
earth. But this year, we would have no solemn, joyous ritual for
peace. I was too sick.

By evening I was staggering when I walked; my tongue was
thick and clumsy when I spoke, and I developed loud hiccups.
These were clearly alarm signals for Michael. He didn't tell me
what they could mean, but said that we probably shouldn't be
stuck in the middle of the Vermont woods when we didn't know
what was going on.

Michael: At 9 p.m., while giving you some tea, I noticed
that your right eyelid was drooping, and your tongue
deviated to the right. You were having some trouble swallowing due to simultaneous choking and hiccups. You
had an unsteady gait, profound weakness, an up-going
toe on the left with rhythmic oscillation in that ankle.
These are brain-stem and vestibular signs — not subtle.

I was upset. I knew where the trouble was located: all
those signs are related to one small area in the brain stem
where there's a series of nerve centres and tracks all
crammed together. But I didn't know what the cause was.
I certainly didn't think stroke — although the symptoms
were stroke-like — because you were so healthy. There
was no hypertension, no family history, no reason for it.
I wanted to believe it was atypical migraine, or at worst
food poisoning from the chips or fruit juice. Botulism
affects those areas. For about an hour or so I was thinking of that.

But regardless of the cause, I was terrified because the nerve centres in that area are right next to the centre that controls the respiratory system. All of those life-maintaining and control structures are right there within millimetres of each other. You could stop breathing.

Michael decided we had to get to an emergency room. Burlington, Vermont, was less than an hour away but he didn't know where the hospital was. He figured it would be better to drive like crazy the extra eighty kilometres to Montreal, than to get lost in Burlington in the middle of the night. He telephoned the Jewish General to say we were coming and then called the kids.

By this time it was midnight. Michael helped me up the few stone steps from the cabin and into the front of the station-wagon. I wasn't sure I could handle the trip. I begged for some anti-nausea or sleeping medication, but he was afraid to give me any because of his unspoken worry that I might go into respiratory failure.

I travelled with plenty of throw-up bags, face-cloths and tissue, with my head stuck out the window for the fresh night air. It was black as only the country night can be. The road was narrow and twisty through the mountains of Vermont. I don't remember any conversation except about how I was doing. Nothing hurt specifically — I was just all over miserable. I was even too miserable to be scared of Michael's driving, which must have been terrifying because he made what was usually a one hour and forty minute trip in fifty-five minutes. I suspect I dozed off, though I do remember the drama of whether we would have enough gas in our tank to take us all the way home. There were no open gas stations between our cabin and Montreal at that hour.

When we got home, I was worried about scaring Seth and
Naomi. They were waiting for us; I don't know if they had
been in bed before but now they were ready to go.

Seth: I can't remember who got the phone call. I guess it
was fairly late. Dad said he was coming home to pick us
up and then we were going to the hospital. I don't think
we were worried at first. You and Dad came home, and
we let Lucy out and helped Dad unpack the car to make
room for us. Dad saved a couple of those juice contain-
ers to take to the hospital. He said you might have botulism. I didn't know what botulism was. The only thing
that I knew from my first-aid training was that slurred
speech was one of the symptoms of a stroke. I think I
started to get worried at that point.

Naomi: I remember that night was really hot. The fan in
my room was on and my boyfriend was over. The house
looked the way it always looked when my parents were
out of town: my stuff was all over the place; probably
some alcohol and cigarette debris was around, and
maybe even some evidence that my boyfriend and I had
been sleeping in my parents' bed. Bad stuff. So when my
brother told me that Dad had just called, that earlier
reports of my mother's "stomach flu" were getting more
serious and they were on their way home, my reaction
was simple: Destroy the evidence. Clean the house.

By the time the Taurus pulled up, the house was clean
and the boyfriend was gone. My dad said that we should
all go to the emergency room together. I came outside and
saw my mother hanging out of the front seat. Her body
was limp. I didn't remember sickness like this. Sickness

that my dad couldn't fix with supplies from one of his medical bags: constipation, diarrhea, nausea; he would fix it. This he couldn't fix and I was scared.

I waited in the car, barely able to focus my eyes. I wanted to hurry up and get to the hospital and have them cure me. I expected a diagnosis and a quick solution. I never imagined that I wouldn't set foot in my home again for many months.

EMERGENCY ROOM

The emergency room was a confused blur — too many people moving too fast in too little space. The last time I had been there was when my mother had some kind of infection related to her Alzheimer's. She spent several days in the corridor because there was no hospital bed available. There had been no room for a chair for visitors, and no privacy when she was examined.

JGH — Emergency Record: August 6
Subjective: 46 y/o WF. Previously healthy, no meds — 2 day HX
started with nausea, later blurred vision, diploplia, slurred speech.
Drank imported peach juice.
Objective: Right ptosis, disconjugate gaze, double vision, discs

sharp, sensation II intact, tongue to R, strength full in extremities, decreased sensation to light touch in L arm.
CT head: WNL
Diagnosis: Atypical migraine

I was seen by the emergency-room physician, a very young man who'd probably only been there a few months. He ordered a CT scan. Michael was sure I had botulism and gave them the fruit-juice cartons to be tested.

Michael: I wasn't *sure* it was botulism. I just thought it was a possibility that should be checked. I didn't know what it was. I thought it might be vascular. But you weren't sick enough to have had a stroke in the usual sense of a hemispheric stroke.

At the same time it could have been atypical migraine. But you only had a little bit of headache. Everything was wrong. The tests showed nothing. By then it was 2 or 3 o'clock in the morning and you were stable and it wasn't progressing further. When you were lying down in bed in a safe environment you were your usual cheerful self.

I wanted to take you home. I didn't want you to be in the hospital. If you weren't in the hospital, of course you'd be OK.

Michael told the emergency-room physician that he would bring me back in the morning for more tests. The ER doctor thought I should stay. Michael insisted we go home. According to Naomi, Michael was bullying the poor guy, who was wildly outranked. Naomi rolled her eyes at me, long established short-hand for those "Father Knows Best" moments. I rolled mine back at her and we stifled our giggles.

Naomi: I stayed with my mother behind the curtain in the tiny examining cubicle. With my father arguing with the other doctor outside, we were suddenly relaxed. Something passed between us like a silent pact.

We'd been fighting since I was twelve.

"What do I do that's so wrong?" I asked her once. "Do I fail school, do I get in trouble with the police?"

"You don't talk to us."

"We're talking right now. What exactly do you think there is to talk about?"

"You don't tell me what's going on in your life."

"Yeah right, Mom. Secretly I deal heroin. Is that what you want to hear? Are we friends now?"

Since I was an impeccable liar and rarely got caught, our fights were less about actual transgressions than about my silence, my sullenness and, as my dad was always fond of putting it, my "refusal to be a part of this family."

But now there would be no more bullshit between Mom and me. We would stop fighting and be allies.

Meanwhile the ER doctor had the good judgment to call the attending neurologist, Joe Carlton, a physician whom Michael respected too much to bully. He gave me the first of what was to become hundreds of neurological exams.

Joe Carlton: When I heard that you had a problem and were in the emergency room, I sort of hoped against hope that it would turn out to be one of those minor things that just show up and then disappear, and you say in retrospect, Oh maybe it was just a migraine.

I had met you before at various JGH social occasions
and we always talked. We shared many things that were
difficult for me to share with my colleagues in medical circles. Literature, art, a certain way of looking at the world.

We kept saying we should get together for tennis dou-
bles someday. I always hoped we would get to know each
other better. But not in the emergency room.

I remember the sinking feeling in the pit of my stomach when I recognized that you had sustained clonus —
involuntary shaking — in one of your ankles, which is a
very serious finding usually associated with damage to the
central nervous system. It could have been caused by a
number of things, including a stroke.

Michael: I said to Carlton, "Why don't I just take her
home and I'll bring her into your office in the morning."
He didn't hesitate, he just said, "Nonsense. We don't know
what's going on here, but you're not taking her home.
You be the husband and I'll be the doctor."

Michael relaxed then and so did I. Joe's presence changed
everything. "Just wait," he said, "we'll be playing tennis soon."
It was a joke, I knew it was a joke, but it sustained me for
months. I repeated it over and over to myself: We had a date to
play tennis. No matter how awful it was, Joe Carlton thought
I would play tennis. And I knew Joe Carlton wouldn't lie.

They moved me to a cubicle to wait for the test results. I
was feeling surprisingly calm considering the suddenness of
this bolt from the blue and the apparent confusion surround-
ing it. I thought I was in good hands — the doctors could
surely sort it out — and my family was closing around to protect me. Naomi held my hand. She had refused physical con-

tact with me for years. But here in the hospital, it was truce time. I told her that I had finally decided what I wanted to be when I grew up: a witch. It sounded funny, even flaky, but I had been reading about women's spirituality.

Naomi: When we were in the cubicle, my mother told me that she wanted to be a witch. My mother was always saying things like that. She always wanted to be more of a hippie earth mother than she actually was and would often resolve to become something she simply was not, like a folksinger — an unfortunate aspiration considering she can neither sing nor play the guitar. The Joan Baez fantasy ran deep. It would resurface every few years and she would learn to play "Greensleeves" again. As for being a witch, well, several of her friends from Studio D were getting pretty flaky; they were into solstices and rituals. I didn't like it when she said stuff like that, maybe because it made me think that she wasn't happy with her life the way it was.

Seth: We were in the ER for hours. There wasn't much to do. Hang out. Wait. Get a chocolate bar. Then suddenly you were being wheeled off to some other place where they had found you a bed and we had to leave. I'd never left anyone in a hospital before.

Patient Summary:
August 6 . . . On exam patient showed horizontal nystagmus, worse on the right, deviation of the tongue to the right, right facial weakness, dysarthria, clonus of the left ankle, and decreased pain sensation in the left foot and left leg and thorax to the T2 level . . . A lumbar puncture revealed an opening pressure of 20 cm of

water, only 1 RBC and 1 WBC, the protein was 35 mg, the closing pressure was 13 cm of H_2O. Proposed diagnosis of right medullary ischemia (local lack of oxygen to right medulla — cause not yet established).

≈

SURGICAL INTENSIVE CARE UNIT

The surgical ICU was one big open room, with people attached to machines in curtained-off cubicles and other people walking around with clipboards. I knew and disliked the surgeon-in-charge. He had once threatened to report a friend of mine for child abuse, for breast-feeding her baby while she had mastitis and a breast abscess, which Michael had assured me is harmless to the baby and good treatment for the abscess. Later, I had a personal run-in with the same doctor when Michael was in the JGH for back surgery. Michael was sedated for the night in preparation for early morning surgery. He had done everything to avoid this operation and was nervous. I was about to kiss him goodnight, when a stranger in surgical greens wandered in. With no introduction or greeting, he said to Michael, "I just heard you're on the University Promotions Committee. My application is coming up: will you support it?" Michael, who felt lousy and sleepy, was visibly annoyed. I jumped to his defence and told the man to leave my husband's room immediately, which he did.

That was before everything changed, when I was an important doctor's wife and fighting feminist filmmaker. Now I was just another patient on his ward.

He came by in the morning, a herd of medical students in his wake. The thin muslin curtains around my bed were drawn, but I recognized his voice. He stood just outside my cubicle and read my chart.

"The precise diagnosis is not clear," he told his entourage, "but the bottom line is, it can't be anything good."

I don't remember if I tried to say something. My voice was weak, but I could still talk at that point. I was furious that he would talk about me as if I wasn't there.

I was still too ignorant about the grim diagnostic possibilities to be scared.

My next visitor couldn't have been more different. My personal family practitioner, Irene Kupferszmidt, had escaped the Nazi invasion of Poland when she was nineteen. She was tough enough to stand up to my doctor husband when necessary, but they had great mutual respect.

Irene Kupferszmidt: It was Thursday morning, I was sitting on the chair at the hairdresser's. My son Henry was going to be married that night, a small family wedding, and I was getting myself fixed up. And just as the hairdresser was pouring the water over my head, my secretary called to say you were in hospital. I jumped up and ran — left the hairdresser standing there with her mouth open! — and arrived at the hospital looking like a crazy lady with a babushka on her head, not a respectable doctor.

I looked at you and thought, it could be anything. Maybe some viral thing, one of those sicknesses that we never diagnose that simply disappear. That was denial maybe.

My first thought when I saw her was, if Irene who is a model of impeccable taste and coiffure rushes in looking like this, I must be really sick. That was the moment I knew this could be serious.

Consultation report — August 6
Dr. Carlton: Possible vertebrobasilar ischemia. R/o evolving brain-stem infarct. R/o viral encephalomyelitis.
Dr. Black: Right 7th and possibly 8th palsy that suggests it is secondary to a medullary infarct. Recommend feeding tube.
Dr. Libman: Likely an ischemic lesion of the right medulla. Doubt inflammatory disease.
Dr. Wise: Possible right medullary syndrome with central Horners and divergence insufficiency horizontal and vertical nystagmus involving the 7th cranial nerve. Possible post viral demyelanating disease?
CT scan — negative
echocardiogram — negative
LP — negative
arteriogram — negative

I spent the whole of that afternoon lying on a tall bed and being wheeled through various departments, receiving test after test. I just lay there while they whisked me about and did things to me.

I remember nervously waiting in a corridor for the arteriogram, a diagnostic procedure where they stick a needle into one of your arteries and inject a dye that makes all the blood vessels in your head visible by x-ray. The doctor in charge told me that there was a very slight risk associated with it — in a very few cases the dye can cause spasms in the blood vessels, leading to a stroke — so he was obliged to ask me to sign a consent form. Michael told me it was OK; he knew and trusted this guy. But I wondered what I would have done if I had been alone. How could I possibly assess the risks this stranger proposed I take? If *I* was feeling overwhelmed, what about someone who doesn't happen to have a physician in the family?

I was poked and prodded by everyone from medical students who looked all of seventeen, to all the department chiefs, who each looked at whatever part of the "elephant" they specialized in, and diagnosed accordingly. I didn't understand what they were looking for. Whatever it was, they didn't find it, but the number one diagnosis was stroke — probably caused by some sort of blood clot in my brain. This was the first time I had heard them used the word stroke. I couldn't take it in. It seemed unreal — only old people have strokes.

Joe Carlton: The first thing that bothered me was the lack of precision in the initial provisional diagnosis. You were fairly mildly affected at that point and I wanted to do something to prevent it from getting worse. One thing that's often used in cases of stroke caused by blood clots is anticoagulants. We did a CT scan to make sure that there was no evidence of bleeding — because in a stroke caused by bleeding, anticoagulants would increase the bleed and worsen the stroke. I remember still being concerned and I consulted with the Chief of Neurology, but we agreed that since the CT scan didn't show any problem, an anticoagulant would be a reasonable thing to use. So we put you on Heparin overnight. Based on the available information, it was the right decision.

I was too exhausted from two nights of sleeplessness to sort out, let alone participate in, the medical arguments about my diagnosis and treatment. Instead, I worried about my current film. *Mile Zero* documented the cross-Canada high school speaking tour of four students, including my son Seth, from SAGE (Students Against Global Extermination). They believed that teenagers could work towards peace rather than accept the fear and hopelessness that affected many young people in those Cold War years. After months of preparation they set off on a fifty-city tour, joined from time to time by a film crew and an anxious mother/director.

Both the tour and the shooting had been finished in May but the long, demanding process of editing had only started. What would happen to the film if I had to stay in the hospital for a few weeks, or even a month? We would get hopelessly behind schedule. On our slim budget, we had hired Sidonie Kerr, a freelance film editor whose work I admired, on a six-month contract with the assumption that I would be there to work full time beside her. I didn't want to lose her.

Sidonie Kerr: I had just started working with you a month before, as the editor of *Mile Zero*. I hardly knew you, and I felt — as I always do as editor — a certain guardedness. We had planned simultaneous vacations so we wouldn't lose time from the film. And then my son Robbie phoned me with the news that you were in the hospital.

On my return I found a note dictated by you, written by Naomi. It said how badly you felt for me coming home to an illness, but that you trusted me to forge ahead without you. I think that was the beginning of my real commitment. What was just an interesting assignment became totally involving. It was a decision that wasn't even a decision. I was going to do whatever it took to help you finish your film.

NEUROLOGICAL INTENSIVE CARE UNIT

The next day I was transferred yet again, this time to the neurological ICU. Late that night I received my first ever acupuncture treatment.

Bernard Coté had treated Michael's back pain with acupuncture on and off for the past three years. Michael had attended the birth of Bernard's last child. Sometimes they had worked together, as doctor and acupuncturist, assisting difficult births. They had become colleagues and close friends: an odd couple, given most Western physicians' professional chauvinism.

When Michael told me Bernard was going to give me a treatment, I was surprised. Although I knew acupuncture was useful for other conditions — smoking, muscle and joint pain, insomnia — I never associated it with serious illness. Bernard had just returned from Tianjin, where, it turned out, he had been studying acupuncture techniques for stroke patients. In China, acupuncture is an integrated part of hospital medicine, and the primary treatment for stroke, but Bernard had never expected to use his new skills in an acute-care setting in high-tech

Montreal. Because Bernard wasn't an MD, Michael had to obtain special permission from the Medical Director.

Bernard: I have trouble explaining acupuncture. I try to talk about the scientific aspects, but they are very incomplete and not totally satisfactory.

It was hard to create the right space in hospital, because acupuncture is considered illegitimate. I find it disturbing if there's lots of crowding around during the treatment, because it's more difficult to concentrate at the moment when the needle goes in, and then the inside doesn't get touched that much. You have to pay attention to the breathing, but also the discomfort; you need concentration to be able to cope with it.

I think therapy has to do with love. One has to feel with you the joy when things are going well and the fear when they're not going so well. I was fearful, just like you were. But obviously, I wouldn't spread it all over the place, and certainly not to you.

I was delighted to see Bernard. When he came into my dingy cubicle, he was sweet as always, saying "What a silly thing to happen on your vacation." Bernard and Michael had plotted it all out. Bernard wanted to use moxabustion, which involves burning a bundle of herbs — moxa — to intensify the effect of the needles. The hospital room was equipped with a hair-trigger smoke detector and sprinkler system which Bernard did not think would enhance the treatment. Michael climbed on my bed and dismantled the smoke detector, while I, good girl that I am, froze in fear that a passing nurse would catch us. What did I think would happen? We would be expelled? Yelled at? Fired?

The fact that moxa smells a lot like pot didn't help my fears, but there was also something delicious about being naughty.

I was a bit apprehensive — I was afraid of needles. I had always chosen chiropractic or massage for my own low-back spasms; I couldn't imagine how needles could ever relax anything. And what if Bernard "missed" and made my condition worse?

Bernard examined me by taking my pulse, first in one wrist then in the other. He looked at my tongue and asked me to breathe in and out. After swabbing my skin with alcohol at the first acupuncture point, he inserted a thin steel needle. I looked away. I don't remember the exact points he punctured — I think there were needles in my ears and legs and in my tongue, which felt weird. Some needles were shallow, just through my skin. Others were up to an inch and a half deep. Mostly they stayed in for ten minutes or so. Every now and then he would twiddle them a few times. Some needles were like a jolt of electricity, a deep tingling or a dull ache. Others wouldn't feel like much at first and then *thong!* — a big hand tightening like a fist. Others felt like nothing at all, and I was afraid to turn over without asking Bernard if it was OK, in case these phantom needles were still in me.

I remember a great peace after the treatment, followed by a burst of energy. My speech was clearer and I was choking less. Michael says my right eyelid lifted dramatically — a good sign. We all committed to continue. Bernard would come twice a day while I needed it, which I didn't imagine would be long. He wouldn't let us speak of payment.

I fell asleep calm and optimistic. Being in the hospital seemed like an interesting interlude, a strange country I would pass through like a tourist, curious and unaltered.

August 7

00:00 Received pt awake in bed.

Heparin drip at 22 cc/hr. infusing well in forearm.

09:15 Neurology:

Pt claims speech is more difficult. Diplopia more prominent.

Pt complains swallowing more difficult.

10:30 Infusion dye injected.

CT scan, shows hemorrhagic infarction, right medulla.

Stop Heparin drip, D5W to KVO.

Joe Carlton: The next day you seemed a bit worse. We got another CT scan which looked more closely at the posterior of the brain stem, and this time there was evidence of a bleed: a hemorrhage in the medulla. Which meant that, in retrospect, an anticoagulant like Heparin had been a very bad choice. It was a minor miracle that your condition did not deteriorate more. That was my first heavy piece of baggage.

The cold intimacy of the hospital notes. I have become Pt (patient) instead of a person with a name. Pt complains ... Pt claims ... Pt refuses ... I watch myself sink into the institutional limbo: no day, no night, just rounds and meds and tests and restless snatches of sleep.

I don't know where to start, why I remember so poorly. My best guess is that my body and mind were too sleepy. I must have been a bizarre sight with all the equipment I was fastened to: IV lines, suction tube, feeding tube. But I have no image of myself, and Michael, usually an obsessive documentarist, didn't take photos. The IV for meds was inserted early — I don't remember who did it. I always look away from needles.

I got so used to the IV needle I didn't even know it was in, except when the tubing and the stand got in the way — tangled up with other tubes or the cord on the earphones I wore for music.

I was given a patch to wear on my left eye to alleviate my double vision and the dizziness it caused. I didn't recognize myself in the short hospital gown, ugly white anti-embolic stockings and eye patch.

The tube was a plastic suction tube used to remove the constant mucus and saliva from my mouth. I never realized how often you have to swallow until I couldn't do it. I felt as if I would be choked or drowned by my own secretions. My lips were parched from the suctioning.

In the bathroom, the nurse catheterized me "in-and-out" because I had trouble voiding. In-and-out means that the tube is removed after the bladder is emptied, unlike with an indwelling catheter, which I had later. I remember being relieved that it didn't hurt much, although that would vary with the nurse; some were gentler than others. I remember being impressed that urine could be removed in this impersonal way. After a few days I was able to pee by myself again, but by then I had developed a urinary tract infection.

I had a few toys that Bernard gave me. One was like a little wooden rolling pin with spikes, to roll around with my foot for stimulation and practice in control and intention. He also brought a few small, Chinese wooden balls, apricot size. You could see the grain in the unfinished wood — it smelled like cedar. He suggested I squeeze them in my hand as often as I could. As with the acupuncture, I didn't really understand, but I did it all faithfully. I liked having something active to do to care for myself. The medical doctors were into diagnosing; if they asked me how I was feeling, it was only as a test to figure

out what was going on, not to address the symptom and pro-
vide a practical way to cope with it. The Chinese balls also
gave me the feeling that somebody had been here before me,
that this was a very old, very simple technique for a fairly common problem.

The hospital was stifling in this typical Montreal mid-August.
It smelled like piss and industrial strength cleanser. It was also
very dry, and I felt as if I couldn't breathe. Michael brought a
small humidifier from home and Irene Kupferszmidt brought
me Evian water in a beautiful spray-mist bottle. I had never
used a mister before. It made me feel like an exotic plant, and
I used it constantly. I don't know how Irene knew, but it was
exactly what I needed.

The nurses often rubbed my back with something like alcohol. I think it was supposed to prevent bedsores or help me
relax so I could sleep. There are many nurses' notes about
sleeplessness. I don't think there was a specific reason, though
one note says "anxious." Probably it was everything that was
going on in my traumatized brain. I was fatigued yet I couldn't
sleep, a vicious cycle. It was better when I had late-night acupuncture treatments. The other big help was music. I became
addicted to music. I always wore earphones. Michael brought
all our favourite tapes and friends made me personal tapes of
music they loved: Yiddish classics from Adrianne Sklar, Sidonie's
La Traviata, flute meditations from Kathleen Shannon, my
long-time boss at Studio D.

During these first few days in hospital, I felt strangely peaceful. Whatever was going on in my body was clearly out of my
control. I didn't believe in any Divine Plan, but neither did I
believe this was a random accident. I didn't ask "why me?"
but felt rather that it was my turn — I who had always been
so privileged and lucky.

Irene Kupferszmidt: Over the next week I was in and out. You were getting a little better every day but you were still very tired. Your friends kept walking into your room, especially ones who worked with Michael. I resent very much that custom. I feel it's barbaric. They make a social event out of illness and they disturb the patient. So I put up a sign for you after the first few days. NO VISITORS — AND THAT INCLUDES MICHAEL'S FRIENDS IN WHITE COATS.

There were so many doctors, high-powered specialists. I would think to go see you but then I'd tell myself I have nothing positive at this moment to tell her. But when you were asleep, I sometimes came in and looked at you. I tiptoed because you were having trouble sleeping and I didn't want to disturb you out of your rest.

Naomi: The summer of the stroke, I had a job doing clerical work at the JGH emergency room. When my mother got sick, I went into my boss's office and told him that I was quitting. He was very understanding. I remember exactly what he said: "The recovery is going to be very long and very slow. It could take months, even years. But there is one thing about stroke: It only gets better. It doesn't get worse." I was very moved by what he said and very excited. I told my mother: "Dr. Afilalo says that it will only get better. It can't get worse." I repeated that phrase to myself over and over again like a mantra. "It can only get better. It can't get worse."

Michael: It wasn't as terrible as it might have been. You were alive and your functions were coming back. You were able to use the toilet, to transfer from the bed to the wheelchair. But you were still very sick.

I was the director of Herzl at the time, the family medicine outpatient centre at the JGH. But I stopped working. I stopped doing the office practice; I stopped doing administration. There were sixty people on my staff at Herzl, plus 100 doctors in the Department of Family Medicine that I was responsible for. And they covered for me. They did my work. They looked after me. The nurses, the doctors, people were with me constantly. Those were the people I cried with.

All I did was deliver babies.

I remember each one.

I practise a sort of midwifery, helping people in what is essentially a normal process. Childbirth isn't an illness, and it's rarely life threatening. I was percolating between your room on the third floor and the delivery suite on the fifth floor, selfishly using attendance at birth as psychotherapy: a break from my concerns for you.

What I couldn't do while you were sick was sit still and listen to somebody's minor ailments, which of course to them are major. And I couldn't deal with administrative work at all. I had no patience for it.

That was one of the consequences of your illness, which is not necessarily beneficial. I had zero tolerance for bullshit.

Naomi and Seth visited frequently, but most of my friends were held at bay by Irene's sign. They phoned or sent cards instead. Shul friends said prayers, and Studio D pagans performed rituals on Mount Royal. As my energy improved, I started to make a few exceptions to Irene's rule. Ron Aigen, the rabbi at our synagogue came every day. I assumed that he was just drop-

ping by while giving "spiritual succor" to older people in the
hospital. Then I realized *I* was sick and he was visiting *me*.

Rabbi Ron was more important to me than either of us
would have anticipated. When I told him several years later
how much his presence had meant to me, he revealed that he
had felt hesitant to impose himself. He did not want to take
advantage of my situation to suddenly bring me religion.

Ron connected me to the piece of my life which I felt had
been short-changed in my relationship with Michael, the son of
left-wing atheists. It's a piece of my childhood, my upbringing
in a traditional Jewish family. Ron is low-key, very warm and
calm. He fits no stereotype of a rabbi, which is why Michael
likes him as much as I do. He has nothing to "sell." His spiritual leadership is by unpretentious example. I always loved
going to shul to watch him pray. He exudes a quiet joy.

Ron told me that he had said a Healing Prayer for me in
shul — the prayer said at the high point of the *Shabbat*, when
the Ark is open and the Torah is being read. It asks that the
One who blessed our ancestors (traditionally it names our fore-
fathers, Abraham, Isaac and Jacob, but our Reconstructionist
synagogue adds our foremothers, Sarah, Rebecca, Rachel and
Leah) bless and completely heal whoever is sick, in my case
Bat-Shira, Daughter of Song, the Hebrew name I made up for
myself when I was a teenager at a Hebrew-speaking summer
camp.

Though he seemed relaxed on his visits, Ron later told me
he was devastated by my stroke. "I did a lot of pastoral work
with older congregants, but you were close to my age, a peer
and a friend. This wasn't supposed to happen to you."

I was in the neurological ICU for four days. Most of the other
patients were too sick to talk, but the staff was like one big

dysfunctional family — intimate and inescapable. It had its good side, however. There was one orderly named Georgio with a moustache and an accent that was Greek or maybe Italian. He treated me with old-world gallantry and made me feel like a queen. I learned to stand (with help), lock my knees and pivot from the bed to the wheelchair, or the wheelchair to the toilet, a move which Georgio translated into a dance. He would say, "Want to dance with me?" And then he'd lift me and sing, "Now we dance" as he helped pivot me onto the toilet. I always looked forward to his shifts. He made something that everyone else treated as a real chore into fun, as though our moments together were pleasant for him as well as for me.

There was another orderly whom I thought of as The Giant. He was bald like Telly Savales and very tall. He didn't talk much, but he would notice when my tray-table had been left out of reach, and push it back without being asked.

Suzi Scott was my favourite nurse. Seth and Naomi already knew her as a familiar face, the mother of children with whom they'd gone to school. The staff tended to ignore Naomi unless she did something they didn't like. She had already argued with a few nurses when she'd taped get-well cards up on the glass wall that separated my little alcove from the main ward. But Suzi welcomed Naomi, teaching her nursing tricks like shampooing my hair in a bedpan.

Naomi: Suzi Scott was like an angel, a loving human being who swooped in and saved us from the heartless, machine-like, nurse androids. She loved us, she gushed all over us. The truth is that if I met Suzi Scott under any other circumstances, I probably would have hated her. I couldn't stand saccharine, manic people, who touch you too much and love you too much and look too deeply into your eyes. When everything is all right, you can afford to hate really nice people. When things suck, they really come in handy.

August 8, 13:40. Dietitians Note:
Pt was receiving 1/2 strength Ensure at 50 mL/hr. via Dobhoff and had diarrhea.
Recommend 1/4 strength Ensure at 50 mL/hr. for today. Pt has also tried semi-solids such as custard this afternoon but she claims she's not up to it yet.
Pt claims to be able to swallow w/o any discomfort but says that "One muscle at the end of swallowing won't do what I want it to do."

I had diarrhea from Ensure, an enriched formula that I was fed by nose tube four times a day. It was a thick, yellowish liquid which came in a blue plastic bottle. My Mom had been fed the same stuff when she was hospitalized. The smell of it nauseated me. I did not want to be my mother lying helpless in a hospital bed, fed through a tube, the same smell, drifting further and further into absence.

Ensure "tasted" sickeningly rich, like the cream on the top of unhomogenized milk. I felt bloated afterwards, especially at night when it interfered with my sleep. I used to plead with the dietitian not to give me a late feeding, and she would counter that I needed the calories. Then in the day I would feel like I was starving. Between my refusals and the diarrhea, I was probably just getting the bare minimum. I worked hard on swallowing but couldn't get much down. They tried to use foods I like: ice cream, custard, chocolate milk. Michael brought me strawberry yogurt and gently stroked my throat to smooth it down.

But it wasn't enough. The dietitian was always after me to try harder, eat more, have some Ensure, until I felt sick. Why did I get into such a tug-of-war with her? Even now as I read the notes, I get angry and impatient. Yet she was obviously concerned. At the time I saw her as cold and rigid. And she probably saw me as stubborn and "non-compliant."

The high point of my day was Joe Carlton's rounds. I could count on him to tell me what was going on. He would sit on my bed in the evening, looking exhausted. I knew his wife and kids were waiting for him, as I had so often waited for Michael, impatient with all those needy people stealing his time from me. But now I felt a desperate dependence. I wanted Joe to stay, to talk, to explain things over and over. My body ached, I was sleeping badly, I was sick of being strong. What I needed from Joe was just the sound of his voice, tired and calm, soothing me with honest, uncertain explanations.

Joe Carlton: I cannot help but feel sympathy for patients whose lives have been transformed by serious illness. Good health is of inestimable value and one day we all must face its loss. Although it is painful not to be able to correct a problem, it is important that caring and competent professionals do their best to help the patient and family readjust their lives as best they can. Even though many neurologic problems are serious and treatments limited or dangerous, I've never regretted being a neurologist.

As a black child growing up in the South in the fifties, I remember feeling angry that the colour of someone's skin could make such a difference. It's just an accident of life. So, too, the accidents of health can leave one feeling wronged by fate and vulnerable to discrimination. I recognize that feeling in the faces of my patients sometimes.

August 10

04:35 Pt states Dobhoff tube fell out — MD notified — Pt
      hungry. Two small teaspoons Jell-O — Pt spit it out.
08:00 Dobhoff tube inserted by resident.
14:00 Pt refused to sit up in chair. Stated she is too tired.
14:15 Pt transferred to Neuro High Care.

NEUROLOGICAL HIGH-CARE
UNIT

When our long-time housekeeper, Meena Williams, came to visit, I had graduated to the neuro high-care unit. High care was a big room right across from the nurses' station, with a sliding glass door so the nurses could keep an eye on us and still do their endless paperwork. There were four beds; I was next to the window, though I was too sick to look out.

Meena Williams: There were no visitors allowed when you were first sick. So I waited until it was time. When I came in, you grabbed for my hand and we held onto each other. You asked me if I would go and visit your mother for you because you didn't want her to feel she had been abandoned. And I was happy to do it. Your mom and I always got along very well.

By that time, her memory had begun fading and she couldn't remember everybody. I would say to her, "Bonnie

sends her love and she'll be back soon." And she'd just
look. I felt she recognized me because she smiled. I would
brush her hair, trim her nails. I could see there was some
satisfaction. But not being able to move around, after
how active she used to be — I think that was hard on her.
But comes the time, you know.

I had all the possessions which constituted my world arranged around me: cards and mobiles, a small box of hospital
Kleenex, my tape player, the apricot lip balm that Studio D
friends gave me in a basket of treats from the Body Shop. Next
to my bed was the ubiquitous sliding hospital tray-table on
wheels, and a little metal cabinet with one drawer, where they
kept the thermometer, blood pressure cuff, and a kidney-shaped,
turquoise plastic basin for what they called peri-care — tooth-
brushing and mouthwashing which a nurse helped me with
every morning. The bottom section was a cupboard for the
stainless steel bedpan which was so icily ungiving when you
sat on it. There were plants on the skimpy window-sill until
the nurse Naomi called The Hun confiscated them because they
were "unhealthy."

In the NICU, my cubicle had been in a little alcove away from
the other patients. High care was my first real experience of
ward life. It was very quiet as all three of my roommates were
in deep comas. I felt like I was in a roomful of corpses.

The woman in the bed next to mine was named Patricia.
She had been in a freak car accident where a construction
crane fell through her front windshield crushing her skull.
She'd been in a coma for six months. She was totally unresponsive. Her husband, J.P., would sit by her bedside every
day for hours. He just sat there and spoke to her in an endless

mumbled litany; *"Patricia je t'aime. Ma bella fille, ma p'tite, ma cherie…"* I would lie there thinking, what an utter waste of time. As far as I could tell she was gone — dead. But J.P. kept on and on. He never gave up.

I was thrilled when after one day in high care, I was moved to a private room.

INTERLUDE: MOM

Journal: July 30, 1994
I am on the ferry *en route* to Gabriola Island off the coast of British Columbia for the long weekend. The heat wave has finally broken — I am amazed at how well I endured it this time. The ferry is one of my favourite places to work. I feel so privileged to be writing here among the fishing eagles.

Getting ready for this trip was miserable. Some of my behaviour reminds me of my mother. Mechanical incompetence. Losing my eyeglasses. Having to repeat the plan several times so I'll be sure to remember everything. Needing to pee, worrying about when, where. Needing routines, rigidity. Writing notes to myself, lists like Mom had all over the house.

Sometimes I feel that Michael is ordering me around, talking down to me as if I were a child. "Go to the bathroom now because there's a toilet." "Lie down and take a rest;

you're tired." Is it fear I see in Michael's eyes, when he flares with impatience at my constant needs?

Mom. Vacant, trapped. Still but not serene. "Practical" clothes: cheap synthetic housedresses, Velcro shoes, elasticized waists; easy to put on, easy to clean. She used to be such a fashion plate. But always messy, like me. Each of us used to get stains on the best-silked tips of our boobs — but that predates both Alzheimer's and strokes.

I don't want to be her. Her gnarled hands. Her bunioned feet. Her toothless smile. Her breastless chest. Her body like a lost, frail little boy, not the Russian matriarch who once was my mother. I worked so hard to hold onto the memory of my mother, how she was. I tried for so long to make her remember.

She died in slow motion over many years. Years of misplacing keys and glasses, then accusing various house-cleaners of stealing them. Making endless lists of things to do and having to ask the same questions over and over. Piling furniture to barricade the apartment door against the man who had stolen her key and was trying to break in. Michael finally insisting that she give up her driver's licence.

In 1980, my sister Razelle called me back from Michael's sabbatical in England when Mom was diagnosed with breast cancer for the second time. Her first breast had been removed a year after my father died, in 1968. The second surgery accelerated her decline, I think. I had to accompany her to each procedure, to explain and re-explain what was happening, the implication of each finding and each decision. It was the first clear sign I had of her childlike passivity, this woman who had been so sharp and questioning, such a fighter, all her life.

Several years later came the move to Montreal, the painful months of living with us, the final euphemistic "foster home" when she became too paranoid to be left even with Meena.

I felt guilty on days I didn't stop to visit her on my way home from work. I thought she had nothing to do but wait for the joy of my meagre visits. "Where have you been?" she'd say. "It's been a long time." Even when it was yesterday. And then painful goodbyes after pleasant visits. "Are you leaving so soon? I think I'll go with you." I begged her with all my rationality not to make me feel guilty about living my life as she had always taught me: "Your husband and children come before everyone else."

But soon she just greeted me with a big focusless smile and said, "What a nice surprise. I wasn't expecting you," in her most sociable, sweet manner. She would show me off to her housemates, remembering neither their names nor mine. I learned to say, "Hi Mother dear, it's your daughter Bonnie," to spare her the shame of not knowing. She would brag about what a thoughtful, wonderful daughter she had, how I took such good care of her. She used to expect Dad too, forgetting he'd died years ago. Then one day she no longer remembered him, not even when I pushed it. It was as if their long life together had never happened.

Her roommate was always going home. She'd have her coat and hat on, her small purse on her arm, and often she did manage to sneak out the front doors. I think her name was Sadie. She always greeted me with a kiss and a hug, as if I came to see her rather than my mom. She was so smooth I fell for her stories that her husband was coming to take her home, until a nurse clued me in. Why did the nurse feel she had to tell me? What did it matter if I believed in that imminent husband, if we believed together?

And just as I was getting used to the absent, childlike sweetness and obsequious gratitude, my mother forgot me entirely.

Sometimes I would think that she was purposely not recognizing me, to punish me. That she was angry I'd abandoned her, contrary to the wish she'd expressed in earlier years never to be "stuck away in an institution." As she had abandoned the aunt who helped raise her after her mother died and her father deserted her. Tanta lived with us throughout her later years. I was too young to understand what became wrong with her, but I remember my mother shopping for the least awful nursing home and visiting her there. I remember my mother's guilt that she couldn't conduct her real estate business and raise her own family and still care for Tanta.

As I write, I wonder about me and my children. What do you do with a mother who can no longer care for herself? What *do* you do?

A ROOM OF MY OWN

Moving into a private room meant I was getting better. I no longer needed constant nursing care. After five days in the hospital, I still couldn't walk unassisted or swallow, but I could now stand and transfer to the toilet by myself, and the rest would surely come in another week or two. The nurse showed me how my new bed could be raised and lowered and tilted at

many different angles; the head, the middle, and the foot all
moved separately, but I couldn't begin to sort it out. She
showed me the call button to buzz for emergencies since I was
no longer right in front of the nursing station. She clipped the
cord to my heavy pillow case, which smelled of disinfectant
and had JEWISH GENERAL HOSPITAL stamped on its hem, and
placed the button itself in my hand. I was alone and secure.

No sooner had I settled in when a man in pajamas wandered in, noisily demanding a cigarette and matches. I tried to
refuse him politely but he insisted, pacing my room and shouting. I was frightened and pushed the buzzer. The nurse came in
no great hurry. She thought it was funny and shooed him away
with no word to me.

Michael: We were in bed watching television the first
night in your private room. I had a sore back, and your
bed was definitely the place to be. I was frequently in bed
with you. We would hold hands and talk, or we would
watch television. I also read to you. But this one night we
were watching the World Series. I can't remember who
was playing, or how interested we were.

And then, I don't know how it started but we were
making love. We didn't actually have intercourse. But we
were involved in very heavy petting. I remember feeling
that it wouldn't be harmful. In the ICU, you were attached
to too many pieces of equipment. I wouldn't have dared.
But now we could, and we had a mutual need. You had an
orgasm. It was good for both of us, even in the hospital.

Though you were getting better, you were still very sick.
You moved differently. And underneath it all there was
this frightening feeling that it might be the last orgasm
for a long time.

I was totally turned on and totally embarrassed. I didn't
think this kind of thing was allowed in a hospital. Somebody
could walk in and there's the Chief of Family Medicine in bed
with a patient. I had such a mix of reactions. Part of me was
thinking: What kind of sex maniac is he? Is he trying to deny
what's happening? Is he so desperate that I be well? Is he trying to prove our life will be the same?

But past all embarrassment and analysis, he touched me. I
could feel that he loved me. This body that was poked and
prodded by daily strangers like a lump of meat was still lov-
able. He made me feel that this body was still mine.

August 11
23:30 Husband still visiting.
Pt anxious, trying to sleep. Awaking easily.

Over the next few days, Naomi de-institutionalized my new
room. She had always been into nesting, while I was as obliv-
ious to my surroundings as I was to my body. It was one of our
ongoing tensions; I thought she was too concerned with appear-
ances and she thought I was an unfeminine slob. I remember
my horror in the early days of the women's movement to discover that my small children seemed to fall into typical gender
stereotypes, despite our best efforts to raise them otherwise.
Seth grew up playing his version of Superhero (Underpants
Man), fashioning his own crude guns. Naomi, deprived of
Barbie and Ken by the same parents who wouldn't purchase
war toys, loved dressing our first puppy in doll clothes and
tying her tail in ribbons.

But even I could appreciate the transformation she wrought
in that hospital room. The walls ran riot with art cards, nature
cards, seriously drippy get well cards, corny chicken soup joke

cards And every few days a new note from my Studio D col-
league and good friend Terre Nash:

August 12
Dearest Darling Bonnie, Enclosed is an item of extreme
importance — a Nancy Reagan NOSE-MASK.
Whenever you get tired of having people around or of
tests being administered, etc., just put on the nose-mask.
It scares the shit out of people and they will go away.

People want to know what to send you. I've been
suggesting precious jewels. I was going to send
chocolates but apparently it is difficult to stuff them
down that food-tube, so they'll have to wait.

love, Terre

My oldest friend and Studio D office mate, Dorothy Hénaut,
sent a different painting almost every day: orange day lilies;
endless fields of bright apple green; a landscape with purple
cows. The hospital staff would come by just to see the new art.
Seth brought a radio. He wanted me to be able to listen to
"Morningside" and public affairs programs, to have some connection to the outside world. Naomi brought back my banned
plants and I kept receiving new ones, which soon took over the
room.

One of my most treasured presents was a shoebox filled with
the tiniest paper cranes, which had been folded by Muriel Duckworth's granddaughter Danielle. Cranes are a Japanese symbol of healing which came to be a peace symbol through the
story of Sedako, an eleven-year-old runner who got cancer as
a result of radiation poisoning from the bombing of Hiroshima.
Legend tells that if a thousand paper cranes are folded for someone, they will be healed. Sedako folded 640 before she died.

Her classmates completed the thousand, and now children from all over the world place necklaces of paper cranes on a sculpture of Sedako in Hiroshima. A clip of Muriel Duckworth placing cranes from the schoolchildren of Halifax at the feet of that sculpture is one of my favourite images in *Speaking Our Peace*.

August 12
07:30   up in commode x 2 — cloudy foul-smelling urine
           and diarrhea
           Mobility: Sat x 20 minutes by side of bed. C/o tiredness.
12:00   Magnetic Resonance Imaging requested. (Dr. Carlton)
           Radiologist thought MRI not urgent. Over next 2 weeks
           should be OK if pt clinically stable. MRI should be done
           before next CT.
           R/o Cavernous angioma.

Naomi: When you heard about the MRI, you said, "Why more tests — don't we know I had a stroke?"

Joe said, "Just a few more, for my peace of mind."

You asked, "Is it claustrophobic?"

Joe said, "Well, you have to lie inside the machine, perfectly still, for forty-five minutes."

You said, "Do I have to?"

Joe said, "I'm going on vacation; we'll talk about it when I get back."

I knew there was still disagreement among the JGH doctors, but I was ready to accept the diagnosis of stroke. I didn't understand why we needed to know more. I didn't realize that many things can cause a stroke — it could be cancer, or a blood clot, or a hemorrhage that might bleed again. I didn't realize that depending on the cause, the treatment might be different.

As far as I was concerned, whatever had happened was now over and done with, and I was ready to move on to rehabilitation so I could resume my life.

I was put in the hands of the Stroke Team, a trio of women, only one of whom seemed to have a clear and practical function: the physiotherapist, Iolanda Zompa. She had dark curly hair, mischievous eyes, and smelled fragrantly of strong coffee. She seemed confident and calm, as if she had seen many people in my condition. She was the first in a long line of physio cheerleaders with whom I fell in love. Her attitude was "I know you can do it." And when I did, she would say, "*Yesss*, Bonnie, you did it!"

The big job of the stroke team was to teach me to swallow. Iolanda and the speech therapist both worked on that. They would feed me brightly coloured popsicles, then check the tube to see if the colour of the secretions I was choking on matched the popsicles. If not, I was swallowing.

I often begged for a sip of Iolanda's coffee. I had a constant headache, which I thought might be caffeine withdrawal. I joked that she shouldn't come with her cup of coffee if I couldn't have some. It was a big moment when she said I could try it. Of course I choked.

August 17
All exercises to be carried out in the presence of a nurse —
10 consecutive reps, 3x daily.
(1) Phonation
    (a) ah
    (b) ah-cha
    (c) click
(2) Tongue movements
    (a) tip of tongue along roof of mouth

(b) tip of tongue along floor of mouth

(c) protrude tongue

(d) elevate tongue to nose, to chin

(e) lick lips

(f) push tip of tongue against tongue depressor

(3) Cough

(4) Take small sips, with a straw, of a liquid at mealtime. A minimum of 2 oz. to be ingested per meal.

Sip, swish fluid around in mouth for a moment & swallow, then swallow again, immediately (i.e. 2 swallows).

(5) Suckle ice cubes, aggressively, & swallow water (2 swallows).

(6) Chew gum (in presence of family or nurse). (Please note: spit out when too soft.)

(7) Chew on tongue depressor & swallow saliva.

I did my swallowing exercises religiously. I couldn't believe I was *supposed* to chew gum. I always hated gum. Did we have some not-too-obnoxious kind? Sugar-free? Mickey Mouse? (Naomi will remember — chewing gum was another of those trivial issues we used to fight about.) The tongue depressor tasted like dry wood — then splintery wood as it got soggy. But I kept at it. I was such a good girl.

I did physical exercises too: leg raises and kicks in bed or up in the chair. Iolanda brought a walker right away, so I could go to the toilet by myself. It was the kind with no wheels — just a folding frame that gave four-point support when it was open. It gave me enough stability to walk a bit if Iolanda held me too, either by the nape of the neck or by the waist, like I may have held Seth and Naomi when they were first learning to walk. I had to lift the frame and put it down for each step, advancing it and then moving towards it. My mother was using a walker in the foster home. How would the kids feel seeing me look like their grandmother?

Naomi: One day I came in for a visit, but I couldn't go in right away because you were in the hall with the physio and she was helping you walk, like you used to help your mom. So I stopped in the nursing station to talk to Dad and Joe Carlton and some other people I knew. There was glass across the whole front of the nursing station, so you could see everywhere. I guess it was the first time that I was watching you rather than being with you and talking to you. Usually if I could see you walk, I would be right there helping you. But in this situation I was just sort of observing you through the glass, from a distance. As I watched, the room started spinning, and I said "Dad, I really don't feel well." Then I fainted. He lay me down and took my pulse, and I was out for two seconds or something. It was really weird. There was no warning. There was no emotional thing attached to it. It was a purely physical response.

Iolanda and I worked hard. The notes indicate that I was improving a bit every day. We gradually increased the distance I could walk. I was hesitant and bumbling, but I remember when I finally walked from my room to the nurses' station. Joe Carlton and the nurses burst into spontaneous applause, and I collapsed with exhaustion.

Iolanda promised me that soon she would take me to the gym. I didn't know hospitals had gyms. I pictured strong bodies, sweat and laughter. It sounded like fun. I asked Michael to bring my shorts — I would have to wear real clothes!

But my progress was up and down. Some days I could barely reach the door, let alone the nursing station. "You can make it," Iolanda would say. "Just a few more steps, and then you can sit and rest on that bench."

It was the old and continuing question of how much to push, when is enough and when am I being lazy or indulgent? Would one more step make me too tired? Was it good for me? I still feel guilty when I read in the nurses' notes: "Pt c/o [complains of] being fatigued, refused to sit in chair."

Despite my daily confrontations with the limits of my body, I still felt that the stroke wasn't real. It didn't touch me. It was something weird, and temporary, that had happened to my body but not to *me*. I was the same person I'd always been and we were all working hard, so everything would of course turn out all right.

Since we didn't know the cause of my stroke, I assumed it was stress — a common oversimplification, according to Michael. The idea that I'd somehow brought it on myself was hard to shake. Maybe I'd been living too long in the fast lane and was now paying the price for trying to have it all. Or perhaps I was "stroked out" by my work environment, fighting so hard to make a film in which I believed, in an institution which did not seem to believe in me.

Mile Zero had certainly been stressful. I had sought the fundraising help of a co-producer, Irene Angelico. We worked without knowing if there would be enough money to complete the film. We did the first shoot using my VISA card for travel costs. Camera assistants brought us their "short ends," literally, leftover film from officially supported projects. The freelancers worked for deferred salaries and didn't watch the clock.

One of my Studio D colleagues wrote to Star Hawk, a well-known feminist witch who sent me her own personal fund-raising spell:

Out of the nowhere
Out of the air
Out of the darkness
To aid me I swear
Piles upon piles
Of silver and gold
Come without warning
As you have been told

There had been delicious moments when I was reminded what filmmaking was all about: the enthusiasm of a gifted and dedicated crew; the exhilaration of filming a dauntless red station-wagon of high-spirited teenagers crossing breathtaking country from Newfoundland to Vancouver Island; the powerful responses of other young people. But behind the scenes, the SAGE kids were having as hard a time as we were. They were exhausted, always having to be "on," and trying to get along with each other with no privacy, no rest, no time off.

Seth and I had our own difficulties. It was his first year away from home and I missed him badly. In a sense, the film made his leaving less painful, but it also presented complications in our usually smooth relationship. He was my intermediary with the group, which often caused him conflicting loyalties. He felt guilty when he couldn't "deliver" his colleagues as planned. But he also had to protect the tour from the intrusions the film made on their gruelling schedule, from stops for re-takes of scenic "beauty shots" (Do you mind driving up that mountain again?), to my desire to film them doing their laundry (they refused).

Seth was the oldest, the father-figure in the group, doing most of the driving and car maintenance, as well as plotting the schedule and route, and packing the station-wagon each day. It was a heavy responsibility for a conscientious young man of eighteen. When I arrived on the set, he expected his Mom. What he got was the Film Director, a person he'd never met before.

Every shoot ended with Seth and me apologizing to each other for forgetting our primary relationship amidst all the logistics and pressures of the shoot, and promising the next time would be more relaxed.

But the stress of working on a no-budget film was only part of it.

Shortly before the tour, I was in a car accident that shook me badly. I was coming home late one rainy night after an editing session when someone rear-ended me. I had painful whiplash for weeks. It wasn't all that serious, but for some reason I just couldn't get over it. Driving became scary, and then riding in cars. I got panic attacks on bridges and then in basement cineplex movie theatres. Over the next year the list of symptoms grew: sleeping problems, crying spells, asthma.

I suspected that I was being poisoned by the airless offices at the film board: Sick Building Syndrome. After giving me a full physical exam, Irene Kupferszmidt called it situational depression. Rather than being scared or defensive, I was relieved to have a name for what was happening.

The diagnosis made sense. I was living in the same house with a stormy, adolescent daughter and a mother with advancing Alzheimer's disease. Studio D was dying or dead, and the film board itself was floundering. At times my filmwork against violence and war filled me with paralyzing hopelessness.

I was even questioning feminism — my firm identity for almost twenty years. Feminism's gender analysis had opened my eyes, but now that vision seemed to obscure other ways of looking at the world. Many people, women as well as men, seemed to be left out. Kathleen Shannon, executive producer at Studio D, and one of my mentors in feminism, had refused funding for *Mile Zero*, saying the resources for women's film-making were too scarce to support a film that was not specifically about women. My head agreed but my heart rebelled against this limitation. "Doesn't the world need everyone's best energy if we are to heal?" I asked in endless arguments inside my own head. "If violence in this society is mostly male, shouldn't we welcome the voices of positive young men?" My accustomed identity was shifting under my feet. There was nowhere left to stand.

Irene Kupferszmidt prescribed small doses of an anti-depressant to break the cycle of sleeplessness. I was desperate enough to take it despite my usual resistance to medication. She also advised psychotherapy. After meeting a half-dozen counsellors, I started seeing Michele Devroede, a Gestalt therapist whose quiet centredness attracted me. I told her I wanted help to slow down, find balance and start living in the present moment.

I saw Michele Devroede throughout the SAGE tour year, except when I was away on location, which was when I needed her most. I wasn't able to handle the stress of filming as I had in the past. I didn't even recognize myself. Some stranger was directing this film, a cranky woman who couldn't make decisions and had trouble organizing simple things. Whoever she

was, she lacked the sense of humour and perspective that had
gotten her through hellish shoots before.

Lying in the hospital bed, I thought of all the doubts I'd had
about continuing in film. Could this stroke be what I needed
to make changes in my life? My days now consisted of swallowing exercises and the excitement of walking twenty feet
with the walker. Maybe this experience was a message from
my body: its way of telling me something important. I remember joking that *my* body had to shout *really* loud to get my
attention.

Seth suggested that if I couldn't make films, I could become
like the *Speaking Our Peace* women. I think he meant that I
could speak and work directly for the causes I believed in, and
not hide behind the camera. I didn't need a label or job, I could
be a full-time, front-line activist, unmediated by institutions.
The women in my film had become role models for Seth, and
now he was offering them back to me.

> **Seth:** What I remember is always asking you questions.
> Maybe it was inappropriate to try and force answers
> about your future. Maybe it still is.
>
> I was trying to ask what you would do if you couldn't
> direct film — if you would write, or be an activist or
> what. I was applying my own feelings to your situation.
> Like if I were in your situation, I'd want to read more
> and listen to the radio and try to take advantage of the
> time in the hospital for learning things. Maybe I wasn't
> fully appreciating what recovery is about.

Seth tells me he felt helpless and awkward at the hospital,
but for me he was a soothing comfort. I remember worrying

with Seth that neither he nor I had been able to cry yet. What was wrong with us? Didn't we need to cry? Wouldn't it be good for us? Was this what was meant by denial?

Seth: I think my role was to be positive. I always assumed that whatever had happened was over and now you would get better. I would hang out in your room discussing the parallels between the peace movement and your recovery. We agreed that the greatest challenge was overcoming the sense of "What difference can I make? It's out of my hands." Approaching the problem with the right spirit seemed to be as important as finding solutions. In both cases no one could know where things would end up; just moving in the right direction had to be good enough.

Seth kept saying how much worse it could have been: my mind was not affected. Although my speech was slurred, I was able to communicate. And I would surely get my strength and balance back with enough perseverance and hard work. Maybe I'd have to go to a rehab centre for a few weeks, or maybe I could do it all at home.

Michael: By that time, we weren't really scared any more. You were still weak, but you were able to get up and your speech had improved. I thought you would be out in another couple of weeks and then you'd have to go to rehabilitation, probably as an outpatient, probably for a couple of months. And you were saying, "A couple of months? I don't have time for this!"

I was getting itchy about how little you were up with the walker. I felt that strengthening your arms and trunk would be useful. So I asked the physiotherapist to hook up a trapeze-like arrangement over your bed. I thought at the very least it would be useful to help you shift yourself in bed. I encouraged you to do some chin-up type things just to have some exercise. Nobody questioned it.

August 19, 1987 was our twentieth wedding anniversary. Our tradition would have been to go out for a nice dinner with Seth and Naomi. Anniversaries were never thought of *à deux*. In fact, we joked in our family that we might never have been married without Seth, so celebrating with the kids seemed only right.

When I was a teenager, my girlfriends and I agreed that being pregnant was the worst reason for getting married. But the road to hell is paved with such correct ideas.

When I was twenty-six and working in New York City, I was invited on a camping trip to the Virgin Islands with my friends, Bob and Sandy Erickson and their two-year-old Andrew. They had already invited some mutual friends, plus this guy Michael, whom they knew from medical school, and his little girl.

"That sounds OK, but you'd better tell him that you've also invited me," I said. They checked with him and he said "I don't want some single woman along; I don't want a two-week blind date!"

"Well, fine," I said, "I'll go somewhere else. It's no big deal to me." Bob and Sandy were always trying to fix me up with doctors, and I always refused because doctors were too boring. So I didn't have any big plans for this guy.

But Bob said, "No, damn it, I'm not going to let Michael Klein tell me who goes on my holiday!"

Bob eventually worked it out that we'd both come (but *not* as a date!) Meanwhile Sandy told me a bit about Michael: he was divorced, political, and had a three-year-old daughter who lived with her mother on the West Coast.

At the airport waiting for the plane to Puerto Rico, I finally met Michael. I gasped. No one had told me he was beautiful (or that his eyes matched the green of his Ethiopian Airways bag).

So there we were on the "vomit comet," the midnight plane to Puerto Rico, full of people going on holiday with little children on their laps (vomiting). His daughter Misha waltzed up to me and flung herself on my lap, grasping a book by P.D. Eastman called *Are You My Mother*. She sat with me all the way to St. Thomas, but Michael made a point of ignoring me. A plane ride to Puerto Rico, another plane to St. Thomas, a ferry to St. Johns, a stop for food at the camp store — and still not a single word.

At the camp store there was a guy buying hamburger, a lawyer who turned out to be from Philadelphia like me. He invited me to come to their campsite for dinner. (I didn't know he would turn out to be a famous conservative senator!) "Sure!" I said.

Setting up our camp, Michael broke his vow of silence to tell me that I shouldn't have made this date, because our group had been expecting me to be there for dinner and he had bought food for everyone. I went on my date anyway, but came back early. Our gang was sitting around the camp fire. Michael was playing harmonica. Soon, the two of us wandered off to the beach to talk about our anti-Vietnam-war activities. We ended up in the sea, and later in a camp cot. I didn't know if this would turn out to be a vacation fling where we would never see each other again in the real world, and I didn't care, although this wasn't my usual behaviour even in the sixties.

As it turned out, we saw each other daily back in New York. After a few months of romance, I started wondering if it was smart of me to get so involved with a recently divorced father. Half-remembered magazine articles fuelled my fears. I was on the verge of calling it off when I discovered I was pregnant. We were using a diaphragm and spermicidal jelly which are supposed to be ninety-four per cent effective. But someone has to be in the other six per cent.

Our immediate reaction was to try to get an abortion. But these were the bad old days when abortion was not available — even to medical interns — except in back alleys. We were given the name of some minister in the East Village who knew someone who did abortions. It was a kind of underground church-basement thing, and it felt so creepy that we couldn't go ahead with it.

These were also the bad old days of the Vietnam war, and like so many others, Michael actively opposed it. He had been refused conscientious objector status because, as a doctor, he wouldn't have to kill people. But as far as he was concerned, to be in the military keeping other men in good health so that *they* could go out and kill people was not much different. There was no way he would serve in the armed forces; he had decided that if he was drafted he would either go to jail or to Canada.

I said, "If you make the choice to go to Canada, I will marry you and go with you and have the baby." I was a little hesitant about going to Canada with a guy I had almost broken up with two weeks before, but there was no way I would marry him if he was going to jail. Michael chose Canada.

I think it was Michael who dreamed up the anniversary party; he was always pushing the rules, but this time I don't think any staff minded. We had staked our claim to life in my room.

Seth: I remember that party. It was just the four of us. You wanted to try the ritual your friends had done on the mountain. Everyone had a hand out and a ball of yarn would be passed criss-cross through all our hands. Every time someone took the yarn they would keep a corner, and they'd say the name of somebody they wanted to call into our circle. It was like a web of yarn and friends. You said your mother's name, and Dad said his parents'. I named all the women from *Speaking Our Peace*. I was on a big evangelical peace kick, just off the SAGE trip, riding the optimistic wave I had been preaching all year. You and I shared that optimism, Naomi was a total cynic and Dad was Mr. Reality. But they still got into the ritual.

I was amazed that Michael and Naomi let down their guards and participated so wholeheartedly. Afterwards, Michael gave me a delicate cross-section slice of amethyst-coloured quartz. I couldn't believe it — my tough-minded spouse, indulging a belief in the healing power of crystals. Whether it was my belief or his he was indulging, I don't know. On one of my purple-flowered notecards, he wrote:

What a celebration! It is a celebration, wonder at survival and wonder at how good I feel about you, us, the kids in the face of such a terrible event. I know you, we will get

through it — better than ever. Love is not strong enough
to explain what I feel. It is that and awe and warmth.
You are my friend.

That night I was giddy and wild and happy to be alive.
Twenty multicoloured balloons bobbed over my bed. Bernard
and his partner Isabel joined us and I held court in my hospital bed, with a rubber feeding tube dangling from my nostril,
and an IV tube hanging from my wrist, showing off my chin-
ups on the trapeze device that Michael had found. He said I
looked like a buccaneer with my eye patch.

I remember the food! Baguettes and brie from a good French
pâtisserie, caviar, dark bittersweet Belgian chocolate. And champagne! Naomi had organized it all, and was delightfully pleased
with her expertise. Unfortunately, eating was a purely voyeuris-
tic activity for me. Ensure served elegantly down the nose was
my only choice. But Isabel gave me a tiny sip of champagne
which I managed to swallow without choking too much. We
joked that it made me even more unbalanced.

After dinner, Michael projected slides onto the wall at the
foot of my bed. He'd been going through our old pictures for
days, late at night when he got home from the hospital. He
said he wanted me to be able to hold an image in my mind of
the active woman I had been, and all I had to live for. But at
first the slides just made me sad. I looked so young and athletic
and healthy.

CLICK: January 1967. Michael teaching me to snorkel in the
    Virgin Islands National Park.
CLICK: August 19, 1967. Our wedding portrait: me in a white
    dress, confident and innocently joyful. We were married in
    Hamden, Connecticut, by the rabbi who had supported

Michael's conscientious objector application. He was the only rabbi with whom Michael was comfortable, a good excuse for circumventing all the decisions and preparations of a traditional Jewish wedding at home in Philadelphia on five days' notice.

CLICK: The wedding party: Only a few intimates made it to Connecticut. Michael's parents, Annie and Philip, arrived breathless, direct from Expo '67 in Montreal. I worried (needlessly) that they weren't very pleased that Michael was marrying me, because I wasn't from an intellectual or even educated family. My parents were (very) small business people, while Annie was a retired elementary school teacher, and Philip was a screen animator, blacklisted from Hollywood for his left-wing politics. In the slide they look healthy and relaxed.

Next to Annie and Philip, my own parents look miserable. My father, recently recovered from yet another heart attack, is white and drawn, a ghost of the fat and gregarious Nat of my childhood. He has endured a four-hour car trip from Philadelphia because his baby daughter is suddenly marrying a man he hardly knows.

Next to my father is my brother-in-law Bill Frankl. He is not smiling. A physician himself, he is worried that I'm throwing my life away because Michael will never be able to practise medicine as a draft-dodger. Next to him, my sister Razelle, nine years older than I, looks equally solemn. Their two boys, my nephews Victor and Brian, stand uncomfortably hot in their suits. Michael's younger brother Henry is not in the picture — he's taking it.

CLICK: September 1967. Michael at Expo, with a view of Montreal behind him. We crossed the border and were welcomed to our new city in the middle of the night as draft-dodgers.

We felt like part of the celebration of Canada's 100th birthday.

CLICK: May 1968. My parents hugging baby Seth. My father died on Seth's first birthday.

CLICK: July 1971. Naomi naked in the wading pool with Seth as Underpants Man pouring water on her.

CLICK: Winter 1974. Naomi and I riding camels on a shell beach in Israel; (CLICK) swimming in the Red Sea; (CLICK) Michael drinking Maccabi beer in a field of poppies near the Lebanese border, the hulking silhouettes of tanks behind him; (CLICK) Seth talking to an Israeli soldier at a machine-gun emplacement.

CLICK: August 1977. Michael and I barging on the Canal du Midi in the south of France; (CLICK) me working locks with lock keeper.

CLICK: 1981. Naomi with her new puppy, Lucy, in her lap.

CLICK: 1982. The New York première of *Not a Love Story*.

CLICK: 1987. Desiree, Alison, Max, Seth and I goofing around at the "Mile Zero" marker bench in Victoria, B.C.

By the end, the slides had worked. I had everything to live for. I felt blessed.

INTERLUDE: WAKE UP

Journal: August 19, 1994
Our twenty-seventh wedding anniversary.

I came outside to do some writing and am now too steamed to concentrate. Vancouver is physically well-ramped, but that doesn't mean all the people are equally sensitive! *En route* to my "office," I encountered a truck parked across the curb-cut by my building, which is my only access to the sea wall. Granted it is not a designated access ramp, but there is no other route I can use. So I reached into my scooter pack for the polite version of my windshield sticker: "You are blocking my access. WAKE UP!" with the universal wheelchair graphic. (The less nice versions range from a pig driving a car that says "OINK OINK" to "Wake up ASSHOLE!" — Michael's style with computer graphics is rather less lady-like than mine.)

Anyway, a nice letter carrier asked if he could do anything to help. Then along came the director of the management company for our condo. He pointed out that there was no reason for the truck driver to know it was an access route. I asked why our condo council hadn't put up a sign as I'd requested, since the curb-cut is frequently blocked, often by residents themselves or service people or moving trucks. He said he had been instructed to write a letter (the meeting was almost four weeks ago) informing me that the council doesn't want a sign. "It would ruin the aesthetic of the front walk. Besides it's not really a wheelchair ramp."

"What is it then?" I asked.

"It's for garbage disposal."

"I can see that. It is too steep to be a regulation wheel-chair ramp. But the fact is, it's all we have, and there are now three people in our building who use wheelchairs on it, so I'd say that makes it a wheelchair ramp." (I hadn't eaten lunch yet; hunger gives me an edge.)

"Well, the council doesn't want to put up signs," he repeated.

"Tell me what their reasoning is, since I haven't received the letter yet."

"Well, it probably has something to do with liability."

He wanted to continue muttering but I stopped him because I was going to explode. How many times have I heard about "liability"? Last month the council decreed I couldn't park my scooter Gladys outside our unit, because it might be a fire hazard (blocking no doors in the six-and-a-half-foot wide hallway) and they would be liable. I can hear myself, my voice becoming hard and shrill. Maybe this is why some people with disabilities become bitter. But being a "good crip" — forever polite and understanding and accommodating — is making me sick.

How do you spell AUGGHH!

I sat on my park bench for hours, trying without success to let go of my anger and settle into writing, and remembering that other anniversary night in the hospital. When I finally gave up and came back home, I asked Michael if we had made love that night after everyone left, our usual anniversary ritual to ensure a sexy year. He replied with an atypical clarity of mem-ory that we didn't. "How come?" I asked. "By the end of the night you were not feeling so great," he said.

STROKE TWO

≈

August 20

Michael: It was a very blurry time for me. All I know is that the day after our anniversary you were decidedly less well. You were having trouble with swallowing, transferring, sitting up, bearing your weight. You couldn't use your walker to get to the bathroom. You took a few steps and then collapsed. We joked that it was the champagne...but I was starting to get worried. No one else was particularly concerned though. These things happen, the doctors said, conditions fluctuate, it's natural she feels a little tired after yesterday.

I don't really remember that day. August 20; another hospital day, my fifteenth. Exercises. Peri-care. Maybe I felt sluggish. I remember telling Michael I was feeling worse. But how do you know whether it's serious, or a temporary setback? A bad hair day?

In the afternoon they sent an orderly with a rickety wheelchair to take me to the gym as Iolanda had promised. I got to wear shorts and a T-shirt instead of my nightgown. The gym was windowless and dark. There were only a few other people in there, lost in their separate struggles, their voices echoing off the concrete walls. I had looked forward to it but the excruciating work made real to me how weak I had become. I was on a mat on the floor, first lying down, then sitting. Arms out. Arms back. It was like being on a little raft on the ocean of the gym floor, hopelessly rowing toward some ever-distant land, with Iolanda, my own personal cheerleader, on board.

When I went back to my room I fell into bed and stayed there for the rest of the day. The medical notes say I "complained" of cramps and nausea. I remember I played Bach's *Suites for Unaccompanied Cello* over and over.

AUGUST 21

Pt doing poorly at physiotherapy —
difficulty finding legs in space.
No headache — no new ocular problems.
R ptosis, R facial weakness, tongue to R.
Speech dysfunction unchanged.

I woke weak after restless sleep. Michael came in early and stayed all day. I did my exercises up in the chair for an exhausting forty-five minutes: raise left knee, up, hold, relax, and again. Raise right knee, up, hold, relax, and again. Yes Iolanda, I'm trying, it's hard. Suck, swallow, cough. Again. The walker — proud achievement of the week before — was impossible without support.

Terre Nash: The first time I was allowed to visit you was a few days after your anniversary. You still had balloons hanging from your bed. You were tired, your speech was quite slurred but you were cheerful. You just couldn't figure out what was going on with your legs. "Look," you were saying, "I can't stand up, it's the strangest thing. And my arm just floats off — see that — I'm not lifting it; it lifts itself."

I remember your doctor, Irene, coming in, and then a million other doctors. Everyone was flummoxed except you. You were in a really good mood. You were sort of calmly puzzled, lying in the bed trying to move your legs. And then your doctor asked me to leave the room.

The medical team must have decided to worry. I was sent for another CT scan which showed nothing they could interpret or theorize. No new bleeding. Nothing. The neurology resident signed out for the weekend. The attending neurologist was already gone, leaving frightening instructions for what to do in case of hydrocephalus or a further bleed. By that evening I was falling over whenever I tried to sit. Falling to the right, always to the right. Michael seemed to find that significant. Me, I was too tired to wonder, drifting in and out of dreams: *something about the border, trying to cross the border.*

AUGUST 22

01:30 pt slept @ short intervals talking incoherently in sleep
04:30 induced to urinate
07:00 hair shampoo — slept well afterwards
12:30 acupuncture treatment given
14:00 back to bed — pt very weak

I had been working hard and it had been successful till now — I had made progress. From the morning after our anniversary, the direction changed. There were still ups and downs, but I was losing ground — literally. I could no longer stand. I needed people's help to walk to the bathroom. Then I couldn't walk at all and they had to bring a commode next to my bed.

The medical notes use the words "pt discouraged" several times. I was only now recognizing that this was serious, that I wasn't necessarily going to win. I needed to cry; I knew it would be good for me. But I couldn't. When I wasn't "discouraged" I was "alert and smiling." How alert could I have been when I barely remember anything? Why would anyone be smiling? Was this all conditioned "good girl" behaviour? To be cheerful and uncomplaining, to make those around me comfortable? Was I so delighted at receiving attention — any attention? Or was my mind somehow affected by the stroke too, in the same way my mother became more pleasant and funnier with Alzheimer's than she was before?

Physio was hell. Iolanda's cheerleader act was wearing thin as I struggled through the easiest of exercises. Don't give up. Don't give up. I couldn't handle sucking ice cubes. I could hardly swallow. I was racked by coughing spasms, bringing up disgusting, thick white phlegm. All day I coughed and choked till my throat was raw and my lungs aching. You can do it, Bonnie.

Naomi: The second stroke hit slowly, relentlessly. I remember saying to my Dad, "Dr. Afilalo said it would only get better. It can't get worse." I felt betrayed. I knew something was really wrong.

Terre Nash: Michael told me what was happening. He asked if people from work could go through me instead of calling him, and so I became your film board liaison. Everybody at the NFB would stop and ask about your condition, which was OK for me because I was obsessed with it anyway. People knew I was the one to ask. They saw us as inextricably linked, even before we made *Speaking Our Peace* together. We were the Studio D bad girls — with my film *If You Love this Planet* refused entry into the U.S., and your film *Not a Love Story* censored in Ontario.

I was always waiting for Michael to call with the next news, and the news kept changing — first they thought it was one thing and then they thought it was something else. The uncertainty was difficult. Michael would explain things to me in very clinical, medical terms, then I would explain it very clinically to other people. There was a kind of refuge in that cold language.

That night I skimmed the surface of sleep for hours. Every time I woke up, Michael was there holding my hand. Or maybe it was one time that lasted all night long, or a dream. *We were in a motel near the U.S. border. Michael, Bernard, Isabel and*

*me. The motel felt like nowhere, like a refugee camp, a pris-
oner-of-war camp, with thin gauzy curtains. We couldn't cross
the border. There was this question of infection. We had to
pass the test, the blood test. They gave Bernard a needle. It was
part of the requirement. Or was the needle infected? Was I
infected? Is that how all this happened? We were behind the
curtains. We had to pass the test.*

$$\approx$$

AUGUST 23

24:30 unable to sleep
          neurological signs stable
          tendency to fall to R side
09:00 pt unable to stand @ all
          balance very unstable
          Mrs. Klein seems to be deteriorating . . .

Michael was still there when I woke up. He helped me do
my exercises. I couldn't stand. I couldn't sit. I couldn't stop
choking. Something was wrong. I couldn't pee, it was too
hard. Michael said I had to. He wouldn't leave me alone. The
nurse put a different catheter in and left it. It felt like a piece
of wire stuck up into my bladder. They sent me for another CT
scan. Michael went with me. He looked at the results. He tried
to find someone to argue with. But all the neurologists were
signed out. *I couldn't cross the border.*

Michael: The CT scan was too imprecise to define what was going on. The second one had picked up some kind of bleeding, but none of the others showed anything. We needed a more accurate diagnostic tool, like an MRI, but it was the weekend and no one was there to order one. Joe Carlton had told me to be the husband and let him be the doctor, but he was still on vacation, unaware of what was going on. The ward neurologist was off studying for her specialty exams. The Chief of Neurology was gone, the covering neurologist was gone, and you were signed out to another neurologist from another hospital, who never came and didn't even know anything about you except by telephone. I would have been delighted to drop back to the role of husband if someone had been there to play the role of doctor.

Over the weekend you lost your leg function completely. You were coughing and spitting up frothy sputum and could no longer suction yourself. Up until this time your thinking had been unaffected. Now your mental functioning began to deteriorate. I called the Chief of Internal Medicine to try to mobilize some care and diagnostic skills. He promised to organize consultations for Monday afternoon.

This was the worst time I can ever remember. I stayed at the hospital around the clock, all weekend, but I finally went home at midnight on Sunday. I was emotionally and physically exhausted. I couldn't talk to you. I didn't know whether you could hear me or not. You were slipping away and you were too sick to care. You were too sick to care about anything.

I thought you were going to die. There was nothing further that could be done, there was nobody that I could talk to, surgery was never even a consideration. We didn't have a diagnosis. What were we going to operate on? People don't operate on strokes. I just went home to bed.

The only doctor on call that night was one of my first-year, family-practice interns, Mark Essak, who was cross-covering for the neurology service.

Mark Essak: It was at the beginning of my internship. I had only done a month of family medicine and then I get a call in the middle of the night to come down and cover neurology because something was going wrong with you.

I was anxious because you were the wife of the chief of my own department. My first time covering for neuro and it's the boss's wife. Not good. When I came in to talk to you, your neck was totally stiff, you couldn't even turn it to the right. Your arms were all flexed up and spastic. It was like you were folding in on yourself. It looked like something I remembered from first-year neurology: decorticate posturing.

It seemed serious to me but I was no neurologist. Michael had left around midnight. No one else was around. You were asking me if things were getting worse. You said you couldn't move your left side, and you had been able to before. When you said that I went back to look at the chart again. No one had mentioned that. It seemed like a progression to me. The ward neurologist wasn't on call, so I called Michael.

Michael: Mark Essak called me at 2 or 3 o'clock in the morning. He told me what was happening. He told me what he was doing. He had nobody else to tell. He said he was monitoring your breathing and doing blood gases, and I thanked him. He asked me if I was going to come in, and I said no. I couldn't. I just couldn't get out of bed. Mark was literally alone in the night. But I was incapable of getting out of bed.

Mark Essak: I didn't realize this was the first time Michael had gone home in days. I didn't want to tell him that you were becoming decorticate. On one hand, he's a physician and I wanted his advice. But on the other, he's the husband of the patient. So I tried to be delicate, but also tell him the signs. Essentially he said "You're doing good. If anything gets worse, call the ward neurologist at home." I did your blood gases and then I called the ward neurologist just in case. She said I was doing fine. So I just kept on.

He kept asking me questions and pulling me back. He was a sweet scared young man and I tried to help. *There was a gas or a drug that I had to take. I needed the gas to breathe, but what I was breathing was poisoning me. There was a countdown, like the creeper at the beginning of a film: 10, 9, 8; and a voice-over saying if I breathed the gases from midnight to 8 a.m., I'd be able to stop and go to sleep. But what I had to breathe was something that was killing me. I remember saying, "They promised that it would end at 8 o'clock in the morning. But they didn't keep their promise. They lied."* And then Michael said, "It's OK. You're OK. It's just a nightmare."

AUGUST 24

24:00 Neuro signs deteriorated
        L arm decorticate, grip weak R moderate
        L leg weak, R no movement
        reflexes absent — responds to pain only
03:00 movement in both limbs absent
        MD notified
08:30 lumbar puncture done by Dr. Danys
        seen by Dr. Melmed, seen by Dr. Frank
11:30 portable chest X-ray done
14:00 seen by Dr. Libman

Michael: I slept for about four or five hours and then I went back in. Mark had taken care of it all. I'd had some sleep, and you hadn't died. If you had the will to not give up and die, then I would find the will to keep fighting too. I got on the phone and rounded up a few more specialists for the diagnostic conference the Chief of Internal Medicine had promised me. That was how I stayed sane — by banging on the system.

Naomi: That morning you were a lot worse than the day before, which was pretty bad. I read you a poem I had just written.

Dear Mommy,
        I envision your being.
        A clear light,

It embraces
And warms me

The clarity of your light
Has shone through to my being
As a never-ending source
Of soothing strength

The generosity of your love
Is the sharing of your light,
Softly glowing between
Mother and daughter

Your love
And your light
Cradle my fright
As they sparkle through
    your pained exterior

I give to you now
what you have given to me,
Cling to it with me
As it gives strength to us both.

But you were too sick to really listen. You were having
trouble breathing. Each breath was loud and gasping. I
didn't get much of a response.

I think I sort of deluded myself. I felt that since I had
poured so much emotion into the poem, you would respond, and it would make you stronger or something.
But if someone's really sick, you have to realize when
you're doing something for them, and when it's really for
yourself.

I felt very deeply about that poem. I made people read it to me over and over. I felt a special bond with Naomi. Somehow she seemed to sense how I was feeling more accurately than anyone else, and for that reason I was more honest with her than with Michael or Seth, whom I protected. I worried about laying all that on Naomi, at seventeen, but her poem said she wanted me to tell her.

All afternoon, doctors and nurses and people I loved came and went and I was too tired to pay attention. I think Naomi was stroking my forehead. I think Michael was trying to explain something to me. It was real while it was happening and then it just drifted away. I was somewhere else, a place like a film loop that just keeps playing around and around.

Naomi: I came back for this big diagnostic conference that looked pretty useless to me. I remember coming in and there were like ten doctors, and one of them thought you had a malignant tumour, one of them thought it was a regular stroke, one of them thought it was what it actually turned out to be: a stroke from a vascular malformation, and one of them said it was multiple sclerosis.

For the next few days there were teams of doctors that would walk around in packs. The best of the best from all over the city. It was obvious that nobody knew what was going on. Each time that I went to the hospital, you were worse. Barely any movement. Then barely any speech. It was spiralling out of control. I remember asking Dad, what's going to happen, is she going to die? And he said, I don't know.

Michael: They didn't have a diagnosis for days. On Monday the 24th, the Chief of Neurology returned. He gave a dismal assessment, feeling that it was a very aggressive cancer that was extending and infiltrating up and down the brain stem, knocking out the tracks and cranial nerve centres. He said you were probably going to die. And I argued with that. Maybe it was denial, but I was trying to figure out how he knew that. He said, "That's the way it's behaving." Which was possible. But I didn't believe it.

Another diagnostic possibility suggested was a very aggressive form of multiple sclerosis. So they called in an MS specialist, and he diagnosed fulminant MS. He saw the disease that he knows. He recommended plasmaphoresis, as well as low dose Cytoxan. Both of these treatments are experimental. Nevertheless, without a clear diagnosis, they were started, as were high dose steroids.

Then they called in the vascular specialist. He saw severe vasculitis. It was a joke. I kept saying, "Wait a second. None of these things fit the pattern."

The only hard fact was that hemorrhage in the medulla which showed up on that early CT scan. It didn't make sense to say that there's vasculitis plus the hemorrhage, or that there's multiple sclerosis plus the hemorrhage. I kept saying, "There's one disease going on here. This is a healthy person who has had a single catastrophic event that is worsening. Why are we looking for several diagnoses?"

Cheryl Levitt: I was the Deputy Director of Herzl at the time, Michael's second-in-command. As you started to deteriorate, Michael phoned me at home and cried a couple of times. One morning I was seeing patients and he asked me to come to his office, so I came in and held him while he cried. Usually he was like the rabbi of Herzl, who everyone else came to with their problems. Now he was crying in his office.

And then he'd pull himself together and turn the hospital inside out for you. He was relentless. It's very much his way of handling things. Whenever I get fifty messages from Michael on my desk about things that need to be done right away, I know that he's out there trying to keep something together. He drives some people crazy. But in the end, he gets things done.

AUGUST 25

24:00 heartrate elevated to 128–188
08:00 c/o difficulty breathing — drowsy
11:00 plasmaphoresis 2.5 L exchange
        incontinent
14:30 transferred to NICU
16:00 intubation w/ naso-tracheal tube

I was too sick for my own room. Everything was moving backwards. I was in neuro intensive care again. That day I shamelessly shit my bed. There was no way I could get the bedpan by myself. Maybe I called for help and they didn't get there in time. Maybe I didn't even think to call for help. I had a cheery visit with the orderly as he cleaned me up. Embarrassment was a distant concept. Breathing was more immediate.

That day I got Cytoxan for my alleged multiple sclerosis; plasmaphoresis where they exchanged my old blood plasma for new and better blood plasma; and intubation: a naso-tracheal tube, stuck up my nose, down my windpipe and through my vocal cords, which meant I couldn't talk any more. It's just a temporary measure, they said. Don't worry. The other end of the tube was attached to a respirator. To breathe for me.

The intubation was a precaution — necessary for the long awaited, long delayed Magnetic Resonance Imaging across town at the Montreal Neurological Institute. All I remember is a hubbub with lots of initials — MRI, MNI — an alphabet soup of confusion. I know Michael was pleased that at last I was having whatever the MRI was.

Michael: MRI transforms electromagnetic signals into detailed pictures of the inside of the body. There were only two machines in all of Montreal, one French and one English, both with long waiting lists, so they don't push it except when it's seen as essential. But after everybody came back from their weekends, they finally agreed that it had to be done.

We went to the Montreal Neurological Institute by ambulance. I had to fight to be able to ride there with you. You were a little disoriented and I didn't want you to have to make the trip without someone you knew. I asked the ambulance attendant what method he would use to clear your trach, since without frequent suctioning you could drown in your own secretions. He told me he had an electric vacuum suction device. "What happens if it fails?" I asked. "It never fails," he said. Suspicious bastard that I am, and a firm believer in the many versions of Murphy's Law, I asked to delay slightly while I ran up to the maternity suite to obtain a few De Lee oral suction traps (simple devices powered by someone sucking on one end). And of course halfway to the Neurological Institute the suction machine did fail, and I used the De Lees till we got there.

The MRI facility was in the third basement, and no one knew where it was. We kept wandering down false passages and around the building. You were lying on a wheeled stretcher and I was pushing you. I can remember feeling alone yet again.

My memory is that all this took place in the middle of the night, but I doubt if it did. I had no sense of time or place. Joe had told me that the MRI was like a tunnel. In my mind, I saw it as the tunnel between the buildings of the Royal Victoria Hospital, where Seth and Naomi were born.

I was outside, then I was inside. I was waiting in a dark tunnel between two big Victorian greystones. It was like a bridge, or maybe it was a narrow corridor. Michael was there, then he wasn't there. My voice echoed after him, down the tunnel. But it couldn't have been my voice. I didn't have a voice.

ICU-type patient:
comatose, needs frequent suction.
Pt very spastic — took 1/2 hour to set up.

Gilles Leroux: The MRI machine is like a tube, ten feet long. Inside is the table of the magnet where you're lying during the examination. We transfer you onto a special stretcher, because in that magnetic environment a metal stretcher cannot go in. Even a credit card should not go in because it will be erased.

It was a première for us. A patient on a respirator we normally don't do, because there's too much metal and it's risky with the high magnetic field involved.

You had the breathing tube in your throat which was OK, it's just plastic, but instead of a metal respirator in there with you, we gave you oxygen from a rubber anesthetic bag.

At the beginning, Michael was a bit, well, he was a bit pushy. The atmosphere was quite tense. Maybe because we were groping, we were a bit nervous and he was nervous too.

Michael: I *was* pushy. I wasn't yelling but they could certainly tell how anxious I was. There were a million problems. They don't do people on respirators. They don't do people in comas. You weren't in a coma, but you weren't in control; you had muscle jerks and spasms. They need you to lie very still for a long time in the MRI or they can't get a clear image. They kept trying, but finally the chief technician said, "This is hopeless. We can't do this study. She's moving all over the place."

I basically begged him. I said, "We don't have a diagnosis and my wife is going to die without it, and I want to know what's going on." And he rose to the occasion. He crawled into the tube with you and held your head still.

Gilles Leroux: Your head was right in the middle of the magnet, your feet were just sticking out at the end of the tube. There was about five feet of space at the top, so I had to climb there to hold your head during the examination. Michael was down at your feet handling the respiration bag. The tunnel is so small that I was in a fetal position. We were there for about forty-five minutes to an hour. Your husband said "Tell her what you're doing. She can't communicate with you, but she understands everything." So I held your head still and talked to you.

Someone was talking about credit cards. There were no credit cards allowed in the tunnel. If somebody had a credit card they could get sucked up and turned inside out by the magnetic field. We were in the tunnel, waiting. Why? Waiting for what? Maybe for the ambulance. It was hot, suffocating. I was lying there and the man would tell me the banging was coming, and the banging would come, jolting through my body, filling the tunnel with its hugeness: BANG, BANG. It sounded like a broken boiler, a steel foundry. Maybe it was defective. A high-tech machine wouldn't be so loud and primitive. It was tearing the room apart.

Gilles Leroux: There was a little fan to push air down the tube, but I was filling the whole tunnel, so the air couldn't flow. It was quite warm. When I came out of there I was sweating, my back was sore, my legs all numb. But we were pretty satisfied with the result. Mind you, they were not the greatest pictures we ever produced, but they revealed the problem. To tell you the truth, I think we gave you good service.

Michael: The MRI technicians aren't supposed to tell you the results of the test. They don't interpret the film. Your neurologist is supposed to interpret it. But while I was waiting for the ambulance to come back, I put the films up on the viewing box. Magnetic resonance images are very clear. They aren't like x-rays, they're like sitting in the anatomy lab looking at a cut section of the brain. All of the structures are there, like in Gray's *Anatomy*.

And there it was, this enormous thing right in the medulla, filling more than half the brain stem. It was horrible.

I can remember distinctly having a whole series of different responses. First I thought, "It's just too big. It can't be that big." Then I wondered about cancer. But it didn't look malignant to me. Malignant tumours are chaotic, they have finger-like projections that go off in all directions. This mass was cystic in structure. So I was thinking, "It's a bad location but it's not malignant, whatever it is." And that lasted for about a half an hour while I waited for the ambulance to take us back. I kept looking at the film and after awhile I started thinking. "You know, it's discreet, it's encapsulated, somebody, somewhere, ought to be able to remove it if they could get to it and it's close to the surface, at least part of it, the upper part is close to the surface, under the cerebellum." And that held me for a while. It kept me from falling apart — the idea that some kind of a wizard somewhere could reach that goddamn thing.

Naomi: The night of the MRI was terrible. The house was filled with people who hadn't been to Montreal since my Bat Mitzvah. Old friends. Relatives. Sitting in the kitchen looking awful. I hated it. It felt like a hotel or sitting shiva. I thought you were going to die. I wrote you a letter in my diary:

"Dear Mommy, I am so very very scared. I don't know what to say and I don't know what to do. I love you deeply and totally and I hope and pray for you but I feel so very weak with fright. I wish so much that I had taken all the kisses and hugs that you offered to me throughout my life because now that I need to have them from you, you can't give them. Mommy, please live, you have to, you can't go now. I am still a little girl and I need you."

Seth: While Dad went for the MRI with you, Naomi and I were waiting for the results with Aunt Razelle and Uncle Bill and a bunch of other people. We'd been told that the worst scenario was that it could be a tumour. That would be extremely serious and you would probably die. And then we got the call from Dad that it was a tumour — some kind of mass that had bled. Everyone was shocked. Naomi started to cry. Then we all got in the car and drove to the hospital. I held Naomi's hand the whole way. It was probably the first time I had held her hand since we were toddlers. All these questions were going through my head, "What if she dies? What am I going to do? What's going to happen to Naomi? What's going to happen to Dad?" I wasn't crying, but I was scared. I was trying hard to be steady for Naomi, but in my mind I was panicking. It was only now that I realized this might be the end.

Naomi: When we got back home Dad was really dazed. He went up to his study and came downstairs with a fat medical textbook with a diagram of the brain stem. He showed us where the mass was and explained what the brain stem is. It was like some sick sort of school in our living room. I think that was the worst night. We all felt beaten.

MRI reveals a circumscribed, solitary, intra-axial, vascular, expansive lesion   typical of a cavernous angioma. The pt's neurological condition and the location of the lesion would make a direct, open operation extremely hazardous.

There was no more plasmaphoresis, no more steroids, no more Cytoxan. They finally had their diagnosis and there were no drugs to fix it. Stroke caused by a congenital malformation. I could hardly move my arms, and my legs were completely gone. I was long past dancing with Georgio. He said he was going to send me to the Arthur Murray Dance Academy. I remember laughing. Can you laugh with a tube through your vocal cords? I tried to laugh. Everyone else was leaking panic. I understood about the mass, in a twilight sort of way. Michael explained it over and over. He said it was like a pea in a pod. That image was all that stuck with me — a pea in a pod in my brain. He projected the MRI slide on the ceiling over my bed so I could understand. I couldn't believe how beautiful it was.

Naomi: A vascular tumour is a mass of malformed blood vessels that you're born with. It's not malignant but over the years it weakens and eventually bursts. And the bursting of blood vessels in the brain is one kind of stroke.

AUGUST 26

Michael: The next day, back at the JGH, they were look-ing at your MRI films and saying that it was inoperable, that there was no way to get in there surgically without knocking out critical functions. I told them, "Look, I'm not interested in your negative prognosis. Something has to be done, soon. Because the alternative is death. And that's unacceptable." So then someone suggested stereo-tactic x-ray therapy, which could shrink the lesion over the course of six months to a year or more, and thereby prevent future bleeds. And I'm listening to this, thinking, "You guys are out of your minds — it can bleed again, while it's getting stereotactic treatment!"

At the same time, I was questioning whether I had contributed to the new bleed by encouraging you to exer-cise with that trapeze over your bed. If they had done the MRI study initially, then we would have known what we were dealing with, and I certainly wouldn't have suggested that kind of exercise. So I was angry at myself and I was angry at the system too, for not having made the diagno-sis. The first, milder stroke had been a warning sign which was not heeded. Of course, the reality was that the mal-formation was degenerating anyhow, and if it hadn't bled then, it would have bled another time.

I don't know exactly when the family started to arrive: my sister Razelle and her husband Bill, Annie and Philip, Michael's brother Henry with his new partner Lyn Charlsen, and my college roommate, Norma Zack; everyone except my mother who was lost in Alzheimer dreams, six blocks away. They say I smiled, made small hand gestures and moved my lips in silent replies to their questions. Razelle was wearing a beautiful sweater. I remember the sweater more than I remember going off later for a tracheostomy to replace the temporary naso-tracheal tube. There was a corny doctor with a moustache who said, "I call this the diamond-necklace operation. Michael will have to buy you a big diamond necklace to hide the scar."

The patient was prepped and draped in the usual manner, and given anesthetic through her naso-tracheal tube. Through a horizontal incision a routine tracheostomy was carried out. A #8 Shiley tube was easily inserted into the trachea between the third and fourth rings. The patient tolerated this well. The tracheostomy tube was sewn into place and tied.

When I woke up they had cut a hole in the front of my neck and inserted a trach tube through my vocal chords. Which meant I still couldn't talk. Don't worry, they said. *The sweater was heavy wool, hand-knit in Bolivia, with bold, multicoloured, horizontal stripes. I couldn't tell her how much I liked it.* (Later on Razelle gave it to me.)

Annie Klein: I remember how happy we felt on the day of your anniversary, when Michael called to say how much better you were. And then, I remember very vividly the next call. Michael said "You'd better come to Montreal. I'm falling apart."

I cried and cried. I cried all the way up to Canada, I think. But once I was able to cry like that, then I was able to deal with it.

When we saw you in the hospital, you were surrounded by medical support systems and you looked so weak. You were drifting in and out of consciousness. Your legs were rigid, your arms curled inward. You could only move your fingers. But your eyes welcomed us.

Yvonne Steinert: I was working as a psychologist at Herzl and you and I had been good friends for years, so I was in and out of your room. I remember I met Michael's parents in the hall. Here everyone was, in a state of shock and profound sadness, but we couldn't just sit there and cry all day. So we ended up chatting about your parents-in-law's travels, and how their son Henry had run out of oil on the way to Montreal and totalled their car. I heard all about Henry's previous life-experience with cars and trucks.

Henry Klein: When we finally got to Montreal, Michael grabbed me and immediately took me off to the hospital. He was in a dead panic. I think it was partly because he was afraid that you were not going to survive and he wanted me to see you, and partly because he wanted everybody who was a piece of your life to be there so that you had all of your life to cling to. It was the first time I ever felt that Michael needed me.

Michael: I was losing it. I kept thinking, "There's no choice but to operate on it. She's bled twice. If she bleeds a third time she'll die." Sitting around waiting for the next bleed to kill you was unacceptable.

INTERLUDE: STEPHEN HAWKING

Journal: June 30, 1993
Confusing feelings.

I can pass. I look like everyone else except I'm on top of my sporty paisley scooter, Gladys. I look perfectly "normal." I don't drool, twitch or jerk, though I used to. I thought I'd finally learned to accept being disabled. But "acceptance" is not a one-time event, it's an ongoing process.

I met Stephen Hawking yesterday and I was scared to death. Not because he's a brilliant physicist and I could hardly understand his book, *A Brief History Of Time*, but because he's so severely disabled.

Hawking triggers my fear of being out of control, helpless and dependent. You'd think I'd be better at this after six years. But he reawakens the horrific memories I hold just under the surface of my skin, of when I was totally paralyzed and could do nothing but blink my eyes.

I can't imagine life without movement again. Each step was so hard to get back, I celebrated every one. I find such joy today in sailing, swimming, dancing, making love. So I understand why I was scared of Stephen Hawking. But I also felt compelled to meet him when he came to Vancouver because I wanted to learn what he has to say about disability. Thirty years ago he was diagnosed with Amyotrophic Lateral Sclerosis — ALS — and was given three years to live. He can't speak, move or feed himself. He needs round-the-clock personal assistance. He has just enough movement in his fingers

to steer his electric wheelchair, and to operate a special
computer attached to a voice simulator.

This unlikely man has become a hero in our culture, both
in spite and because of his disability. What a strange twist on
the notion of hero. Typically, heroes are large and strong,
perfectly proportioned. Hawking's body is fragile and with-
ered. There's irony in his name: he's not a hawk, he's a
wounded bird.

In the afternoon before his public lecture, Hawking spoke
to a group of young science students with disabilities. There
was a small press reception afterwards, where Hawking was
to answer questions from the media. I was there for my CBC
radio series, "Bonnie and Gladys," the only visibly disabled
journalist in the room.

Hawking asked his nurse for tea. She poured it into his
open mouth like a mother bird feeding her chick. More than
half of it streamed down a large plastic bib. It was hard for
me to watch. It made me recall when I couldn't swallow and
Michael fed me. But I was moved by Hawking's lack of
embarrassment at the mess he was making. He kept talking
as if nothing unusual were going on, and enjoyed being the
centre of attention.

He spoke by using his slight finger movement to select a
word from a dictionary on the top half of his computer
screen. The bottom half showed the sentence he was forming.
He clicked the completed message to an electronic voice
simulator that speaks without human inflection, and —
Hawking joked — with an American accent. A whole new
etiquette has to be invented around this laborious method of
communication: he told us to talk among ourselves until he
had prepared his answer.

"I am often asked, how do you feel about being disabled with ALS. The answer is — I try to lead a life that is as normal as possible and not think about my condition and the things it prevents me from doing, which are not that many."

When asked if he follows neurological research about ALS, he said, "I tend to avoid following it too closely because I don't want to be disappointed. I would like to hear when they have a treatment, but I will concentrate on other things until then."

That is what I have learned to do, too — with lots of help — to stop looking for a cure and get on with living. But it's easier for me — I don't have a degenerative disease like Stephen Hawking, or like Sue Rodriguez, another person with ALS, who took her demand for physician-assisted suicide all the way to the Supreme Court of Canada. Denied permission, she received it anyway. I was glad when someone else asked the inevitable question about assisted suicide.

"I will answer," the robotic voice said. "People should have the right to die if they want to. It is one of the few rights the severely ill have left. But I cannot imagine I would ever use that right myself. That would be giving in and I don't think one should do that."

Hawking became severely depressed after he was diagnosed — suicidal. When he met the woman he later married, he says he then had something to live for. That "something" doesn't have to be a lover or family, though it often is, and was for me. On the few occasions when I had suicidal thoughts, I dismissed them because of Michael and the children, our friends and family, all of whom were pulling for me. The few people I have met who gave up, either literally or spiritually, perceived themselves to be alone in the world.

Interesting that it was love and not science that Hawking chose to live for.

The issue is self-determination. No one can predict how they would respond in a situation of grave illness, and so we can't judge whether someone else's life is worth living. Assisted suicide is sometimes confused with euthanasia, when someone else — often a parent or child — determines that another person should die. However well-meaning, that decision is often based on ignorance and lack of adequate societal support to care for the person and assist the caregivers.

Even self-determination is not always simple. It's not easy to distinguish between an intense but passing anguish, a conditioned fear of disability, and a considered life decision. If anyone had asked me before my strokes if I could survive so severe an illness and the resulting disability, I would surely have said no, I would prefer to die — a "choice" which now seems almost laughable.

Few would ask if Steven Hawking's life is worth living. Apart from his scientific achievements, he is more full of life than many of us: he knows how to have a good time. I saw him playing poker with Data on "Star Trek." He hasn't lost the edge of excitement about living which comes with closeness to death. Hawking contradicts my great fear of dependence. While not physically independent, he is in control of how he lives.

We folks with disabilities sometimes cynically call a person like Hawking a "supercrip." Most of our images of disability come from myth and media and are stereotyped and extreme: pitiful victim at one end, supercrip at the other. We need many more models to choose from. Most people whose disabilities are as severe as Hawking's live in poverty; many are locked away in institutions — out of sight, out of mind —

leaving the rest of us with the ignorant assumption that a disabled life is not worth living, that it is, by definition, tragic.

The metaphor of flying is common in literature and poetry written by people who can't walk; to transcend gravity is the fantasy, the dream. It's what I feel when I sail or swim or drive Gladys in high gear. I love the idea of the spirit soaring, transcending the limitations of the body. Hawking does just that; his passion for life refuses to surrender to his body's paralysis.

The image of Hawking and his irrepressible grin stays with me. I wouldn't have chosen to have a stroke and live the rest of my life as I am now, but it's what I've been dealt and I'm pleased with myself for making the best of it. While I don't want to idealize bad luck, we are more than our bodies, and there's more than one way to fly.

AUGUST 27

Neurostatus: Pt trying to communicate by moving lips showing
what she wants with R hand.
09:50 Mrs. Klein was provided with a magnetic letter board
    to enable her to communicate.
15:00 Pt seems to be complaining of pain/trach site.
18:00 TF 1 can Ensure tolerated.

Michael: The MRI images moved on up the line to the Chief of Neurosurgery. He was the first person to hold out some hope. He said it might be operable, but not by him. He said we needed somebody who had experience in this particular surgery. And very few people have any experience, because usually patients die a respiratory death before they ever get to hospital. If the patient does last long enough to get into the operating room, they can die from the surgery. It's a really bad place to cut: low on the brain stem. In the brain itself, there's room to move, relatively speaking. But in the brain stem all the structures are tightly packed together. The tracks for sensation and movement, for blood pressure, heart beat, breathing and sleep cycles are interlacing, interconnecting and crossing over. So we had to find the right surgeon. Soon.

Seth: Naomi and I weren't allowed into the intensive care unit. We could only get in when Dad was there; he could get around the rules.

You couldn't talk and a lot of the time you were sort of asleep. So when I was there I would just sit by your bed and listen to the respirator. The respirator was weird because it didn't have a regular in-out breathing pattern. It had a few short sounds and then a long sound, then every once in a while there'd be a really long pause. And right towards the end of the pause, I'd panic that it had stopped. I didn't trust the machines, but Dad was really comfortable with them. He was always adjusting the respirator. I didn't know whether he knew what he was doing or not. I sort of wished that he'd leave it for the nurse to do.

I didn't know I was paralyzed. I remember being surprised every time Michael told me I couldn't walk. It was shocking to hear the word quadriplegic — that was a word about other people surely, not me. When I heard things like this, I thought of them as temporary. They would go away as quickly as they'd come. It's as if the paralysis did not penetrate my inner being. I was blissfully stupid.

Michael: You seemed to understand when I talked to you. At a certain point you were able to do things like thumbs up, thumbs down, for yes and no. Or you would use the letter board to spell out words. You couldn't do more than the first few letters but I could usually guess the word from that. When you lost that ability, you would communicate by blinking your eyes.

Adrianne Sklar: I was the contact person for the synagogue. I arranged for people to take turns visiting you, so you wouldn't be overwhelmed. Michael was there all the time but he also wanted us to be there, to remind you of the things you loved in life. You were lying in a fetal position. All you could do was blink. It was terrifying that you were alert and could understand everything, but I had to act as if I wasn't terrified and try to speak semi-normally.

Yvonne Steinert: I would come down from Herzl and sit with you sometimes. I wasn't sure whether you even knew that I was there. You weren't responding. I remember drawing parallels in my head between you and my infant daughter. Here was this baby, who couldn't communicate what she was crying about. And there you were. I had to try my best to figure out what you were thinking.

Henry Klein: Sometimes it was just obvious, like you would be choking, and pointing to the letter board or the cardboard word chart for the suction thing. Or you made a gesture towards your mouth and it almost always indicated that your mouth was dry and we should give you ice chips. One time Michael got carried away and gave you a popsicle, and it came gurgling out of your trach tube. We had to clean you up and put the suction tube down to kind of vacuum out your lungs. But it was worth it for the expression on your face when you gummed on that popsicle.

You didn't have time for bullshit. Things were basic: scratch my ass, give me a massage, give me some ice, get this asshole out of my space. You didn't have time for any of the niceties. It was very direct and primitive and healthy.

Annie Klein: The phone bill must have been tremendous, because Michael was absolutely frantic. He was calling everybody under the sun, all his old medical school friends and anyone he knew who might know a surgeon who could help you. I was being the secretary — I had this book that Michael gave me and I took messages. The phone did not stop ringing.

Lyn Charlsen: I cooked, Annie cooked. Henry accused us of doing it as a diversionary tactic which was true. It was a strange way to meet my new in-laws for the first time. I remember having dinner, with nine or ten people at the big table telling jokes and drinking . . . lots of doctor jokes, and everybody filled with a kind of nervous energy. It was comforting somehow.

Henry: It was whistling in the dark.

≈

AUGUST 28

08:30 pt alert, smiling, moving eyes

14:30 listening to music w/ husband

21:40 complained of discomfort from trach by non-verbal
       gesture from face

2 Empracet given via Dobhoff

*Which memories are mine and which are Michael's? Which have
I reconstructed from nightmares and medical notes? I steal memories, invent events to fill in those blank weeks.*

I couldn't eat. I couldn't stand, walk, run, dance, sit or speak:
"locked-in", they call it. I couldn't roll over in bed — an
orderly turned me every three hours to relieve the pressure of
lying in one position. I couldn't read. I couldn't turn my radio
on. I couldn't pee without a tube stuck up me. I shit in a pan
that an orderly put under me, or I shit my bed. I couldn't un-
bend my elbow. I couldn't call for help. I couldn't scratch my
nose. I couldn't laugh. I couldn't breathe.

Irene Kupferszmidt: You were confined. You were im-
prisoned in sickness. When you tried to speak there was
no sound. I was your doctor and your friend but I couldn't
follow your lips. Michael understood you — I don't
know how. He just looked at you and he knew what you
wanted to say. He would ask, "Is this it?" and you would
blink yes or no.

Your kids were with you all the time. They were so
good. And they were so angry: that anger of young people. They don't always talk about the things which are
the most important. They don't want to water it down
with words. Sometimes with one glance of their eye you
have much more than ten sentences. You were the motor
of that family. Suddenly they were fragments without the
motor.

I remember Naomi's expressions and the way she
looked at you. She couldn't take your suffering. Often she
was so angry she ran out of the room. She was angry at
God, at whatever, not about stupid things.

Naomi: I was scared. Every day when I came to see you,
I was afraid of what might have happened overnight.
Every time I got to the hallway outside the ICU, I would
wonder if you were still there.

People kept saying Daddy was too positive. But things
were good in a weird way. He and I were getting along
and we were getting so much support from friends and
family that we all felt very loved. Dad's friends from
Herzl would leave food in our milkbox — spaghetti
sauce, potato leek soup, chocolate cake — and there was
a parade of people at our house: grandparents, aunts,
uncles, cousins, friends.

Seth: I decided my role would be to keep the house stable,
playing host to this never-ending stream of people who
were at our house. I could always chauffeur folks around,
even though I couldn't do anything to make you well. It
was very comforting to feel that your friends were so committed to being there. That wasn't true with most of my

friends. They hadn't had experience with major life ill-nesses and tragedies, so it made them uncomfortable, and they steered clear.

Those days there were no days, just a slow torrent of minute after minute: blood pressure, catheter, rest, catheter, blood pressure, rest. Sleep was a shallow nap between one person checking my IV and another person checking my blood gases. Silence was the constantly competing rhythms of the life-support equipment. Night was when Michael went home to sleep.

Night was the nightmare loop. There were bottles of poison gas. You couldn't stop the system; that was part of the torture. It was like a deadly video game, like a closed system and you have no control. Push any button and the same message keeps on flashing: bad command. But I had the feeling that there was a way out. Maybe somebody brighter than me could break the loop; probably Margaret Atwood could figure it out. There was a countdown. I had no one to tell. The nurses didn't know how to listen to me. I can't remember how long it went on for.

What I remember is hearing my sister Razelle cry. She was sitting by my bed and there was the sound of sobbing. It tore me apart. It was like she was coming to my funeral, mourning me before I was dead. Her fear was scaring me. I clutched at Michael's sleeve and said "Please." He took her out of the room.

Seth: I didn't cry at first. Neither did you for a long time. Dad did. I remember once we were going home from the hospital and he asked me to drive, which was unusual. So we were driving along and he started to cry in the car. I'd seen him cry before, but this was different, an uncontrol-lable sort of cry. It was really disturbing. When he was with you, he would be really up. He had so much more energy than anyone else. He would be running around, checking things out. He knew exactly what to say to keep everyone going. And then when he would leave, when he would go home or to his office, then he'd suddenly sink. So I felt that what I had to worry about was him and the hard time he was having. And he would take care of all the rest.

When I finally cried, it was in Dad's office at the JGH. Aunt Razelle was with me and maybe Dad. Then Rabbi Aigen walked into the room. He didn't even say anything. I just walked into his arms and started to cry.

Neurosurgery note:
August 28: There is a favourable experience reported in neuro-surgical literature of evacuation of both brain-stem hematomas and neoplasm via a suboccipital approach. Will follow up.

AUGUST 29

06:00 suctioned several times for s/a of whitish yellowish
       secretions from trach
10:45 pt alert, smiling
       will put out tongue, squeeze w/ both hands
16:00 pt turned and positioned
19:00 pt turned and positioned
22:00 pt turned and positioned

One day. The next day. The next day. Turn and position. Trach care. I remember always being asked to squeeze people's hands. It was one of the things I could do. Grip my hand, they'd say; squeeze my thumb, wiggle your toe. They'd stick pins in me and ask me if it hurt. It didn't.

They swabbed my tongue with glycerin. It was too soft, soft on soft, how could it remove anything? I don't remember the taste. They put Vaseline on my lips — thick, gunky, greasy, petroleum taste. Where was my apricot lip balm? Henry brushed my teeth. He was thorough and gentle; it was much better than the glycerin swabs. The nurse was always cleaning the trach tube. It took hours. Or maybe it took five minutes. I would want her to be turning me, and she'd be cleaning the trach. *There was something about a smell. A concentration camp smell. There was a man. He was bald and old. I said, "You're a Nazi torturer" and he said, "Yes. You got it." There was no subterfuge.*

Suzi Scott: Your trach was infected with a bacteria called pseudomonas. It has a very distinctive powerful smell. All nurses know that smell. Your trach had to be cleaned once or twice every shift. It took a long time. Pseudomonas is very contagious, very easily spread from one patient to another.

Annie and Phil read to me from the book I had been reading in Vermont. Before the hospital. Maybe it was to connect me with my old self. Everyone was worried about my old self. The book was boring, even the first time around. But it helped me sleep. When they reached the part where I had left off, I tried to tell them with the letter board. When they finally figured it out, they were very excited. It proved I was listening. It proved I could understand. It proved my old self was still there inside.

Michael didn't require proof. Every day he would sit by my bed and explain the deeper complexities of my medical condition, while I smiled and choked and the other doctors looked away, embarrassed. I remember when he started talking about the possibility of surgery. He kept talking about London, about a guy in London.

Michael: The neurosurgeons were consulting and searching the literature for some sign of success with a low brain-stem lesion. We were all searching. Your friend Norma was close friends with a neurologist at Tufts, who had a special interest in stroke. And I had a friend from Stanford, who was now a neurology professor. So we said, "OK, let's send them the MRI films. Let's send the films to every neurologist we know." We sent them by Federal Express, to UCLA, Berkeley, New York, Boston. And all these neurologists called us back. And they all said "London, Ontario."

A neurosurgeon in London, Ontario had performed successful, low brain-stem surgery, just a little higher up than your lesion. Nobody had ever done surgery that low, but this guy Peerless in London had come close.

INTERLUDE: YELLOW POINT

Journal: August 29, 1994
Whenever I write these August dates, I can't help but try to
remember where I was on that day in 1987. I had a few tired
and lifeless hours this week when I couldn't get out of bed,
as if my body were reliving those pre-surgery days that I am
now writing about.

I'm not in my "office" today, but by the sea at Yellow
Point on Vancouver Island, where Michael and I came overnight. Michael is finally reading the first draft of our first
chapter, and I'm sitting beside him, fretting and watching
the waves.

I worry that this story will come across as another
"Triumph over Tragedy," like those movies-of-the-week
loathed by many people with disabilities. The flip side of pity
is putting us on a pedestal, praising us like heroes for our
"courage" in overcoming disability. But disability is not a
tragedy and we have simply done what had to be done, step
by step. In the T.o.T. genre, some brave person manages to
win their individual place in the world, while the obstacles
and prejudices which face most of us are essentially unchal-
lenged. How can I write a book which avoids this trap —
and every other possible pitfall too?

Michael sighs, stretches, reads on. I read his slightest
expression. I want him to feel good about the book. It is,
after all, his story too.

AUGUST 30

15:10 pt suctioned around 15 times today for s/a
       secretions colour white to yellow
       rubber on trach changed
17:35 respiration 26–28/min.
       pt coughing constantly — Intern called
21:45 turned and positioned
       family visited

Dorothy Hénaut: On August 30, 1987, my journal says: "I saw Bonnie in the ICU today with Michael. She looked beautiful but a little bit lost. Her thoughts have lost their route to her tongue. She was bright and smiling and then frustrated. My orange flowers were up on the wall. I felt so helpless.

I did a ritual that day, walking all around the outside of the hospital, planting symbolic guardians at the four corners and saying "Stay with her, protect her, no matter where she goes."

Naomi: Dorothy drove me crazy saying, "Everything's going to be all right. We did a ceremony and stuck our toes into Lake Ontario."

Some kinds of faith are helpful, and some are unbelievably frustrating. Like some people cannot deal with the reality of just how bad it is. They say, I know it will be OK, don't worry, everything will be fine, when in fact no one knows.

Michael: It wasn't reassuring, it was ignorant. At a certain point, I had absolutely no idea if you were going to be able to do anything again. I was terrified. And then somebody would tell me not to worry.

Dorothy Hénaut: Part of me was absolutely realistic, but I couldn't stay with that part because I wanted to put my energy into the healing. I was keeping a vision of what was possible. I figured everybody else was being realistic as shit and the vacuum that needed to be filled was the positive possibility.

Naomi: I remember there was one thing that I did. I was sitting next to your bed in the ICU. You were having trouble breathing, and I wasn't getting much response from you. I was looking at all the cards up on the wall — a wallpaper of get-well wishes. I was holding your hand and trying to concentrate my love and all the love that had gone into those cards, and trying to sort of channel it into your brain so that you could heal. I was concentrating very hard on it. But it didn't work. You didn't get any better.

Naomi and Michael's needs weren't always the same as mine. It was important to me that certain people never doubted. Even if it was off the wall, they had faith. There's a difference between that kind of faith and not being able to face your fears.

On one level, people were praying for themselves. It was because they felt helpless that they needed to perform rituals or say prayers in church or synagogue. It gave them something to do, just like twiddling the respirator gave Michael something to do.

But it also helped me. I soaked in the energy from people's dreams and rituals. I experienced this energy in the same way I experienced the medical care. It was another modality — and I needed them all. I don't believe any less in the things you can't see. Why deprive ourselves of miracles? Even if all it did was make me feel positive and hopeful about my chances for recovery, it was important. You need to hear that there is hope.

Michael: As a completely non-religious person, I can't dismiss things like prayer melting tumours. I've seen it... people whom I know are going to die come back a year later alive and well. It happens, and I just have to accept it — not in religious terms, but as sort of a humbling experience that basically says we don't understand everything. I never say to a patient that there's no hope. Because it doesn't help and it also isn't true.

AUGUST 31

Neurosurgery: Will request opinion of Dr. Peerless re: pros and cons of surgical decompression in highly experienced hands.

Seth: That was the worst time, those last few days. We thought you might die. Dad made a slide of your malformation and we all worked at visualizing the different blood cells eating it away and clearing up the clots.

It was hard to keep talking to you with no response. Dad was the best at it. He didn't say stupid things. I couldn't stay in the room with you for very long. There was this horrible smell from your trach infection. Your arms and legs were either pulled in tight or bent at weird angles. Your muscles were so spastic that your fingers were sticking out in all directions. It was really hard for me, that spasticity. It made me flash back to the disabled kids I worked with two years before, at the McKay Centre Camp. That was a good summer; I really liked those kids, but to see you looking the same way, I couldn't stand it. I didn't mind feeding you, or emptying your bedpan or any of that physical stuff. But every time you looked or acted like one of those kids, it was upsetting.

Meanwhile, I was supposed to leave for university in Toronto in just a few days. I remember asking my cousin Brian if he went on to school after his brother Victor died. And he said he did, he went right back and that was a mistake for him. It never gave him a chance to deal with certain things.

I was torn. I felt very guilty. I went to see a psychologist friend of the family. She told me I had to decide what I wanted to do, for *me*. And I realized I wanted to go to school. If I had stayed, I would have been angry.

So after I had sort of made up my mind, I went to your room to ask you. You were not able to speak, but you had that letter board.

Michael: You indicated that you were worried about Seth. I asked if you were worried because Seth was going to Toronto. And you said no. You signaled that it was the opposite — you were worried that he wouldn't go.

I was dying. That's why everybody came. To say goodbye.
Michael Dworkind from Herzl came with his wife, Lesley Levy.
They were my friends and they worked with dying people.
They brought New Age meditation tapes and Kahlil Gibran. I
can hear Lesley's voice telling me to "soften." I wasn't sure
what she meant, but it helped to counter the demons and the
pain. They knew how to be with me, what I needed. They had
experience with death; they were ready to help me die calmly
and peaceably. They were not scared.

I wasn't afraid of dying. I was sad but had no regrets, no
would-have-dones or should-have-dones. I was greatly loved
and had made a difference to some people's lives. It was enough.

Bernard Coté: I had been away on a camping holiday
since your anniversary. I remember I called from a phone
booth in the woods to see how you were doing. And
that's when I found out. I really didn't know what to do.
By the time I got back, things had deteriorated badly. You
were very far away. You had moments of consciousness
between long, long sleeps. I wasn't giving you treatments
any more, I was just being there. Michael was keeping
busy with technical aspects of the situation; otherwise he
probably would have been banging his head on the walls.
He cried with me a few times, but always in a very con-
tained way. It was like he was walking on the edge of a
precipice. There was no time to wonder how deep was the
abyss. He had to get across the wretched thing.

Joe Carlton sat on my bed after evening rounds, just like
before. He was tired and sad. I tried to tell him about the video
game and the poison gas, but he couldn't understand me.

Joe Carlton: When I came back from vacation, you were completely paralyzed. It was a shock. I couldn't help but feel a certain sense of guilt and responsibility, as if I should have known. But I didn't feel blame coming from anyone in your family.

I kept going over and over all the previous decisions and assumptions, trying to make them come out differently. I had assumed we had some time. There hadn't seemed to be a reason to push for the MRI. You were stable. I certainly hadn't been thinking surgery. Brain-stem surgery is just not worth it unless it's clear that function is threatened or the thing is growing. I hadn't anticipated it was going to rebleed so soon, so badly.

Michael: In the end, it was good people making bad decisions, and the system let us down. I do blame the system. If it can happen to us, it can happen to anyone.

In modern medicine we're always blundering along, making both good and bad decisions. MRI had only been around for five years or so. What would we have done in your case before MRIs were invented? Nothing. What are you going to do, cut into the brain stem on the basis of a slightly swollen thing on a CT scan? And CT scans are only ten years old. What about before that? If the lesion had bled out when you were twenty — which is more typical of these congenital malformations — you would have died.

We both use and misuse the technology. We're just screwing around trying to figure out what's going on. It's more or less enlightened screwing around; sometimes it works.

Seth: There was something incredibly naive about my thinking that all you needed was the right attitude. I took for granted the financial and cultural advantages that let Dad call neurologists across the continent and mobilize the best possible treatment for you. When I look back, I think that if Dad wasn't a doctor, then despite all your strength and optimism, you probably would have died. It took a full-time person who knew the system and knew medicine to force everything to stay on track until it was figured out. Dad was like a detective looking at the pieces of this puzzle and saying no, they don't fit; we need other clues. We need to think harder.

August 31
1) London Ontario neuroradiologist thinks:
　　　　the quality of the MRI films is sub-optimal
　　　　recommends repeat studies
　　　　or transfer to London for investigation.
2) Dr. Peerless thinks a small arteriovenus malformation in this area might be approached surgically.

SEPTEMBER 1

Michael told me I had to decide something important. There was a tangle of blood vessels. The man in London was the one person who could try to get it out. He had been practising this

operation on dogs or something. He was ready. He was a surgeon who was waiting for the right patient.

But it was risky. I could die. Michael thought we should
take the risk, but it was my decision. I didn't hesitate. I tried
to cross my fingers, but I couldn't. I tried to put my palms
together in a gesture of prayer, but that was impossible. I think
I finally managed a thumbs up. It meant, yes, we have to take
the chance.

Naomi: In a way, the best night was the night before we
went to London. It was euphoric. It was me and Dad and
Seth and Henry. Just close family. It was about two in the
morning and we were suddenly starving but the only
place open was Mac's Milk. Henry and Seth and I drove
there and we bought every junk food imaginable, the
stuff we weren't allowed to eat as kids: Doritos, Oreos,
Alphagetti, Pringles, Chef Boyardee Ravioli. Dad walked
into the room and said, "What is this dreck?" Then he
grabbed the Doritos and ate the whole bag.

So there we were having an impromptu middle-of-the-
night kitchen party. After all of the fumbling diagnoses,
suddenly a decision had been made.

Seth: I like it when there's a plan. It gives you something
to do, so you don't keep dwelling on hypothetical situa-
tions. Once the decision was made to have surgery, I never
had any doubt that it would be successful. I wasn't going
to spend my time thinking about what would happen if
you died, because we had something else to work on.

Sidonie Kerr: Terre told me you were going away for
surgery. I didn't know what would happen. I just kept

working. Apart from anything else, I wanted *Mile Zero* to be a good film. It was *your* film, maybe your last film, and it had to be strong. I felt like a guardian or something.

Lyn Charlsen: The last night I was there, I had a dream. I came by the hospital and told it to you before I left. There was a shower of gold, kind of like rain, and somebody told me it was you. And in the dream I thought, "Well, anybody who is manifesting in a shower of gold is going to be OK." The alchemists used to try to turn shit into gold and it seemed to me like this stroke was the shits. And it was going to be turned into gold. I remember you smiled.

SEPTEMBER 2

Terre Nash: I came over to the hospital just before you were flown out. I remember it very clearly. We were all hysterical, including you. We were making stupid jokes with Skip Peerless' name. "How could anyone named Skip perform brain surgery?" Seth was calling him Skippy and Naomi was calling him Mr. Peanut Butter and Michael was calling him the Cowboy Surgeon and you were making signs with your one finger that was all you could move. We started the Montreal Chapter of the Skip Peerless Fan Club.

Razelle: We kept thinking of that cult film, *Buckeroo Banzai.* The hero is a rock musician, race-car driver, particle physicist and neurosurgeon. And that was Peerless. He was the fantasy hero rescuing the maiden.

Naomi: We made up songs about him. "Skippy Peanut Butter, he's good enough for me." We were delirious and fixated. "Do you think that's his real name? No one's real name is Skip." And *Peerless*? What more is there to say? It was so perfectly waspy. "I bet he plays golf," Seth said.

How could anything go wrong?

Terre Nash: And then you were leaving and Naomi was holding your hand and crying and saying goodbye. You knew what was happening. The life behind your eyes was the same life. It was like you were trying to communicate everything you were feeling through your eyes. Everybody was taking turns holding your hand. You looked at Michael at one point and your eyes were desperate. I didn't know if it was the last time I would see you or not.

Michael: We were scheduled to go to London, 700 kilometres southwest of Montreal, shortly before the Labour Day weekend. Seth had to begin university the next week, so Henry said he'd help Seth pack and drive him to London to be with you before going on to Toronto.

Quebec had an ambulance jet with a built-in respirator, and the hospital arranged to have you transported. Provincial medicare didn't fuss about sending you to Ontario because nobody in Quebec was willing to do the surgery, and they agreed it had to be done.

We went to the airport in the ambulance, but they

wouldn't let me go on the plane with you: "No room, no insurance, no family members allowed." Naomi and I had to take the damn commercial flight — first to Toronto — and then change planes for London. You got in about noon and we got in around five. It was the first time I'd been separated from you.

Naomi: We didn't know when you were going to London until the day you left. There was no notice. And then we found out Daddy couldn't go on the ambulance jet. I said I would fly with him as soon as we could get a plane.

When we were finally on our way, Dad said, "Thank you for coming. I need you." I remember thinking: "He thinks I'm here for him. She's my mother, not just his wife." I mumbled something to that effect, but I was also happy that he appreciated me. That's how my dad deals with a crisis. He knows what he needs and he makes people feel useful because he's concrete. But sometimes he doesn't see what *they* need. The truth is, though, that he was right, the best thing was to be useful: he made himself useful medically and choreographed everyone else to be useful to him. What an administrator.

I can hear the drone of the jet engines. I can see the skinny doctor and the blond nurse with too much make-up. I remember thinking, isn't this interesting: there's a plane that's also an ambulance, with a doctor and a nurse and a respiratory therapist. . . . It was like being in some kind of television drama.

I can still smell the nurse's perfume. It made me choke. I didn't know what to do. We were stuck in this small space and I was choking and choking and I couldn't tell them it was the perfume. There was all this emergency technology but no one talked to me. The doctor kept going somewhere, some place where I couldn't see him. No one told me where we were, or how long it would be, or what they were doing, or who they were, or who I was. I was something between just-a-job and a-big-pain-in-the-ass. I was a bundle of cargo.

INTERLUDE: FLOATING

Journal, May 10, 1994
I went swimming this morning. I was alone in the pool and the sun was flooding through the skylight. I was floating face down with my snorkel and face mask, vaguely wondering how long I could stay like that. The light made never-ending, ever-changing ripples in the water. It was hypnotic. I remembered being in the hospital, floating further and further away. The snorkel brought back the sound of the respirator. This was a new remembering, opening sudden and whole out of those blank weeks, seven long years ago. My throat was dry from the respirator and I felt heavy in my chest. Each breath was a decision. I remember thinking: Is this all there is to dying? Is this how it happens — breathing gets harder and harder until it's easier to stop?

Back then, I was so sick it would have been easy to let go, except for the voices and hands, holding me, calling me. Or maybe it was a physical thing where my body still demanded the breath it needed; or perhaps Michael and Seth and Naomi were with me, pulling me back.

Our culture is so strange. We're taught to see life and death as absolute states: either you're alive or you're dead. But when I was there, hovering between them, there was no sharp border. It was nothing like the near-death experiences I've read about. No wondrous white light, just an easy letting go.

Most of the time we pretend there is no death. And I live that way too, now that I'm seven years away from it. It makes no sense.

LONDON

≈

SURGERY

I just want to get this part over with. I was unconscious in London and I don't remember anything. I wasn't there, I wasn't there. I have nothing to say. All I know is what other people told me afterwards. Let them write about it.

Writing this, my chest is tight and breathless. My head hurts. My shoulders and neck are stiff. I remember this feeling. My body remembers. I was *there*.

I have a sensation of being on the stretcher. Tubes. Bottles. Oxygen. I'm trying to think if I felt pain. I can't remember what I was feeling. Fear? What do you feel when you don't have the energy to feel fear?

I don't remember being transferred from the airplane to the ambulance. I have a vague memory of frustration because things were taking so long. Somehow I thought the plane would take me right to the hospital and I would land on the roof and be there, like in the movies. I had no idea where I was. Then I was there. Orderlies, doors, hallways. A different cubicle in a different ICU with different doctors and the same antiseptic smell.

Skip Peerless: When you came to us, you were trached and on a respirator. I don't think there was any movement in your legs to speak of, and just a bit of movement in one arm. Minimal. But your eyes were moving in that crazy double-vision way, and I could see the humanity of you coming through your eyes. You were what we call locked in: paralyzed but conscious.

It was a long time before Michael could get to me. It could have been an hour. It could have been eight hours. I had no anchor in time and place.

There was a countdown. It was a closed system. It was a film loop. You couldn't stop it. That was part of the torture. The film went around and around, like white noise: the breathing machine, the heartbeat machine. There was no way to break the loop.

And then Michael was there.

Michael: I was tense and angry on the plane, but the minute I got to the University Hospital I calmed right down. I couldn't believe the ICU. It was staggering. They had a nurse for every patient, and a respiratory technician for every three patients. They had extra beds! It was so different from the overcrowded facilities, marginal staffing and chronic under-funding I was used to in Montreal. There were more than two hundred unfilled nursing positions at the JGH.

Bill Frankl: Razelle and I flew to London and went to the hospital. It looked like you were basically dead. I had a very bad feeling that you might not recover. Or if you did recover, you would be severely impaired.

The medical records tell me I had a CT scan the first day, a cerebral angiogram on the second day, and an MRI on the third.

This time there were no nightmares of tunnels and credit cards. Somebody in London had invented a respirator with no metal parts that could go into the MRI. I remember the grinding noise, like in Montreal. Then you hear the clanging. And then there are silences. You don't know what's happening in those silences — whether it's over or it's going to start again. And then at last it's over.

Michael: After the MRI, we had a conference with Peerless. Naomi, Razelle and Bill were there, and also my friends Mickey Brennan and Linda Spano, two family physicians. We were all staying at their house while we were in London.

Mickey Brennan: Do you remember what the success rate for this procedure was? It was dreadful. I think Peerless had done six similar operations, all of them higher in the brain stem. Only two people pulled through well; one died and the other three were left seriously disabled. This was a very, very chancy thing.

Michael: I don't remember the exact statistics, but Peerless said it was dangerous. But it was also in the midline, a millimetre below the fourth ventricle. There was a possible entry point. None of the others had been that way. That's what I paid attention to, not the numbers.

Mickey Brennan: Michael was in denial, which was fine. The normal process is to start off with denial and hang onto it as long as possible. If there were two out of six, then you were going to be one of the two. There wasn't any alternative: surgery was risky but no surgery was death.

Naomi: It's called the brain stem because everything stems from there. The way Dr. Peerless explained it is that the brain stem is the source, and if you lose something at the source, it's permanent. Some of your paralysis could be a result of swelling and bleeding pressing on the nerves, and if the pressure was removed, the paralysis could be gone also, but any nerves that were actually damaged in the stroke would not recover. And if some nerves got cut in the surgery, it could kill you. I was just numb when he said that. The reality didn't hit; I couldn't make myself think it was going to happen.

I remember Michael sitting on my bed; he drew me a diagram, and explained how Peerless was going to open my skull, elevate the cerebellum, peel away some other part, and delve into something else. I think he used the word "elegant" about the approach. I couldn't take it in. I didn't know the anatomy. I didn't know anything about how you open a skull. And it was my skull! It was *me* they were going to carve and peel and delve into, my body that would lie unconscious on the operating table, my brain in Michael's diagram.

But Michael needed to tell me. So I listened and smiled for him. He was so pleased to have a plan! After all those weeks of waiting and uncertainty in Montreal, someone was going to do something. It was a kind of big, desperate hope. Science can fix it.

I don't think I felt fear. I was swept along by Michael's enthusiasm and his confidence. I trusted Peerless. He didn't fit the arrogant surgeon stereotype. He was calm and quiet and very much a gentleman. And everyone kept saying, "If anyone can do it, Peerless can." There was this almost God-like faith.

Michael: The conference was on the Friday before Labour Day. Labour Day weekend everybody goes away. So when the final decision for the surgery was made, Peerless said, "We'll do it first thing Tuesday morning." And I said "That's a long time from now." He said, "It's not a good idea to operate when we're short-staffed, especially a major operation like this. It's best to do it when all of the services are there." I said, "Yes, I understand that. But she could bleed again before Tuesday, and she won't recover from the next one." Peerless said "That's true. Okay, we'll do it first thing tomorrow morning if I can get an anesthetist and assemble a team of people." Adrian Gelb, the anesthetist who had devised the plastic respirator for the MRI, immediately volunteered. The chief resident said he'd come too, and so on. And it was decided right there that they would in fact do it the next day.

September 5, 1987. There was a full-page article in the Saturday *Globe and Mail* called "The Death of Documentary?" It was about the future of documentary filmmaking and included a picture of me and Kate Millett from *Not a Love Story*. Peerless posted it in the ICU. I was confused by the word "death" so close to my picture. Was it my obituary? The headline kept spinning in my head. But I was glad it was there for all the doctors and nurses to see. It proved I was a person, not just a body attached to a bunch of machines.

Do I really remember that? Did I see the article, read the headline? Or is it something Michael told me about later?

Michael says he and Naomi came to the hospital early and were with me until I was wheeled into the operating room. He told me the operation would take eight hours. How could anyone mess with my brain for that long?

I have a vague memory of Peerless coming in before the surgery. There was something I wanted to ask him about the anesthesia. But I couldn't talk. Maybe I wanted to tell him not to give me too much because I was afraid I would never wake up.

I can almost remember the operating room. Or I remember the memories my imagination supplied later. For weeks afterwards I kept meeting people who said they had been at my surgery. So I "remember" that it was in a big stadium filled with doctors and nurses and technicians. Michael kept saying that this operation had never been done before and was historic. So it seems to me that there must have been seats — rows upon rows of students. And big lights and video cameras. I was lying on a stretcher in the middle of the stadium. The notes say I was in the "park-bench" position, lying on my side so that they could get to the back of my skull. They must have had me strapped in because I was unconscious and paralyzed. In my made-up memory, Peerless is very cool and calm and surgical.

Skip Peerless: I remember telling Adrian that I was worried about whether we might destroy the respiratory centre when we manipulated there. Adrian convinced me to press on.

Adrian Gelb: It was one of our more memorable Saturdays together...

Michael: You went into surgery very early in the morning. What the hell were we going to do, hang around the waiting room? We all went downtown to the market for breakfast. And then we went shopping. I bought a blazer, and Naomi picked out two ties for me, the most expensive I've ever owned, that I wore for years afterwards. She bought a long dark coat for herself, a real lint collector, which she has never worn. I also bought shoes, desert boots, or whatever they're called. They didn't fit.

Razelle: I bought two sets of Teflon pans. I still have them.

Naomi: My dad hates to shop. He shops like someone who wants to get it over with and for that reason he is easy prey. We went to Ports for Men and he bought two $80 silk ties, a blue blazer and pants. They were outrageously expensive but he didn't even notice. He was like a walking zombie as the sales clerk frantically circled him, sticking pins in the pants and sleeves. It was fun. It was a way of not thinking about what was going on.

Henry Klein: On the day they decided to operate, Seth and I were driving from Montreal to London in your station-wagon. We had all of Seth's gear packed in the back, because after a few days in London, Michael was going to drive him to Toronto. He was pretty wired about your surgery, and also about going away to college for the first time. It was the long weekend and there were lots of other families on the road driving their kids off to university. You could tell; there'd be the boxes in the back, the nervous teenager in the front. Seth was checking them all out, because *of course* all the other kids had exactly the right number of boxes. He was getting himself into a frenzy thinking he had too much stuff and that everybody would think he was a geek. He was afraid he wouldn't know how to make friends. He said he didn't know how to make small talk, he only knew how to talk about nuclear war.

September 5, 1987
University Hospital Operative Note
S. J. Peerless, Division of Neurosurgery

With the patient under general endotracheal anesthesia in the park-bench position, the head secured in the Sugita frame, the back of the head was clipped, scrubbed with soap and prepped with tincture of Savlon. Through a midline incision in the skin, subcutaneous tissue and para-spinal musculature was reflected from occiput and arch of C1. A small craniectomy was then performed, removing the posterior ring of the foramen magnum and the arch of C1. The dura was opened in Y-shaped fashion and Sugita retracting system assembled to elevate the right cerebellar tonsil.

On first inspection using the operating microscope there was little obviously abnormal except that the right side of the open medulla was clearly swollen and slightly discoloured with brownish tinge. It was then apparent that this swelling extended up to the restiform body and had obliterated the markings in the region of the tuberculum cinereum and acoustic area of the open medulla.

A 3-mm incision was then made over the mass in the open medulla and at a depth of about 3 mm below the surface. Old brown hematoma was encountered and removed with fine suction. The opening was then held apart with two micro retractors and under 25 to 40 times magnification the cavity was cleared of old hematoma.

Working more deeply we came first upon a large aneurysmal dilatation of a thin-walled vessel which bled immediately when the clot over it was removed, causing what appeared to be arterial blood but not under particularly high pressure to escape into the cavity. This was controlled with bi-polar coagulation, the dissection carried further to uncover a raspberry-sized mass of coiled, rather large vessels surrounded by numerous small arterial vessels. The small arterial feeding vessels were individually coagulated and cut, the large mass being shrunk down with the bi-polar coagulator. The whole mass was finally removed in two pieces, staying always entirely within the confines of the cavity.

During the dissection on the lower pole of the mass we recorded two episodes of marked cardiovascular change with, on the first occasion, a marked bradycardia and hypotension lasting some 15 seconds and the second occasion, periods of tachycardia and hypertension. These responses appeared to be related to manipulation of a single large arterial feeder but in that it clearly went directly into the malformation I finally coagulated it and divided it with no further changes in heart rate or blood pressure.

When I was confident that the complete hemostasis had been affected, the wounds were thoroughly irrigated with saline and bacitracin, the dura tightly closed with running and interrupted silk and the para-spinal musculature closed in layers with dexon and ethilon for the skin.

Mickey Brennan: After eight hours, the surgery was due to be finished, and everyone went back to the hospital. Here's this little room, filled with people waiting, getting quieter and quieter. We knew that what was coming was the moment of truth. And there would be absolutely no way that anything could protect us if the news was bad.

Then in comes Peerless. I remember the broad smile on his face.

Bill Frankl: Peerless indicated that in clipping off the malformation and then excavating the blood clot, the amount of brain involved was not extensive. He felt that you were going to come through. I wasn't sure if he was just trying to make everybody feel good or if this was the truth. But there was just something about him and the entire atmosphere that made me more optimistic.

Mickey Brennan: There was no great "whoopee!" There was just a kind of stunned, "Are you sure? What's going to happen now?" And in fact at that point people started to become more worried, more concerned about what the degree of recovery was going to be.

My head was aching. Somebody was there, talking to me. One of the nurses. I remember that feeling of disoriented awakening, that process of going in and out of anesthesia. I was in the recovery room with strange nurses. Or maybe Michael was there. I remember wanting him to tell me how it went. I think he reassured me that he had seen Peerless. Yes. That was it. He told me Peerless felt it was very successful.

I was still alive.

INTERLUDE: A SILENT STROKE

There was a stroke before the stroke. The year before, that terrible year of shooting *Mile Zero*, panicking while crossing bridges, taking drugs for depression. I remember walking up long flights of stairs because I was afraid of escalators. I remember the night I went to hear k.d. lang at the Spectrum. The club was crowded and smoky, the concert wildly exciting. I couldn't fall asleep that night. I started to wheeze for the first time in my life. I couldn't get enough air. I snuck out of bed and sat on the rocker by the open window. Still I wheezed. Must be all that smoke. I couldn't seem to remember how to breathe. I had to keep thinking about taking the next breath or I would die. I was careful not to fall asleep.

The next day I felt better, and the day after that, worse. I didn't know what was wrong. I talked to Michael, Irene Kupferszmidt, and later Michele Devroede. We looked for reasons and there were reasons enough: my mother, my daughter, my work, my life. Situational depression — the shoe fit.

But Skip Peerless found another reason. When he opened my skull he saw the two recent bleeds plus the remains of a previous bleed, maybe a year old. A "silent stroke" he called it, small enough to go unrecognized, large enough to make me tear off most of my clothes in a fit of car-wash claustrophobia, and wheeze with asthma that never responded to the asthma medications because it wasn't in my lungs but in my brain stem.

I don't remember when Michael told me. It must have been soon after surgery because I slowly came back to myself with this new information already in place. The "depression" of the previous year, the current strokes, were all related, all caused by a malformation with which I had been born. I felt a sense of relief: I hadn't brought it on myself. There. That's solved.

At the same time, I felt slightly disappointed. It seemed as if a random accident of birth had determined that I would have these strokes. It was as if they had nothing to do with me. But I wanted a message from them, a metaphor about how to live my life. In the end I decided the strokes had many possible levels of meaning and I could use whichever I needed.

POST-OP

Seth: Henry and I got to London that night, after your surgery was over, and Dad took me to see you. The ICU was very glistening and high-tech, each patient in their own glassed-in cubby with all of their machines and hardware. You were lying there, your limbs all twisted up, still completely paralyzed. Maybe I was expecting a miraculous post-surgery transformation. That's when I realized the recovery was going to take a long time. I remember being very comforted having Dad with me.

The noise of the ICU never changed: soft hissing like radio static and a kind of disembodied, sucking sound. After a while you couldn't hear it. The whole place smelled like disinfectant and rotting flesh. The rotting flesh was me, the stink of infection from my trach wound. I have no memory of the other patients. It was as if I was the only sick person in the world.

Michael: That particular ICU was a place where most people stayed only briefly, and during that time they would be heavily sedated with Valium or morphine. When they began to recover, they would be shipped off to the wards. There were a few long-timers though who'd been there for months on end. Nobody knew what they were thinking. If they were conscious, there was no way for them to show it, because nothing moved. Sometimes they had visitors who would talk to them, but mostly they were treated as if they were in a vegetative state.

I remember the headache. Constant headache. There were tests with hordes of residents and medical students coming through and poking me with pins and asking me to move things. "Wiggle your toe." They were always asking me to wiggle my toe. I would try very hard because I wanted to please them, but I couldn't actually tell if my toe moved or not. The testers didn't tell me so I never knew if I was doing it right. "Do I pass?" I was good at fingers but they wanted toes.

Naomi: They were obsessed with your toes.

Annie Klein: When we went to visit you after your surgery, your eyes were bright and alive and you were moving your right hand, and even your left fingers a bit, which you hadn't been able to do for a long time. When I was telling all this to Mickey Brennan, he asked if you were moving your legs at all. I said no, not yet, not that

we know of. And he said, "That's not good. It could mean
the nerves are permanently damaged and she'll be para-
plegic." I guess as a physician he was preparing me for the
worst. I don't know. But when we went in the next day
and your legs still hadn't moved, I started to get scared.

Michael: We couldn't predict the results of your stroke.
No two strokes are alike. The recovery depends on so
many things, especially the location where the damage
has occurred; sometimes a fraction of a millimetre makes
all the difference. Sometimes there are multiple sites damaged.

Most strokes are hemispheric. They usually cause weakness on one side of the body, and often aphasia — the
inability to access language — again depending on the
severity and location of the damage.

Brain-stem strokes are relatively rare and there are few
survivors. Even among brain-stem strokes, there are variations, depending on how low it is, and how close to the
midline. The symptoms are not principally cognitive. They
involve areas like breathing, swallowing, movement of
the trunk, arms and legs. The kind of paralysis you experienced was typical of a brain-stem injury. We had no
way of knowing how much of the damage would be permanent.

Norma Zack: I remember going down to the cafeteria for
coffee with Michael. As we sat down, he looked around
at all the people in wheelchairs, and said that he didn't
know how he would cope if you ended up like that. We
sat there quietly drinking our coffee for a long time and
then he said, "Well, actually, it doesn't look *that* bad."

222

2

The legs are not moving. That's what the doctors said. The legs. The body. How could it be *my* body, when I couldn't send messages for it to move, when I couldn't feel sensation when it was touched. It. When I touched myself, I didn't know if it was my own leg or some object in bed with me. My flesh felt to my fingers like a piece of dead meat from the butcher shop. My vulva and clitoris felt like strange accessories.

Michael: After your surgery, I didn't spend all my time at the hospital like I had in Montreal because London was so competent medically. I developed a routine of swimming, playing tennis with Mickey Brennan, or doing a little work in the morning. I would come in around 11 o'clock, when visitors' hours officially started. If I came in before that, some of the nurses would get upset because that's when they'd be bathing and changing you. So I stayed away until 11 a.m., which was a long time for me but it was also time I needed for myself.

Naomi: To say that we made ourselves at home at the Brennans' doesn't begin to describe it. We took over. Relatives were in and out. We were constantly picking them up at the airport and setting them up in what seemed like an endless number of guest bedrooms. And when we weren't at the hospital, my dad was on the Brennans' phone, keeping everyone in Montreal, California, Philadelphia and New Jersey up to date. The Brennans were incredibly generous with their home and they were really good at making fun of Dad. One Friday night, Linda made this amazing *Shabbat* dinner including the best matzoh-ball soup I've ever had — there were tiny quail eggs in the middle of the matzah balls. And she isn't even Jewish! Anyway, she set this beautiful table in the dining room and at one place she put a pink telephone right on the plate. "OK, Michael," she said, "guess which seat is yours."

Compared to dark and dreary Montreal, London felt like a resort: tennis courts and new cars, winding, tree-lined streets, and a quaint downtown with renovated movie theatres and indoor markets that sold only gourmet food. It was like "President's Choice" everything.

University Hospital was London's crowning jewel. If London was a resort, University Hospital was a Club Med for sick people. Everything was brand new and completely high-tech; all the doctors looked like they had just stepped off a golf course and taken an exhilarating shower. The nurses were big, healthy, strong, unbelievably attractive people who all seemed to love their jobs and love each other. Bottom line: they were not burnt out, unlike at the understaffed JGH.

The gowns that visitors had to wear into the ICU were crisp and yellow, more like the kind you get at hair salons than hospitals. The walls were brightly painted yellow and turquoise. The cafeteria had not just good, but *really* good food. "Do you know, Naomi," my dad would say as we sat looking out at the woodsy view behind the hospital, "this cafeteria does outside catering. I mean, that's how good this hospital is."

And then there were the legends about Skip Peerless and his boss, Charlie Drake, how they had saved the lives of movie stars and presidents and oil sheiks. It was their out-of-country money that financed this uber-hospital. Suddenly, we were really big fans of private medicine. Hurrah for huge hospital fees!

The nurse with the blond hair sang to me while she made my bed. Something about a bird, "with a wing on the left and a wing on the right," complete with flapping elbows. The other good nurse was Rick. His voice was very calm. My head hurt.

The nurse Rick talked to me. "Now I'm going to brush your teeth. What flavour toothpaste today? Hmmm, mint. Do you like mint? I hope so 'cause that's all there is. Is that too hard? Blink your eyes if it's too hard. OK, now I'm going to swab it out. There. So when do you get to start eating steak?"

It's very intimate to have someone else brush your teeth. Rick knew I was alive.

Seth: A few days after your surgery, Dad drove me to Toronto. I was nervous about going to university. Looking back, I don't know how I did it, or if it was the right thing to do.

When we arrived, Dad helped me move into my new room in residence. It was a small space, and without any posters or books it looked a lot like a prison cell. We stepped into the room, then Dad sat down on the bed and started to cry. I guess it was a combination of many things: his son starting university combined with the relief of the surgery.

Michael: It was a long drive to Toronto and back. So when I got to the Brennans' around 11 p.m., I called the hospital and asked how you were doing. The nurse said your condition was not good. You were less responsive and you had fixed and dilated pupils. Fixed and dilated pupils means brain-dead. It meant some catastrophe had occurred; there'd been another bleed. It didn't make any sense to me, in light of how I saw you when I left, but these things do happen so it was not inconceivable either. I said, "I'm coming right away," and hung up.

Mickey was upstairs, asleep. I don't think I made any noise, but the next thing I knew, he was downstairs in his pyjamas, asking me what was wrong. Then he was getting dressed and we were driving like crazy to the hospital. I remember this kind of empty feeling in my stomach. The nurse was waiting for us at the door to the ICU, crying. She was a mess. She said, "I'm very sorry, I made a mistake. It was another patient; your wife is fine."

Naomi: Eventually I had to go back to Montreal for school. It was really hard to leave. I got home the night before my boyfriend left for college. I spent the evening with him and he left at about one in the morning. Then I went to the kitchen to get something to eat. It was really quiet. All of a sudden I realized that I was totally alone. Our dog Lucy was at our friends the Ushers' house, you guys were in London and Seth was at school in Toronto. It was too late at night to call anyone. I started to get spooked. I was hearing noises — like footsteps on the stairs. I went into your bedroom and locked myself in. Finally I fell asleep and the next day I went to my new school, Brébeuf, where everything was in French. I was a total mess. The only good thing was when that afternoon there was a message from Dad saying you were starting to get better.

I seemed to have moved my left big toe. They said I did. I couldn't feel it, but they were very happy. I passed the test. I could move all my fingers and one toe. I could lift my right forearm off the bed. I wore moon boots. I had a dream of shit.

Or maybe it wasn't a dream. *There was an ocean of diarrhea all over my sheets and bedclothes. It was sweet shit. That's what we used to call it when I was breast-feeding. When it's your baby, it's not repulsive. It was like swimming in a warm, sweet ocean.*

The moon boots were blue styrofoam splints. The physio prescribed them to straighten my feet which were rigidly turned in. I had hand splints too, to straighten my wrists and thumbs, but I used to wiggle out of them. I guess they were uncomfortable.

The Blue Chair was another torture device I was put into at intervals throughout the day. I remember dreading that chair. Sitting in it was enormous work. There was always a big deal about how long I could stay in the Blue Chair. The nurses were so excited when they could say, "Ooh, she sat in the Blue Chair for half an hour today."

Michael: The Blue Chair was a pretty standard lounge chair, like a Barca lounger, with a high back for neck support since you couldn't hold the weight of your head yet. The nurses would either get a couple of orderlies to lift you into it, or they'd use the hoist which was like a derrick that winched you into the air in a kind of sling and swung you over and down into the chair. Rick couldn't be bothered with that. He'd just schlep you over in his arms.

Sitting in the chair was an exercise to help you develop trunk control. You were having a hard time just staying upright. Even when you were in bed, you had to be wedged and propped, and every two hours they would turn you. Even in the middle of the night they would wake you and turn you; otherwise you would have been bearing weight on your buttocks all the time and would have gotten bed sores, which are hard to get rid of, extremely painful and can become seriously infected.

The nurses in London had a clever way of turning me: it was like that trick you see in old movies, where they pull the table-cloth out and leave all the dishes in place. Two of them would grab the edge of the sheet and flip me like a pancake on the count of three. (There was a more complicated variation for changing the sheets.) Between turnings I would just lie there, unable to move my head to look at someone or shift my weight in any way.

Michael: I remember one time you were trying to tell us that something was hurting you. We thought you were saying it was a headache. The chief neurosurgical resident came down and did a careful examination but she couldn't figure it out. You were too uncoordinated to use the letter board. Then somebody came along with a diagram of the body, and we started pointing to different parts and asking you if that was what hurt. That's how we found out it wasn't your head. As soon as that was clear, the neurosurgical resident was no longer interested and left the rest of us to figure out what the hell was wrong. We went down the diagram with you mouthing the words: no, no, no. Until we got to the pelvic area and then you were saying: yes, no, yes, no. We were totally confused until we realized that the diagram showed only the front of the body. We turned you over and, there was a big red sore spot on your bum.

In spite of the morphine they gave me, I was often in pain. I think I kept my eyes closed most of the time. I know I was dizzy from double vision and a condition called nystagmus where my eyeballs kept bopping around. Smell was much more vivid than vision. Certain odours caused my throat to go into spasm. I choked at the smell of cigarette smoke on people's clothes. I could tell what they had eaten for supper. Strong foods were offensive, but I loved the smell of sake.

I could lift my arms off the bed for seconds at a time, and even though my right foot was still disconnected, I could wiggle my left one like crazy. I still couldn't breathe, eat, pee, sit up, or dance, but surely those would come soon. Meanwhile the nurses did practically everything for me. There was skin care, back care, mouth care, bedpans, massage, bed baths. There was constant checking of blood gases, spirometers, IVs, feeding tubes, catheters and trach tubes. The best time was Rick's shift. He had a flat, nasal, Ontario kind of voice, but to me he sounded handsome and sexy. In the warm current of attraction, I remembered I was alive. He'd tell me about his day and what he was doing and what he was going to do next: not profound talk, just talk.

"I'm thinking of buying a windsurfer. What do you think? Last weekend I tried Steve's. You know Steve? The RT's boyfriend? Anyhow, a bunch of us went out to the lake and I was windsurfing. Man, it was amazing. Just zinging over the water. And falling. Did I mention falling? OK, OK, so I'm a klutz. But should I get one? Blink if you think I need a windsurfer. All right! I knew you'd be on my side."

I understood everything. People would talk to each other and my imagination would piece together stories from the fragments. There was an ongoing soap opera in my head: *Rick*

and the pregnant occupational therapist were some kind of
number. Whenever they were both off duty, they were together
windsurfing. But it was all in my mind. It turned out she was
married to the orthopedic resident.

Michael: You used to laugh with Rick. You didn't make
the sound of laughter, but you laughed. That's why Rick
liked looking after you — you were responsive.

A lot of the nurses didn't even talk to you — you
couldn't talk, so you weren't worth the bother. But in fact
when something was working well, I could see it in your
face. You'd be shining. That was real feedback if people
chose to see it, and the difference with Rick was that he
saw it.

Seth: I used to talk about you to the staff every time I came
in from Toronto. I felt a strong need to tell them who you
were — about all your films and friends. I wanted them
to know they were dealing with a real person, not just a
paralyzed body.

I remember one of the nurses giving me a bed bath and saying to the respiratory therapist, "She used to be a filmmaker."
As if I wasn't there, as if I couldn't hear, as if my life was over.
I wanted to shake them and say, "Don't talk about me like I'm
dead!" But I couldn't shout or shake anyone or even explain it
to Michael on the stupid letter board. I remember my finger
wobbling around, not able to reach the right letter. I remember the blur of the board in my double vision. I remember the
letter board getting lost, over and over again. Why the hell
didn't they have an extra one?

Skip Peerless: The letter board is considered a minor item overall.

It was my life line.

Interlude: Finding Memories

Journal: January 1989, Costa Rica
I asked Michael to help me find memories from that lost limbo time after surgery. Michael is more interested in watching the sunset. He is casual about memory, prefers the present. But I am always working, worrying at that hole in my life. I'm afraid of what's there, but I feel I won't heal without finding out.

"Why were those splints called moon boots?" I ask him.

"I don't know. They just were."

"Did I go somewhere for the moon boots? Some kind of theatre?"

"Theatre? There was no theatre. Hey, look at that fishing boat out there. What do you suppose they're after?"

"What about for suctioning?" I persist. "I remember some other place, a big place they took me to for this stuff."

"No, it was all in your cubicle," Michael says. "Splints, suctioning, trach cleaning, everything."

"I don't remember," I say, but suddenly I do. I can see the

clear plastic around my bed, hear the soft shush of the respirator, choking, footsteps, voices.

"We'd suction you out constantly," Michael says. "A couple of times an hour. I used to take turns with the nurse or the respiratory technician. You would start choking and bubbling, and we'd have to disconnect you from the respirator and connect you to a self-inflating bag that would take over breathing for you. Then we would put distilled water or a saline solution down the trach tube to make you cough."

He's on a roll now, explaining the procedure, and the memories are flooding back. "It was awful," I tell him. "I would cough and sputter and they would say 'good.'"

"Coughing kept you from getting pneumonia and it also cleared the tube. Then we would suction out the trach and bring up all of the pus, mucus and debris. It had to be done thoroughly."

"I hated it."

"Yes, because it made you choke."

I remember that all right; my body resounds with recognition. But I still want to know more.

"Do you remember being weaned off the respirator?" Michael asks. "They put you on a schedule where you spent an increasing amount of time every day practising breathing on your own."

"Was that in the theatre?" I ask.

"Forget the theatre! There was no theatre!"

"OK, OK, tell me," I say.

"We would unplug the respirator and hook you up to a T-tube — an accordion-like tube that attaches to the trach and provides oxygen. But it doesn't inhale and exhale for you like the respirator does. As you breathed this dial would turn and indicate if you were getting enough oxygen and whether you needed to go back on the respirator. Sometimes it was clear that you'd been off for too long and were exhausted."

"I think I remember. I couldn't breathe. And you would clean the T-tube with Savlon, that horrible smelling cleaner."

"No, that was for cleaning around the trach tube. The gauze would be impregnated with all this smelly pus. It's a disgusting smell: overpowering and sickly sweet. I remember you complaining about that smell on your letter board. I think it had something to do with the panic attacks."

"I don't remember," I say.

But I do.

PANIC

Does torture have a smell? My foot was caught. In the sheet, or maybe in my nightgown. I tried to move but couldn't. I was paralyzed. My leg was far away. I couldn't find it. It was caught in a trap. I was trying to scream. The nurse said "There, there, it's all right." But it wasn't all right. I was trying to tell her. I was trying to scream. "You're fine," she said. "It's nothing."

Michael: Almost two weeks after the operation, you started having panic attacks. Some days you'd just have two or three, but other days they'd be coming every hour. You'd be dozing and then you'd become suddenly alert and there'd be a look of total terror in your eyes. You didn't have very good control of your arms, but you would clutch at me, you would clutch at the nurse. And the nurse would say, "Calm down. It's nothing."

It was not nothing; I was choking to death. I couldn't breathe, I couldn't swallow. I was drowning. What did they know? The goddamn letter board was lost again. *I was in the concentration camp with a torture device on my head. It was squeezing my skull. Even morphine didn't help. There were circles and squares and something about blood gases and oxygen and numbers. I could smell the cyanide.*

The singing nurse was stroking my head. Mary. Her name was Mary. I wanted to tell her about the bald Nazi. I wanted to ask her if I was dying. I wanted her to stroke my head forever. "You're going to be OK," she said. "It will pass." Michael got a big green magic marker and made a new letter board on the back of an old file folder. The letters were messy, but it worked just as well as the lost one.

Michael: I remember you trying to tell me about the nightmares, but it was a concept that I couldn't get. All I knew was there was something terrifying. I was always waiting for the next panic attack. And when it came I would try to reassure you that you were OK and you were going to be able to breathe. I would try to acknowledge what you were going through by saying, "Yeah, it's scary. It must be absolutely terrifying. But it will pass. It has never not passed. Just let me hold you." That was the litany. It was only marginally successful.

Rick: It was as if you were trying to tell us something, but you weren't able to. You'd get a worried look, and then you'd start getting physical symptoms — sweating, agitation, laboured breathing. But there was no actual physical problem. There didn't seem to be anything we could do to keep you from going into a panic attack, but once it started, if the nurse didn't take the right approach, it would just get larger.

Michael: The phone was next to your bed so that if you got particularly anxious, the nurses could call me and put the phone to your ear and I would talk to you. You couldn't talk to me, but you could hear my voice.

I was afraid to sleep because that's when the film loop would start. But I wouldn't get well unless I slept. It went around and around. Michael was gone.

It took me a long time to get the nurse's attention, and a long time to tell her what I needed. She refused to call Michael. She told me I was being a baby, that he had to eat and sleep and play tennis, so I would have to wait until he came back. She smiled and patted my hand. "He needs some time for himself." "No," I wanted to yell, "I don't care what he needs. If he knew how desperate I am, he would want to be with me and save me."

I knew he was staying at Mickey and Linda's. I tried like hell to remember the phone number, but I couldn't even remember their last names. I couldn't look up the number, I couldn't even dial, and the gatekeepers wouldn't help me. I was trapped. I would die in the hospital while Michael was playing tennis.

Panic attacks punctuated my days, feeding off the ICU atmosphere of constant hysteria, of life and death. My skin was too thin to keep it out. There was no distinction between myself and the outside world. It jolted through my nerves, made my heart race, constricted my chest. The ICU melted into the nightmare concentration camp: constant lights, constant noise, constant routines. All day and all night. I was desperate for sleep and the rock of Michael's presence.

September 18. The nurse's notes say, "pt mouthing words: 'Help me, I'm going crazy.' Settles with comfort, or at times a firm hand." My body tenses against the memory. There was a psychiatrist, someone Michael vaguely knew, who just happened to be in London. He came to see me at Michael's request. I pulled at his white jacket, saying, "Help me." I knew he was a psychiatrist, the kind of doctor who is trained to help frightened people, the kind of doctor frightened people are trained to ask for help. He pulled away, almost ran for the elevator. I could see his terror — she's insane, she's off the wall. I'm getting out of here, fast. I'm a busy man.

> **Michael:** You let me know that you were afraid you were crazy. I said that anybody going through what you were, had every right to be crazy. It was no big surprise and nothing to be afraid of.

I suppose I was crazy. Something was going on that I couldn't control and it was driving me mad. Although it was based on a physical reality, what I experienced and the way I acted is commonly labelled insane. I crossed the line and discovered there really is no line. The division between myself and those other people, those crazy people, was gone. They were me.

I tried to pull myself together for Michael. I desperately wanted to give him a good reception, to show I was OK. Sometimes I could do it, but more often I would fall apart. I would try to tell him what I had been going through and end up making dry soundless sobs. I was angry at him for abandoning me.

Everyone kept moving around: London, Montreal, Toronto. They were just words to me, not real places. Michael would tell me very carefully who was where, trying to keep me oriented. "This afternoon, Naomi is coming from Montreal, and tonight Seth is coming from Toronto. I'm picking him up from the train." It seemed like a complicated choreography of comings and goings; planes and trains and cars and cities; today, yesterday, tomorrow. I couldn't understand why everyone wasn't there all the time.

Seth: My whole first term of university was awful. It scares me now when I think how cut off I was. There were only two people who knew what was happening with you, Alison and Sheila, friends from SAGE. I resolved to tell no one else. At school, I would concentrate on my studies and try to have a social life. If I needed to talk to someone, I would go to Alison or Sheila. On the weekends, I would take the train to London and focus all my attention on you and Dad and Naomi. I guess I felt guilty for leaving, especially after the panic attacks started. I came to hate those train rides, doing my homework and trying to shift my brain from one compartment to the other. When I think back on it now, going to school was probably a mistake. But it was also good for me in a way, to be able to give you all my attention for those two days, and then escape.

Carol Zavitz: On the day of your first stroke, I was in Toronto, giving birth to Natty, our first child. In the weeks

that followed, I was entirely absorbed with that inscru-
table little being who had been part of me. I was looking
for other mothers who would rejoice in the baby in the
way that I needed, so I called you — a long-time friend
and ace rejoicer. Naomi answered the phone and said you
were sick.

I think you had just gone to London. We got in touch
with Michael who suggested that Dan and I come to visit
you; he was concerned that you not lose touch with the
world outside intensive care.

When we got there, Michael saw us through all the
gowning and washing. We knew that according to the
rules, we shouldn't both go in at once, and certainly not
with the germy baby, but it was clear that Michael made
up his own rules for your care.

You were lying on a very high bed in the middle of a
bristling nest of machines. I wouldn't have known you.
You were asleep and looked flattened out, obliterated. I
felt I was seeing you from far away and that you were
dying. It looked impossible to get close to you through the
beeping equipment, to make any kind of human contact.

Michael woke you and ushered us in closer. I held up
the baby so you could see him, and all at once your face
came alive with an expression of joy and wonder and
welcome that made the ICU recede into irrelevance. There
you were after all. Excited to see a new baby, you started
to talk; you had no voice, of course, so Michael interpreted for us. You got tired very quickly; two or three
times you dropped back to sleep and vanished again, but
now I knew you were there, just hidden sometimes.

I didn't believe you were going to die any more. I was
vividly aware that you were going to have to learn, all

over again, what Natty was just starting to learn: to eat, use your hands, balance, sit, walk.

We spent some time with Michael after we left you. The total integration of physician and loving husband in him amazed me. Every part of him was activated to care for you, and to organize the rest of the world to care for you better than it would have dreamt of without his example.

The baby was nursing in my cubicle. They were friends, and they were sharing their baby as if I was alive and well, as if they wanted my blessing. It situated me back in a world of which I was not the centre. The focus was clearly on the baby; how could it be otherwise? It was a moment of peace between the panics. Michael and Rick decided that newborns should visit the ICU all the time, as a standard therapy.

The Nazi came at night. I asked him if I was going to die, and he said yes. I couldn't get away. I was struggling, choking, dying, grabbing out for someone to help me. "Don't leave. Please don't leave." Only Michael could talk me down. He would breathe with me until I fell asleep. The literal meaning of "conspire" is to breathe together. We were conspirators against the night terrors. He would hold my hand and breathe deeply and steadily, till I could drift off. Only then would he go home.

Twice a day, the doctors came on their rounds. Skip Peerless with a small army of penguins following him. It was like a hurricane with everyone scurrying around — "The doctors are coming! The doctors are coming!" They would look at my chart for five seconds and tell me I was doing great. "Good stuff, good stuff," Peerless would say. They were delighted with my progress. I was a success, I could be checked off. This psychological stuff was trivial and there were lots more patients coming in from all over the world, needing dramatic surgery. No one wanted to know how bad I felt.

Michael: Once the panic attacks began, I had to start playing doctor again. You were at the mercy of whatever nurse was on duty. If it was someone like Rick or Mary, you would be in relatively good shape. But if it was one of the punitive ones, you'd be a mess. They way they would treat you drove me crazy. "Don't be a crybaby," they'd say, "There are people who are much sicker than you in this unit." Meaning unconscious people. They were great with unconscious people. I would tell them "There *is* a problem. She's in pain, she's paralyzed, and she feels terrified. You can't talk her out of it because it's real." I had to constantly reassure you that you weren't being too demanding. You didn't need to feel guilty on top of everything else.

I asked one of the nurses, "Why are you looking after my wife if you really don't like to?"

"It's the shift rotation," she said. "There's nothing I can do about it. It's not that I don't like her, but she's recovering. I want to work on the transplants, I want to work with the livers and the cardiacs. There's new machinery that goes along with each new procedure, and I want to learn to use it."

Luckily, Rick was ready to take the panics seriously. He and I agreed that we needed a case conference to develop a workable approach that could be applied consistently on every shift. He spoke to the head nurse and got permission to organize a meeting. I brought literature on panic attacks. Out of the discussion came a very clear and sensible plan — you would be looked after only by the nurses who wanted to work with you and learn about panic attacks. We outlined specific relaxation techniques that everyone would apply. It made a real difference. It didn't stop the panics, but at least people were not being cruel to you.

A year later I saw an article about something called "ICU psychosis." People who spend long periods of time in intensive care often have uncontrollable fears and hallucinations, frequently related to torture. It wasn't a new concept, either; it had been studied for years. Why would highly trained people identify your problem as "acting spoiled"?

At Michael's urging, they started me on a minor tranquillizer, Xanax, and an anti-depressant, Ludiomil. In my old life, I would have been wary, resistant, but now I was willing to try anything to keep the nightmares at bay.

I yearned to be put in a room full of furry puppies — wiggly little golden retrievers, like our dog Lucy when she was young. I could feel their puppy-down tickling me, their exuberant licking tongues as I rolled around laughing with them. I breathed the earthy smell of their wet fur. If I could go into that room, I would get better.

Michael: I was sitting on your bed, and asking you if I could get you something. I was reading your lips or the letter board, I don't remember which. You told me that you wanted to talk to Michael Dworkind and Lesley Levy. They had experience working in palliative care and had been very helpful after your second stroke. I called them on the phone by your bed and held the phone to your ear as they talked to you.

Lesley Levy: We'd never done anything like that before — panic management by long-distance telephone, but Michael sounded pretty desperate. It was really hard to know what to say because we couldn't get any feedback from you. If we could have seen you, we could have read your facial expressions, but there was just silence. What we did with you was a technique we were just learning — meditations from a book by Stephen Levine. We hadn't used them with many people yet, but we thought they might work for you. We mailed Michael photocopies that he could read to you, and a tape of us reading as well. It was our way of dealing with the fact that we couldn't just hop on the plane and see you.

Michael Dworkind: You were completely dependent on others. You were being passively handled, without being able to speak your own needs. It's a horrible situation. No wonder you were scared! But the meditations were telling you that no one can take away your mind. Your mind is a tremendous, powerful tool. Even though you're paralyzed, not able to talk, you can still do something. If you pick up an ember in your hand and hold it softly, it hardly burns you. But if you clench it, it hurts much more. So there are ways of accepting your pain. It doesn't go away, but it doesn't burn you, and you can live with it.

Michael: It used to drive me nuts to read you that stuff. I despised it, it was so banal. But in fact the meditations helped. I read them day after day, night after night. What did I care if they sounded like New Age bullshit? They worked.

It is a cliché to be looking towards "spirituality" on death's doorstep — the old life insurance thing that says just in case there *is* a god... or when all else fails, pray. I don't think that was true of me, however. I wanted wisdom, help to smooth my way through the pain and the fear and to accept my illness. I had died and come back to life, stripped to the bare essentials. No speech, no movement, no breathing. What is the Self then? Who am I, with none of the usual human accoutrements, let alone my particular labels and roles? I was de-constructed, literally. How post-modern of me! It sounds pompous now, but I wanted to live through this experience well. With meaning and grace. I never considered not struggling to survive. Too many people were in it with me to give up.

Michael: I made a list of all your friends in Ontario and showed it out to you, asking who you wanted to see. You pointed to Rosalie Bertell, so I called her up. She came all the way down from Toronto and prayed by the side of your bed.

Rosalie is a biostatistician who has done brave and lonely research on the cancer-inducing effects of low-level nuclear radiation. She is also a Catholic nun. As Terre and I selected the women for *Speaking Our Peace*, we didn't realize that they all had deeply-rooted spiritual beliefs, even church affiliations. Muriel Duckworth and scientist/philosopher Ursula Franklin are Quakers; writer Margaret Laurence was a United Church goer; Marion Dewar, then mayor of Ottawa, is a practising Catholic. While we chose not to correlate their religious beliefs with their peace-making, I knew they were not coincidental either.

So when I needed spiritual guides, the *Speaking Our Peace* women became even more important to me. And true to form, they were all there for me, with letters, visits, phone calls.

I remember Rosalie sitting by my bedside in London. She knew how to sit with the sick. "Do you mind if I say a nun's prayer?" she asked. She waited for my answer. I was a little nervous. Was it like the last sacrament before you die?

She began by "thanking God for the clean air and sparkling water, and for the precious life of Bonnie." There was also something in the prayer about God taking me under Her wing. Rosalie slid back and forth between female and male pronouns and imagery in the most natural way. I know that's not easy to do, because we stumble through it in our synagogue. "What is Woman that thou art mindful of him?"

Much as I appreciated Rosalie's prayer, I kept thinking there must be Jewish sources of knowledge about sickness and death. I longed for the illuminating humour of Jewish spirituality. Why was I so unprepared? Where was the wisdom of my own elders? What could I do to sanctify this moment? It's strange that at a time when I couldn't remember where Montreal was, these questions were so clear inside me. I was thinking of Sholom Aleichem, the Yiddish writer whose stories are so bittersweet, and all those Hasidic stories about consulting Reb Nachman of Breslov or Reb Zusya of Anipol about the ultimate meaning of life:

> ...and Reb Zusya said: When I arrive at the gates of judgment, I will not be asked "Why weren't you more like the great Moses?" I'll be asked "Why weren't you more like Reb Zusya?"

I knew these stories existed but I couldn't remember any, and without language I had no way to explain my need.

Michael: You somehow indicated to me that you wanted me to call Rabbi Ron back in Montreal, and that I should ask him to tell you something funny. All through your phone conversation, you were kind of snorting and choking with laughter. I still don't know what he said!

INTERLUDE: ROSH HASHANAH

Journal: September 7, 1994
I feared from the uncertain weather of the last few days that my "office hours" were over. But I'm sitting here on my bench, after several days of Rosh Hashanah services, watching some bare-chested (male) canoeists go by. I should be writing about panic attacks in London, but my head is full of last week.

New Year's began not so sweetly.

Michael, Seth and I went to Or Shalom Monday evening for Rosh Hashanah services. I was looking forward to this New Year like never before. I was keen to show off our synagogue to Seth who has just moved to Vancouver to go to graduate school after teaching up north last year. Or Shalom is a community where I am at home, where the most diverse group of Jews I know feels at home.

Services were at the same address as last year — the Talmud Torah school. Last year, my first, I had carefully checked the venue beforehand, but by now I'd learned to take access in Vancouver for granted. What a shock to see the flight of stairs leading down to the auditorium which the synagogue had booked because the school's gymnasium, which had been used last year, was so cold and unaesthetic.

Michael scurried to the side and rear of the building, confident there'd be another way in. We are used to service entrances and freight elevators. No such luck. It was completely inaccessible. Ellen Frank, my friend and disability buddy, limped over on her cane, looking like death. Our eyes met. Ellen uttered three words: "NO ONE NOTICED." It turned out that she had been there earlier and even *she* hadn't noticed. There was no "them" who forgot; them was us.

By then, many others had arrived. Some people rechecked the building in disbelief. There was visible pain on the faces of several members of the shul, probably the people who'd worked so hard to create these wonderful High Holiday services for us. They were horrified to see me in my scooter at the top of a flight of stairs.

And probably ashamed.

And my reaction? Hurt. Isolated. Then a rush of other feelings quickly pushed those away. I was stupid for not checking it out beforehand. After all, I hadn't been to synagogue all summer, so why should other people remember? I hadn't been able to volunteer for any of the committees; other people had been doing all the work—how could I complain when they were doing their best? Most of all, I felt guilty for making them feel guilty on Rosh Hashanah.

Then I remembered I had invited my friend Pat to join us the next day. She hadn't been to synagogue for years, since

ALS put her in a wheelchair. She was thrilled to be coming. I felt like shit.

I parked Gladys unobtrusively and struggled down the stairs, using one cane and clinging to the railing. I tried to let it pass and get my spirit into the services, but my head wouldn't stop buzzing. I wasn't really part of this community; I was Other. And how would I tell Pat? I was robbed of my holy day peace.

The phone was ringing as we got home. Pat wanted to make arrangements for the morning. "You can't come. I'm sorry, it's inaccessible." I fumbled with excuses. Pat leapt in: "They're good people. We have a year to teach them — this is good." I learned later that she wheeled down to the ocean and cried.

The next day, I parked Gladys right at the top of the steps so everyone would have to walk around her. People kept suggesting that they carry her — with her great weight and delicate electronics — down the stairs. A crowd of six or eight kids gathered around us.

"How does it work?"

"Why do you use it?"

"Who painted it?"

"Can I have a ride?"

As we were conversing, I caught sight of another child, standing at the top of the stairs, leaning on two canes exactly like mine. I watched him struggle down the stairs with his mother in front of him. The railing I had used the day before was too high for him.

The day after Rosh Hashanah, I flew to the Okanagan Valley to attend a workshop of the B.C. Coalition for People with

Disabilities. The others had gone by bus two days before; I had stayed for the holidays. At the end of a stimulating three days, with a sense of belonging to this community of people with disabilities, I stood up as a Jew. I told them that just as I would speak in my synagogue about "reasonable accommodation" for people with disabilities, I needed to call their attention to the fact that they continued to schedule major events on our most important holidays. Maybe they could make "reasonable accommodation" for people's religious priorities.

Afterwards, though, I was plagued by doubts. Was I too demanding? How much is too much to ask? How much should Or Shalom or the BCCPD have to give up in order to accommodate just a few people?

Why do I still feel that it's asking too much to want to be included: as a person with disabilities and as a Jew? Our rabbi spoke about stretching ourselves that extra bit when we thought we'd stretched as far as we could. I will use this Rosh Hashanah to commit myself to speaking my piece, "making a stink," as Marsha Saxton, one of my disability mentors, says, wherever and whenever I can, even at the risk of being a nag. I will invite people to be our allies, not out of guilt, but in the spirit of the Mitzvah of Tikkun Olam, re-building the world. Maybe literally.

September 1995: Update
This year's High Holiday services will take place at the wheelchair accessible gym.

LEAVING

Anne Usher: Michael phoned me and asked if I would come visit in London. He's usually so strong and analytical and together, but this time he sounded really lonely. I think he probably hadn't been sleeping much. I jumped on a plane and flew out to London.

It was a few weeks after your surgery. The last time I had seen you had been just after your second stroke, and you looked a lot better now. Rick got you out of bed and into a wheelchair for the first time. I think he wanted to get you out of that square box of a cubicle and remind you that there was a big world out there, just waiting for you.

They packed me up and wheeled me out, with my IV tubes, tracheostomy, respirator, my friend and my nurses. They thought nothing of riding in a crowded elevator, walking down the hall to look at the flowers in the front lobby. We were going for an outing. It's all part of life in the Real World.

But the ICU is its own world: tiny, intense and extremely limited. I would lie in my narrow white bed in my narrow white cubicle and have nightmares. I kept my eyes shut. There was nothing to see. I'd been in one hospital or another for a month and a half. To suddenly be out in a crowd was culture shock.

I couldn't handle all the motion. It was like an assault. I couldn't tell if I was moving or if other people were moving around me. If someone walked towards me, I felt like I was falling into them. And there were lots of people and they were all walking and they were either staring at me or going about their business trying not to. I saw myself out in the world for the first time in the lobby of that hospital, and I realized I was not normal. I was a Freak.

I had no control over my body, my mouth was hanging open, my hands were twisted and shaking. My legs were shamelessly jumping with clonus. A grim mental image rose in my mind, of pitiful creatures with their heads drooping and drooling. Vegetables. And I was one of them. That was me.

Anne Usher: You mouthed the word "freak." I felt awful that we hadn't thought about how you might react. You had trouble sitting up and you were tied into the chair, but as a nurse myself, I'm used to seeing tubes and machines and people flailing around. All I could see was how much better you were than you had been.

Michael: The ICU administration decided they needed your bed for somebody who was sicker. As soon as you were completely weaned off the respirator and onto the T-tube, they transferred you to the ward. It was all decided in the course of a few hours and then off you went, with no chance to say goodbye to Rick or Mary.

Unlike the ICU, the ward was badly understaffed, with only two nurses per shift covering a large number of patients. During the day, they would come into your room periodically, and turn and suction you on a sched-ule that fit in with all their other tasks. It was not great.

But at night it was much worse. The head nurse thought you were demanding, neurotic and taking too much of his time. When he handled you he was rough and abrupt, never talking to you, or explaining what he was doing. Every time that nurse walked in the room, you flinched.

The panic attacks got worse. His response was to pump you full of Valium, which was prescribed for you as a PRN — to be used as required at the nurse's discretion. He said the best way of dealing with you would be for me to go away and leave it to him. I was considered part of the problem as if, by taking your fears seriously, I was contributing to your "neurosis."

After two days on the ward I said, "We might as well go home to Montreal." Even if the care was no better at the JGH, as a member of the hospital staff I could at least do a better job of manipulating the system.

I remember Skip Peerless' last rounds, the day I left London, three weeks after my surgery. I thanked him for the hundredth time and then I asked The Question. The question I had been too sick and then too scared to ask. "When will I be well again?" I fumbled with the letter board in my nervousness and in the end Michael had to read my lips.

"I'd guess you'll be standing by Thanksgiving and walking by Christmas," Skip answered. Standing by Thanksgiving: less than a month. Walking by Christmas: three months. It became my mantra. Repeated by Michael and all my friends: "Standing by Thanksgiving, walking by Christmas."

Michael: There was a doctor and nurse from Quebec who came with the air ambulance, plus room for one more person. I thought I was going to get to go with you this time. But the Ontario bureaucrats said "She's our patient until she reaches Quebec. We have to send an Ontario nurse." So a nurse who didn't even know you went on that plane. Ontario had to pay her plane fare back from Montreal, and you had to fly with a bunch of strangers at a time when you were suffering from panic attacks.

No one told me how long the flight would be. Again, no one even spoke to me. After an eternity, we landed. I was wheeled through a confusion of corridors and then we were outside and there was Michael Dworkind popping out of an ambulance. I know I was glad to see him, but I have a vague, guilty memory of being nasty in some way, sharp and unappreciative.

Michael Dworkind: You were uncomfortable and obviously you'd gone through a rough trip. I understood that. I was trying to be jovial and welcoming. I sat in the back of the ambulance with you for the ride to the JGH. You couldn't see out the window from your stretcher so I was telling you where we were, sort of like a guided tour of Montreal. "Now we're turning on Décarie Boulevard, there's the Orange Julep building. . . . We're stuck in the usual traffic at Cote-Ste.-Catherine. Now we've moved about another three feet. Here we are coming back to your hospital, to your bed in your room in the neuro ward . . . returning to a safe place." I wanted you to feel like you were coming home and everything would be OK, even though I was saying in my mind, "Gee, *is* this a safe place? Who am I kidding?"

JEWISH GENERAL HOSPITAL

≈

BACK AT THE JGH

Night after night, all night.

Pt awake and agitated. Pt flailing both arms over head. Pt asking
to have husband called.

*I couldn't move my legs. I was trapped in the sheets. My arm
was falling through the slats of the guardrail, flattening and
stretching, like Elastic Man or Rubber Man, some guy from
Seth's old superhero comic books. Mr. Fantastic, that's it. My
whole body was going to be flattened and squished through the
bed rails until I strangled. The nurse was mad at me.*

Pt demanding attention. Given Xanax. Ludiomil. Haldol.

Michael: You were racked with panics every night. You
were nearly delirious from lack of sleep. And the nurses,
shortstaffed as they were, had a hard time dealing with
you.

Naomi: We were back in the high-care unit with the
Hun. I hated her. You would have panic attacks and she
would get mad at you. She was terrifying.

The Hun was the worst. She thought the panic attacks were a bunch of nonsense and I should pull myself together and stop being a baby. It didn't help that she had a German accent. She evoked all the deep-seated Jewish fears and prejudices about Germans which were surfacing in my nightmares. She had such power over me. She was there after everyone left for the night. Every day I would ask Michael if she was on duty, and I'd beg him not to leave me if she was. I used to fear Michael alienating her, that she would take it out on me after he left.

Michael: I was very angry with her one day and I said, "You know, I notice that you do much better with comatose patients. I bet you prefer them." And she said to me, "You're right, I do."

Patricia was still there in the bed next to mine! She was still in a coma and her husband was still sitting by her bed talking to her. Michael would talk to me and J.P. would talk to Patricia. *"Ma chere. Ma fille. Ma belle que j'adore. Ma belle marie."* They must have been in their fifties, but he kept talking about her as a young and beautiful girl, his bride. Had there really been a time when I thought her good-as-dead and him a fool? Now I knew she was listening, as I was listening. We were rooting for each other.

Suzi Scott: The whole time Patricia was in high care, she never even blinked. Then one evening, J.P. comes running up to me and says, "Suzi, she talked!" And I think, "Oh yeah, I'll believe anything." But he says, "No, no, Suzi, you have to come see." So I go over and sure enough, her eyes are open and she's mouthing the words,

"I love you." J.P. starts crying. I start crying. "She's back! She's back!"

My right leg was still completely paralyzed. Every day the doctors stuck pins in my toes and shook their heads. I was still tube fed and incontinent. I wasn't having much success with the bedpan. There was a green, plasticized pad underneath me, which used to get all bunched up and stuck to my body. It reminded me of the diapers I used to put on Mom. For peeing I had a catheter and bag. My vagina and rectum were sore. Everything was sore. They wiped me with some kind of cloth that felt like sandpaper to my heightened sensitivity.

Everyone said I was improving. I graduated from bed baths to tub baths. The orderly wheeled me down a long corridor to an endless row of tiny bathtub rooms. In my mind it stretched out for miles. Then he would park me beside a big winching machine, and the nurse would take my gown off and wrap me, diaper-fashion, in a rubber sling attached to cables. Then the orderly would turn on the machine. It would start up with a horrible grinding sound, and lift me into the air. I would hang there, my limp body like a dead fish in a net. I think my eyes were closed. I have no memory of the bathtub below me, the nurse standing by to guide me down. *The grinding went on and on, and then the warm water closed around my body. The water stroked me, soothed me, terrified me. I knew I didn't have the strength to keep my head from going under. I heard someone screaming; maybe it was me. The nurse bathed and shampooed me. Then there was the shower sound. The screaming and the shower; the bald Nazi, the concentration camp.*

The days hung on Michael's visits. No matter how mistreated I felt or how awful the panics were, I knew it would be better when Michael came. Michael would put me to bed every night. He would read to me, and stroke me and breathe with me until I dozed off.

Michael: Your panics kept getting worse. I was at my wits' end. I asked Bernard to resume your acupuncture treatments. You were calmer after seeing him, but only temporarily. I asked Michael and Lesley to come in. I implored my psychiatrist friend, Laurence Kirmayer, to work with you, even though he had largely given up clinical psychiatry for research. I went to the NFB and explained the panic attacks and asked your friends to come see you.

I was exhausted, but it was nothing compared to what you were going through. People kept telling me I should go see a shrink. But that wasn't what I needed; I needed you to get better.

I got my support from colleagues at Herzl. The nurses, the doctors, the secretaries. They looked after me. I had started seeing a few patients again at this point, people I'd known for a long time who had concrete illnesses that needed monitoring. I couldn't deal with anyone who needed a lot of emotional support, or with the day-to-day administration of Herzl, but my colleagues understood and filled in for me.

Cheryl Levitt had taken over as Acting Director. Some days I would just walk into Cheryl's office and say, "I'm not coping." She never talked much, or asked questions. She would just sit down and hold my hand.

Cheryl Levitt: I remember one night I dropped by high care on my way home, and walked into the middle of a panic attack. I was terrified. I'd never seen anyone going through that. Your eyes opened up and you had these weird, spastic movements of your hand. You were mouthing words but there was no sound. You were asking me to get Michael. But when I called him, he said "I have to sleep. Just for a few hours and then I'll come."

I felt terrible, because I wanted him there nearly as desperately as you did, but he was at the end of his strength. So I said to you, "I don't think Michael can come in, but I'll stay with you for a while." I couldn't leave because the nurse on shift was someone you were scared of. You were panicking for nearly an hour and a half before you fell asleep. Nothing seemed to help. You kept mouthing the words "I want to die. I want to die."

I don't remember asking to die, but it's there in the nurses' notes too. I don't think it meant I wanted to commit suicide or wished someone would do it for me. It meant: I hurt, I'm scared, get me out of here.

Kathleen Shannon: We had worked together for years at Studio D, but we weren't close. You always radiated a kind of cheerful confidence, as if you had your life just the way you wanted it. I wasn't exactly jealous, it just never occurred to me that you would need anything from me. Then Michael came to the film board and asked us to visit.

When I walked into your cubicle, it was hard to tell whether you were greeting me with delight or freaking out. Your body was speaking a whole other language that I had never seen before. Your facial expression was all untuned. It struck me that it would be stressful for you to have to welcome me, or entertain me. So I said, "I'm just going to keep you company while you rest. Don't worry about saying anything; you can say it later." I stroked your arm and kept telling you, "Don't worry about anything, everything can wait." You seemed to fall asleep at that point, but then someone else dropped by and you got all anxious trying to talk to them.

Michael: It soon became apparent that this chaos of visitors was only adding to your anxiety. We needed to create a delicate balance between your need for rest and your need for company. Sara Lazzam, my secretary, started setting up a schedule where you would see only one person at a time, for half an hour. Each morning she would create a list of the day's visitors for you.

I loved Sara's schedules. I don't know if I ever thanked her enough for the diplomacy it required to retract "appointments" from the people I decided I didn't want to see. I quickly learned who gave me energy and who drained me. Conversations with anyone but Michael or Naomi or Seth were exhausting and sometimes ridiculous. Michael says I usually communicated sympathy for folks who couldn't understand me, but in truth I was sick of the letter board. Often when someone correctly guessed the letter I was trying to point to, they would jump to conclusions about the rest of the word and even finish my sentence on the basis of that one letter. I watched in helpless frustration as the game of charades spun out of control in the wrong direction.

Michael: The reason you couldn't talk wasn't because you couldn't remember or access language, as happens sometimes with hemispheric strokes. It was because, for a while, you were unable to breathe. One needs breath to speak, and your breath was being provided through a tube in your throat. The major concern of the neurologists was to protect your airway, and the fact that you couldn't talk with a tracheostomy was considered to be a temporary state that I shouldn't get excited about. I, on the other hand, was very concerned about your ability to talk, especially in light of your panic attacks. I was trying to bridge the importance of the medical concerns, which I didn't deny, with your psychological well-being.

The solution was to decrease the size of the trach tube, so the opening gradually got smaller and smaller. Then you could cover the trach tube with your thumb, for short phrases.

Seth: I was home for the weekend the first time you spoke. I don't remember what you said; I just have this picture in my mind of Dad's hand covering the trach tube, and you making noise through your mouth. And then you smiled. It was a tremendous relief. We're all big talkers in our family.

Pt is learning how to cover her trach to communicate w. voice. She needs some direction as to where it is. The closure she maintains is adequate for intelligible voice. Should this not be possible, a nurse may cover the trach for her. She needs to be reminded to take a deep breath before closing.

The first sounds were breathy, less than whispers. My Jackie Kennedy voice, Terre called it. The therapists called it "not functional." It was hard work. I learned the economics of speech.

To measure my words, as the cliché goes. When it's so difficult to get ideas across, most of them seem hardly worth it. A lot of self-censorship occurred: "Never mind, it's not important."

The speech therapist said that I would never regain normal speech. I could try, and she could help, but we were doomed to failure. The damage had been done, and we had to be "realistic" in our expectations. She was cool and brisk, as if she had just stopped off at the hospital on the way to doing something really important, like preparing to give a dinner party.

I was devastated. How could I be me if I couldn't speak? Who the hell did she think she was? Who taught her it was her job to make me "realistic," to dash my so-called false hopes? I *was* talking! Real words. I had no strength to project them, but they were all there. Or mostly there. I could only get out a few words at a time, so my phrasing was weird and irregular. My thick tongue made my words slurred and people had trouble understanding me. I had to repeat everything as I became more fatigued. Requests came out as baby talk or one-word commands: "Radio," not "Would you please turn on the radio?" Sometimes I grunted. But it just wasn't conceivable that this weak voice would not strengthen with time and practice.

I can't remember the speech therapist ever coming after that. Maybe she just gave up on this hopeless case. I don't think she did any speech exercises with me, not even the tongue movements and clicks I had done after the first stroke. And she never had the decency to admit I was doing better than she had predicted, or to congratulate me.

I didn't know why I had trouble speaking, that the stroke had damaged my cranial nerves, paralyzing one vocal cord and half my tongue and palate. Michael says he knew, and maybe he told me but I didn't understand.

I talked slowly because I was thinking slowly and my breath was slow. I wasn't able to be glib and just rattle things off like I used to. But some people really listened. They had to be quiet to hear me. There's something compelling about such speech, something sacred in the silences.

My hearing was painfully acute. I could hear people whispering about me from the nursing station across the ICU, or at least I thought it was about me. I recognized everyone's different footsteps. Loud voices frightened me. The paging system was the worst — intrusive and insensitive, going about its business in flat tones as if we weren't sick and sometimes dying. "Dr. Swift to the ICU! Dr. Swift, stat!"

I would become confused and overwhelmed if I was supposed to do two things at the same time, like have my lips swabbed with glycerin and listen to a conversation. If there was talking, there could be no music; if there was music, there could be no talking. I couldn't separate them into channels, as I had without thinking before my stroke. Now I became the music that I heard; there were no boundaries. I could follow all the various instruments, as if I were inside the heads of the composer and the musicians, participating in their creation. I would laugh at a trumpet improvising, or nod to a flute responding to cello. But anything with a strong beat was painful. The rhythms pounded in my whole being. Ladysmith Black Mambazo, my favourite group from the summer before, became scary. Orchestral extravaganzas and Renaissance fanfares were frantic. Opera was too noisy. Violins were too shrill. I became addicted to Mozart and Glenn Gould's rendition of the *Goldberg Variations*, as well as the New Age music that I had previously scorned. Environmental tapes of running streams and bird sounds were mainlined through earphones to create my own private island on the hospital bed. Music soothed my frayed nervous system.

The nose tube went through my nose all the way down to my stomach, and it irritated the whole tract. My throat was always sore. I would pull the tube out, usually in the middle of the night. I'm not sure if I was pulling it out on purpose or in my sleep. I remember one of the nurses yelling at me, "Bad girl! You pulled out your tube!" She wasn't allowed to put it back in, so she had to call the neurology resident. And of course I couldn't eat meanwhile, so the dietitian — that same one I fought with before — would be there scolding me about dehydration and malnutrition.

Reinsertion was painful, probably because I pulled it out so often. I remember exactly what it felt like. It goes down your throat and into your esophagus, and then you have to kind of swallow it down. I would always ask for Michael to reinsert my feeding tube because he was so gentle and smooth with it. It was the resident's job, but if he didn't come, Michael would just do it.

I was a perfectly terrible patient, a royal pain in the ass, and so was Michael.

The hospital was short on nurses, short on orderlies. They couldn't turn me at my discomfort, they had to turn by the clock. No one seemed to know the "sheet trick" the London nurses had used so it was an awkward procedure. Each time I was turned, they also had to "position" me, wedging me into an elaborate nest of pillows. I felt like a flower arrangement or maybe a corpse. I lacked the control to lie on my side unsupported without flopping over. There was one pillow in front to keep me from rolling, one doubled up against my back, and one between my legs. I used to beg to be repositioned because I would get numb at the pressure points. My body was a dead weight and I didn't know where my limbs were. But I had trouble remembering the word "position." I would ask for "posturing" or "placing" or "set-up." Exact words often eluded me, forcing me to invent approximations.

Gerry Rogers: I remember on my first visit, going up the elevator, so afraid to see you. The first thing you said to me was, "Hi, I missed your birthday." You were smiling but kind of shaky, and your eyes were rolling around. You were desperately skinny, like a concentration camp survivor, and your muscles were like jelly. One arm kept floating off in the air, and you would say, "No control." This was going to be the first night when Michael wouldn't be sitting with you until you fell asleep. I would be there instead. It was a big deal and we were all nervous. You were so afraid that you weren't going to be able to sleep, but you kept saying, "Michael has to rest."

Pt coughing up thick yellow mucous. Pt restless and noisy.
Pt really demanding, wants to change position every 30 min.
Given Haldol.

One panic melted into the next. I begged the nurse to untangle my legs from the sheets but she was busy charting. They were always charting.

Annie sang me a lullaby to help me sleep; something about flying, one of my favourites. She used to sing that same song to Seth and then Naomi. She always sang it with hand gestures, in a soft voice:

My pigeon house (fingers interlocked)
I open wide, (hands twist, fingers unlock)

And set my pigeons free. (fingers fluttering...)
They climb so high
Till they reach the sky
And they light on the nearest tree...
Ku-ru, Ku-ru
Ku-ru, ku-ru, ku-ru.

I was the baby now. That was OK. It was good.

Annie Klein: I sang "My Pigeon House" for you, and when I got to the Ku-ru's, you sang with me. It was soon after they fixed your trach so you could talk a bit, and your voice was so sweet. I'll always remember that.

My leg was stuck in the bed rails. My bad leg that Bernard said wasn't "bad," only lethargic. My body was infinitely distortable. It was squished flat. It was a melted coke bottle. I called and called with my weak voice. I banged on the bedframe, over and over, with my numb fists.

Pt confused, waving her arms about. Haldol 0.5 mg.

In the morning I noticed that my knuckles were blue.

Annie and Phil came and went so often I lost track. Were they in New Jersey, or had they just gone out in the hall for a minute? They didn't talk much about feelings. Their focus was on what needed doing and how they could help. They stayed in the background, cleaning, cooking, shopping.

Annie brought me long, elegant nightgowns which she had bought on sale to replace the skimpy, scratchy hospital gowns. I loved the feel of the flannel, but my feet kept getting tangled up in them, which would set off panic attacks. So Annie took them back and hemmed them up short. I was sad at this dese-cration, but lo, she had just folded their length into giant hems which she then let down when I was well enough.

I hated that I had missed Rosh Hashanah. It's a time to reflect, reevaluate life and make resolves for the coming year; a time to appreciate life and its blessings. We had always cele-brated with my mother — she would come from Philadelphia for the High Holy Days and for Passover, even before she came to live with us. Annie and Phil were less into the holidays, having rejected religion as the "opiate of the masses." "Gibber-ish," Philip would mutter under his breath. But they were always into good food and any excuse for a party.

One of the few good things about being back at the JGH was that Jewish holidays were acknowledged. Two men came around to blow the shofar just after sundown on Yom Kippur, the Day of Atonement. I loved the idea that they were coming to me because I couldn't go to synagogue. But the wild, primeval notes quickly became too shrill for my super-sensitive ears. I anxiously waved them away.

Interlude: restraints

Journal: July 3, 1990, Black Lake
I was lying in bed just now, for an afternoon read with Robin Morgan's *Dry Your Smile*. The narrator was describing her

mother's violent attack on her under the influence of L-Dopa. The hospital staff rushed in and put her in restraints. RESTRAINTS! I shot up in bed like in bad movies. The memory of restraints washed over me. I cried out, sobbed, shook, wanted Michael. I'm amazed that with all my remembering, this particular horror has not come back to me until now, almost three years after the stroke, and has come back with all its original terror. I fear that I will have this kind of flashback forever. For the first few years, a smell, a sound, a phrase would trigger vivid replays of painful events. But beyond the pain, there is a deep relief in exhuming these memories.

I remember the feeling more than the details. I am at the JGH, in a panic attack and thrashing to pull out a tube — is it the tracheostomy or the nasal feeding tube? In my panic, I grab at one of the nurses or aides, begging her not to leave me, and she gets scared or angry. Orderlies are called to restrain me. I think they just use pieces of sheeting, tying each of my hands to the bed rails. I continue to thrash, my paralysis now exaggerated by this physical leashing. I feel like a prisoner. But no, I must be crazy — this is a reliable hospital. The staff must be acting appropriately. I wondered before if the panic attacks meant that I was going crazy, and now I know they do.

I don't know how often I was put in restraints. I only know that I lived in fear of them. I remember being threatened with them if I didn't behave, if I pulled out the tubes. They were the "or else."

My family seemed to know nothing of this part of my experience; it happened at night after Michael had left. But the medical notes tell the story.

Pt needs to be restrained . . .

Wrist restraints applied for safety so the pt will not pull at her
trach or feeding tube . . .

Pt sleeping quietly, arm restraints removed. . . .

SCREAMER

I remember a voice. A woman howling, "Nurse, nurse, help
me, somebody help me. Don't leave me alone." It went on and
on. Her voice ripped me apart. It was as if I were inside her
body. I could have been her. Sometimes I was her.

People crying, walking around drugged out and drooling:
I got used to it, like the nurses were used to it. "She's just a
screamer, don't bother about her. We have a few on every
ward." Who was this new self who could hear someone beg for
help and accept the nurse's verdict that it was "nothing"?

22:00 Pt awake and crying out.

Saying she wants to get up and get out of here,

asking for nurse's help.

Haldol given with little effect.

My limbs were numb and distant, like strange objects lying
in my bed. I remember the soft rubbery texture under my fingers. *This is not my skin.* I remember my hands spasming into

claws, fingernails digging into my flesh, leaving marks that I couldn't feel. *I remember Mom digging marks into her hands because they didn't keep her nails short. I would cut her nails and try to stretch her fingers out, but it would hurt her. Finally I had to accept that her fingers couldn't be straightened.*

Joe Carlton quoted Shakespeare to me:

The lunatic, the lover, and the poet,
Are of imagination all compact:
One sees more devils than vast hell can hold,
That is, the madman ...

I loved the self-aggrandizement of seeing my panic attacks as artistic imagination working overtime.

Joe Carlton: You asked me if you were going crazy and I said no, you were hypersensitive. Small things seemed life threatening. It was understandable. Often it's only after a crisis has begun to resolve that one can really look at what is happening. It's then that we are most susceptible to terror.

Eventually Michael persuaded the hospital to hire sitters overnight so someone would always be at my bedside to help with my panics. It was an awful job, I knew that. I felt like I was imposing on them, asking these underpaid women to stay awake and take care of me. You can't pay somebody to love you. But the people who loved me were already strained to the limit.

Every night I'd somehow ask the sitter to pat my head. It was a hypnotic motion that calmed me down and helped me sleep. It was very awkward. Why was I asking a total stranger to do this weird and intimate thing? Often I would outlast her ability to keep patting without falling asleep herself.

I remember asking one woman to read from Kahlil Gibran's *The Prophet*. She was a francophone who could hardly speak English, let alone read this convoluted, archaic translation. She stumbled through it, missing words and fracturing phrases. I felt ashamed to put her through that, but I was desperate for the words.

> 23:45 Pt can't fall asleep. Wants to die. Attempted to
> reassure. Pt asked us to kill her, wants to stop breathing.
> Haldol 1 mg.

Seth: You were having such a hard time that the rest of us had to pull together.

Your stroke entirely transformed my relationship with Naomi. She and I hadn't been very close in high school. We fought about all the things teenagers fight about: the telephone, her sloppiness. I thought she was a fuck-up. I didn't understand her at all.

Naomi: If someone had told me in grade 11 that I was going to be living alone with my father the next year, I would have jumped off a cliff. There was no way. He and I were at each other's throats. It was a power struggle and I always lost. Every time we'd fight, I'd end up feeling it was a waste of time; it doesn't matter what I say or what I do, he always pulls rank on me, he's my father, and I'm totally dependent on him, why am I even arguing? Mom was the mediator for everything that happened in that house. When she would go on location with some film, I would go crazy.

But after everyone came back from London, it was just me and Dad. Suddenly, we were a family. The two of us. He needed me. And he knew that he needed me. The power struggle was over. When you need someone, you're much more careful with the way you treat them.

Naomi had begun Brébeuf, a classy academic CÉGEP (Quebec's junior college system) in the French-from-France tradition. Most of the students had attended private French secondary school. Naomi's French, while fluent and colloquial, was purely Québecois, learned at a populist summer camp. Seth had gone to Brébeuf for a year before going on the SAGE tour and he had survived, but Naomi was drowning there.

Naomi: Everyone from my high school was going to English CÉGEP but I decided to go to Brébeuf. Brébeuf is an incredibly snobbish school but from a distance it looked like the ultra cool scene I had always been sure was waiting for me somewhere.

But by the time classes started, my mother was in the hospital and I was the walking wounded, an open sore. This was supposed to be a challenge, but I wasn't up for it. Everyone looked like Gitano jeans models. My French, which was considered stellar at my English high school, was a disaster.

I couldn't meet people. I walked around the school on the verge of tears. I was afraid to put my hand up in class because I thought I might start bawling. Brébeuf is two blocks from the JGH and I shuttled back and forth so many times a day that it seemed like the two buildings were attached.

I don't know when I stopped going to classes. I convinced myself somehow that I had dropped out, that it
was official. The only problem was that I didn't tell anyone. Every day that I missed, my teachers were busy giving me zeros on assignments that I didn't even know I
had. I "officially" left Brébeuf at the end of the term. The
highest mark I got was a 16 per cent.

Naomi spared me this information. Instead, she told amus-
ing anecdotes, and I chose to be proud of her going to such a
tough school. Once she said she wanted to quit because she
was doing badly, but I brushed it off saying surely they would
understand and she probably wasn't doing as badly as she
thought. It was a long time before I understood that she was
seriously failing.

All I knew was that I was dependent on Naomi, and she was
my unfailing confidante and advocate. She insisted on absolute
honesty. Her poem on my wall told me she could take it, and
it was true, she could. But it was a difficult position for a
seventeen-year-old. Lacking any status in the hospital, she
would do her best to shield me from the Hun and anyone else
who mistreated me. After all those years of trying to teach her
to be "nicer" to adults, I now needed her to protect me against
them.

Naomi: Suzi Scott and I ganged up on my captive mother
and did a complete beauty makeover. I had my mother
wearing more make-up in the hospital than she would
wear to an awards banquet. I had always desperately
wanted her to look like one of the suburban Hampstead
moms. This was my chance, I suppose. My friends whom

my family had always dismissed as useless airheads came
in to do facial masks, even lip treatments. We were useful
for the first time. Thank God for *Mademoiselle* magazine.

Naomi had spent years locked in the bathroom, valuable
years when (I thought) she should have been acquiring the
skills and competence she would need as a female in this society. Math. Sports. Automobile mechanics. Instead she was
becoming an expert in hair colour and make-up. Her nagging
feminist mother and her doctor father both managed to miss
the fact that her bathroom hibernation also included long bouts
of bulimia.

For Naomi to swab apricot balm on my parched lips, to
bleach the dark hairs on my face (the result of those mispre-
scribed steroids), to do something as intimate as shave my
armpits, sounds natural between mother and daughter. Hadn't
I wiped her sweet baby bum, combed her little-girl braids,
nursed the bumps and bruises of body and heart? But daugh-
ters — and mothers — forget, and it had been so long since we
were comfortable with each other's bodies. She wore a loose
sweatshirt for the entire year in which she grew secret breasts,
and demanded that I not make a "big deal" when she informed
me that she had begun menstruating at camp. (There went my
fantasies of a family menstruation celebration.) Naomi's discomfort had made me become more inhibited with my own
body, which had previously hung loose in our Vermont sauna.
I accepted all this as probably "appropriate" modesty — but
with sadness.

So it was doubly — no, triply — sweet to share Naomi's
new Sultry Peach lipstick. My skin was blotched, my features
lop-sided, my limbs slack and wasted, but my daughter made
me feel pretty.

I remember the smell of her hands stroking my face during an anxiety attack. It must have been hard for her to watch me twitching and gasping, but she never pulled away.

I felt confused and betrayed when Suzi Scott announced she was now Wanda the Witch. I guess she thought she was being cute, but I had no sense of humour about it. Suzi was the only nurse who loved me, and now she had decided to get tough with me. She refused to untangle me when my nightgown attacked my legs. She said I should learn to wait. She refused to help me find CBC on my bedside radio. She said I could do it myself. Why now? Had I done something wrong? Was she only pretending to like me?

Seth had given me that radio to keep me connected with the real world, the world outside the hospital. CBC was all I listened to, but somehow it always seemed to be tuned to some Top 40 station. I had great difficulty learning how to operate that simple machine — not just physical but mental. There were countless hours of having to listen to the wrong station, with annoying commercials and brainless deejay banter piped directly into my brain through the earphones.

Suzi Scott: When you started to be able to move your fingers, that's when I started playing with your radio. Once a day I would move the dial as far from CBC as possible. It was a way to get you to use your hands. You needed to realize you could do things for yourself. I think you knew I was doing it, because you used to call me "Bitch." It took you awhile, but you learned to change the station.

Panics continued to come suddenly and without provocation. I would be with a visitor and suddenly feel like I couldn't

swallow and was going to choke and die. I seemed to be on a
million different drugs, which confirmed my fear that I was
going mad. Fortunately the psychologists from Herzl were my
friends, people who knew me when I was OK, who thought I
would be OK again. Michael had asked them to help me with
daily relaxation exercises. I remember Yvonne's hypnotic voice
counting backwards. Judy had me visualize ocean waves.
Morrie added gestures: tapping my left hand, which was more
spastic, with my right one as I was saying "Calm. Relax." There
was deep breathing associated with it. Breathe in relaxation.
Breathe out tension and fear.

As soon as I felt the shortness of breath, the constricting
chest, I would start the exercise:...calm, relax, calm, relax,
ten, nine, eight...I struggled to remember the exact words and
motions. Breathe in — inspiration? Breathe out — what? Per-
spiration? If I got it right, perhaps it would save me.

Morrie Golden: The words didn't matter. What mattered
was the notion that you didn't have to lie there and let it
happen, that somehow you could fight back. You needed
some sense of active participation, of control. It would
usually work, if you caught the panic soon enough. If it
was a full-blown attack that had already overtaken you,
then nothing would work. But I remember watching the
panic start to roll over you, and you take hold and dim-
inish it.

Many of the high-care staff didn't take what we were
doing very seriously. Sometimes I would show up for our
appointment and the nurse would say, "This is not visiting hours." And I would say "This isn't a visit." But as
far as she was concerned, we were just chatting. It wasn't

important enough to write on your chart. It wasn't hard-core medicine like drugging you would be.

Laurence Kirmayer: In the end, Haldol may have been part of the problem, rather than part of the solution. It's not a good drug for anxiety; it can add to your disorientation. It can cause odd symptoms, like stiffness, drifting arms, and phantom limb stuff. But it's a very common medication, and probably used too often with unclear or minor rationale.

You seemed to be displaying those typical Haldol side-effects, so I wrote a note on your chart asking that Haldol be avoided if possible, and suggesting Cogentin to counteract some of the side-effects. But I was just a consulting psychiatrist — it would have been up to the attending neurologist to write the orders. That night you had an extremely bad time and were given the full dose of Haldol. The next day I left a stronger note, recommending that Haldol be discontinued. It was replaced with chloral hydrate, for treating your sleeplessness rather than some supposed psychosis.

How long had it been since I had a real night's sleep? Two weeks? Three? Michael decided that maybe if I didn't nap during the day and stayed awake well into the evening, I might be able to re-establish a normal sleeping pattern. That made theoretical sense, but in practice it was horrendous. My entire roster of visitors was recruited to keep me from dozing. Again and again I would start to drift off, only to be forced awake. Michael would program my evenings, trying to keep me entertained while I waited for the hour when I was finally allowed to shut my eyes. He would lift me from the bed and wheel me downstairs to the Herzl conference room. There he would project some of the family slides he had assembled after the first stroke. After the slide show came the telephone. Michael would pull out my little phone book and say, "Who shall we call tonight?" I usually had enough energy to make one call. It was like a game: Michael would dial and hold the receiver for me and I would surprise the hell out of somebody.

I remember calling Norma, my college roommate, who lives in Boston. I said, "Hello, Norma? This is Bonnie," and she started crying. The next night we called Razelle. She screamed. "It's my sister! I've got my sister back." I understood for the first time the extent of her fear of losing me.

Phone calls seemed to require even more vocal projection than talking in person, and I was self-conscious about my lengthy pauses, knowing there was a long distance bill to pay. But they would leave me feeling happy and loved, ready for my bed and a good night's sleep — which would last all of a few hours before it was panic time again.

02:00 pt noisy & confused.
States she had "bad dream" where she was "paralyzed."

Gerry Rogers: I brought a floral brocade writing book to the hospital for your visitors to write in. (Maybe it was that compulsive documentary habit we were all into at Studio D.) I called it *The Friends' Book of Healing*. I thought, "Recovery is going to be slow, and probably the hardest thing for Bonnie will be to remember how bad it was and realize what a big victory each new movement is." The changes were so apparent to us on the outside and yet for you it was like a sea without markers in terms of time and space and change.

My other thought was that probably some people wanted to say things to you but weren't quite able to say them out loud, so the book would be a safe place to communicate. In the back of my mind, I was also thinking that if things didn't turn out, then this would be really precious to your kids and Michael.

The Friends' Book of Healing:

It is so good to see you — you told me this is the "improvements" book — so, this being my first visit, I've got to say you are a lot better than I thought you'd be — such good smiles — and much activity with your arms and lots of secretions which you're spitting into recycled Kleenex. Yucky. I'll bring you some fresh Kleenex next time I come. Thanks for the brownie someone made for your guests. Love you a lot. Try to be calm — better times will come, and we'll be bitching together in the halls of the NFB.

Love, Gloria

I loved the message you left on my machine today, ("If you think I'm getting better just to talk to your machine, you're mistaken!") I'm so glad that you're well enough to be silly. Now it's time for you to blow this joint and get back to work! I miss you.

All love, Terre

It was a funny time. On the one hand, I was constantly anxious; on the other, I felt bathed in love. My hospital room was a melting-pot where Catholic nuns met feminist witches, and physicians met acupuncturists and deep muscle massage therapists. I remember watching one of my NFB friends in animated discussion with Ron and wondering, "Does she know he's a rabbi? Does he know she's a lesbian?" It was gloriously mixed up.

The stroke had restored my love and faith in men, erased my knee-jerk prejudices that were an easy but unnecessary side-effect of the pain of sexism. My women's networks had rallied around me, from sacred rites on the mountain and inventing *The Friends' Book of Healing*, to domestic details like bringing me real food and nurturing my family. I had a special closeness with women who were mothers during my worst weeks. They were at ease with my physical helplessness, they knew how to dress me, feed me. But I couldn't separate my women friends from the men who also formed my "net" in this crisis. Until my stroke, Michael and Seth had been the only "exceptions" allowed into my women-centred life. But now my life embraced gentle healers like Joe Carlton, Rabbi Ron, Rick; Bob Usher who cried with joy at the foot of my wheelchair; male film colleagues whom I had previously excluded from my "inner circle" but who were brave enough to include themselves in my healing; Bernard, who was there almost daily and ended every acupuncture session with a kiss — it was part of the treatment.

But not every would-be healer was as helpful. One night a man snuck into high care. I thought he might be a rabbi. He certainly wasn't my rabbi, but he was dressed in Hasidic garb. I don't know what the nurses were doing at the time, but he waltzed right over to my bed and stuffed this dry, crumbly matzoh into my mouth. I was still being tube-fed, so of course I started choking. He said he wanted me to swallow it all, and

I kept trying to. I was totally passive and accepting. I guess I was used to people coming by and doing mysterious and uncomfortable things to me. Michael walked in while I was choking and chased this guy down the hall, returning to suction the matzoh crumbs out of my trach tube. It turned out that he was a patient of Michael's. A former hippie, he had become an Orthodox Jewish schoolteacher and had been trying unsuccessfully to convert Michael for years. (The matzoh had apparently been blessed by the holy Lubovitch rebbe in Brooklyn six months before.) Later he sent Michael a very contrite letter about how he only meant well and asking to be forgiven. Michael was furious.

But Seth said, "You know, she did start to feel better the next day."

TURNING POINT

The Friends' Book of Healing:

Every time I come, you keep looking better — calm and relaxed. Now you're sitting up and getting ready to go to the gym. If you could just get that tube out of your nose!

All in good time — as Kohelet said, "To everything there is a season and a time for every purpose under heaven." Now is the time for healing.

Love, Ron Aigen

What changed? It was probably a combination of factors: stopping Haldol, relaxation exercises, Michael's forced wakefulness regimen, the simple passage of time. According to the medical notes it happened very quickly; one night was solid terror, the next night was broken and restless, and the next was smooth sleep with a single short-lived nightmare at dawn.

Being able to sleep brought an immediate turnaround on all other fronts. Each day was a benchmark. Suzi Scott taught me to turn myself, carefully isolating each step in the process. First I had to reach for the metal bed rail; then, using my arm strength which was greater than that of my legs or trunk, I had to wriggle myself face-down on the bed. Then, after a rest, I could reach with the other arm for the other side of the bed and slowly worm the rest of my body over until I was facing the other way.

This exercise was complicated by the piles of pillows that kept me in place. I didn't have the strength to move them out of my way, let alone set them up for my new position. I couldn't distinguish my own limbs from the pillows, and often floundered around trying to rearrange or remove my legs. Suzi wouldn't help me until I had completed all the steps I was capable of, and struggled for a while with the ones I wasn't. It was a Big Moment when I rolled over entirely by myself. No more waiting on the every-two-hours schedule.

I started physio again, with Iolanda. It was gruelling work. I don't know if I can adequately describe the fatigue: it was profound, blinding, literally unspeakable. When fatigue hit I could no longer form words in my mind or my mouth. I stammered and my tongue got in the way. All my new skills deserted me and I cried for my bed.

I remember collapsing in misery when I tried and tried but still couldn't lift my right leg; when I couldn't sit unsupported on my gym platform; when I couldn't get my toothbrush into my mouth but smeared toothpaste across my face for the millionth time. Iolanda would counter my despair by reminding me of all the things I now took for granted — like breathing — and how hard they had once been.

Learning to use the bedpan was a long and complicated process. It had been months since peeing was something I decided to do rather than something that happened to me. I had lost the ability to recognize when I needed to go. It's painful and somewhat humiliating to remember it now, but at the time, pee and shit were simple facts of life.

Kathleen Shannon: All the rules of privacy that people keep between each other had changed. One time we were talking very seriously about film board politics and you suddenly said, "I'm shitting," and asked me to get the bedpan. I kind of blew it because I didn't move fast enough and I didn't know how to slide the bedpan under you. In fact I failed entirely, and you shit in the bed — very tidily, I must say. I stood there with the bedpan in my hand, wondering how to clean you up. I felt embarrassed at my embarrassment. I would have liked to have taken everything in my stride.

Gerry Rogers: One time when I came to visit, you were sitting up in the chair, showing off your new exercises. I remember your feeding tube was hanging down from your nose and every now and then as you were talking you would pick it up and swing it around and we would both crack up. Hospital humour.

But then you started to get tired. You told me: "I want to get in bed, I have to get in bed." I went and asked the nurse and she rang for the orderly, but he didn't come. You were starting to shake from sitting there, because sitting up was still a hard thing for you.

Finally, the orderly came in and without saying a word he swooped you out of your chair and plunked you on the bed. It was almost violent. Then he walked out the door, without even looking at you. I thought I should say something to Michael about it, and then I thought, "No. When you are dependent like that, if you alienate any of the staff you are really helpless." The main thing I could see that would help, was for you to get out of that place.

When Michael told me that I would probably go to a rehabilitation institute after I left hospital, I thought he meant to rest up before diving back into normal life.

The only Anglophone rehab institute was way out in the suburb of Chomedy where I would be isolated from my friends and family. So Michael applied to the Institut de Réadaptation de Montréal, a French institution, founded by Dr. Gustav Gingras, after he became internationally famous for his rehabilitation of Korean war veterans.

Iolanda described it as summer camp, a live-in gym run by the physios. Summer camp was my favourite childhood place. I was euphoric.

But the Institut only accepted people who stood to gain by rehabilitation. If you were too far gone, you were doomed to stay that way. If "they" believed there was room for improvement, you were accepted. Plus you had to have reached a certain level of independence to be admitted. Nose tubes and tracheostomies did not meet their dress code. The scarce beds came up only rarely and unpredictably, and when they came, you had to be ready.

Naomi: My dad was losing his mind because they couldn't find a bed in a rehab institute and he didn't think that my mom was getting sufficient physio at the JGH. He felt like we were losing time. One morning my dad and I were having breakfast in the kitchen and he started talking about bringing Mom home. He said we could put a hospital bed in the dining room, have round-the-clock home nursing and therapists visiting the house. He wanted to set up an ICU in our dining room. He was back at work full time at this point and really wanted everything to return to normal. As if Mom being home would mean everything was OK. I got really mad, telling him I didn't want an ICU in the dining room, that I had to go to school and everything. I was chain-smoking boyfriends at that time: one after another with some very messy overlaps. I was very needy and my judgment was sometimes a little off. Dad made me feel like I was incredibly selfish, like I didn't care. We had a huge fight, and I remember telling him that no matter what happened, I was never going to have my mother again in the same way. I felt the loss of a comfort, a net, of some level of childhood that I had been planning to hold onto for a few more years. Of course I cared. He eventually dropped the idea of moving my mom home just yet.

I worked like crazy to learn the skills I needed to be admitted to the Institut. Iolanda taught me how to use a wheelchair. I needed to practise pushing and pulling evenly to make the chair go straight. My tendency was to go in circles since my right arm was much stronger than my left. I wheeled into furniture and scraped my knuckles. Stopping was not an automatic reflex any more than pushing the wheels. More often than not, I ran into walls to stop myself.

My wheelchair didn't have footrests, probably in order to give my legs more exercise. So I would be "walking" as I wheeled: a slow process with my left foot struggling to keep up and my right foot dragging unwillingly along the floor.

I would get breathless fast. My little coordination disappeared with fatigue till I was going round and round in circles of frustration. But how proud I was, the first time I pushed through a doorway without marking the walls.

I was determined to learn to swallow. I needed to be off the feeding tube to go to the Institut. Besides, I missed the pure pleasure of eating. When the sickeningly rich smell of Ensure seeped through the nose tube and into my brain, I fantasized about water: clear, delicious, amazing water. I felt cheated because I had missed the fruits of late summer — raspberries, peaches, tomatoes and Annie's sweet corn.

According to the medical notes, my first real food was a few spoonfuls of apple sauce and puréed carrots administered by one of the physios. My trach secretions were "rosy" after that, showing that I hadn't been able to swallow the carrots, but had inhaled them instead. I was told I couldn't expect to achieve a "functional swallow" until my breathing was declared out of danger and my trach tube was removed. That night I pulled out the trach tube in my sleep.

Suzi Scott: The trach tube is like a piece of plastic with a hollow finger that's inserted into a hole in your throat. You were off the respirator by that point, but the tube was still in your throat to keep the hole open and allow the suction catheter to be passed in and out. When the tube is removed, the hole closes and scar tissue forms, and then if the patient has to be reintubated, it's a prob-

lem. So until everybody is confident that the patient isn't
going to have any respiratory problems, it just stays in,
tied to the side with a ribbon. But you got tired of it and
I think you just untied the ribbon and popped it out. It
was coming out eventually, but you were ready and you
just took charge. There was a lot of shaking of heads and
clicking of tongues, but in the end, they decided to jump
the schedule and leave it out.

With my trach tube out, I was declared fit for serious eating
practice, usually with a greyish purée of well-boiled vegetables
from the hospital kitchen. At first I would gag back and spit
out whatever I swallowed, but eventually it would stay down.
I could only eat under staff supervision, because of the danger
of choking. Luckily Michael passed for staff in this instance,
and his ideas on nutrition were a little different. I'll never forget the super-thick Haagen-Dasz coffee ice cream milkshake
that was the first thing he fed me, stroking it down my throat
to help me swallow. "Such *nachus*," he said. *Nachus* is Yiddish
for well-deserved pleasures; "such *nachus*" is used with ironic
humour to note the tiny silver linings in immense storm
clouds. It became a family code phrase.

After a while I graduated to beautiful mushed-up chicken
and mashed potatoes that Meena sent from home, and small
bits of solid food. I was drooling a lot and my hand-eye coordination was off. With half my mouth and tongue paralyzed, I
couldn't feel when food dribbled on my face. People were
always dabbing at me, and my nightgowns were filthy. It didn't
bother me. Table manners were not a big issue at the time.

I was still on the feeding tube to supplement my eating practice, and I still pulled it out regularly. Finally, after I had pulled

it out for the umpteenth time, the dietitian decided to leave it and work on getting enough food down me by mouth. I loved eating, but it was heavy exercise and I tired quickly. The dietitian posted a chart where my daily food intake was logged. I felt like a kid with a bad report card every time she came in to check it. She told me I was malnourished and that if I didn't increase my intake by the end of the week, she would order the resident to reinsert the feeding tube. I felt like crying. I couldn't stand the thought of trying to swallow that tube again.

Michael: You were working hard to stuff down those calories, you didn't need threats. "She's a dietician, not a cop," I said. "She has no right to force a feeding tube down your throat. We're going to deal with this very easily. We're going to lie. There's a worldwide tradition of record fudging and we're going to be part of it." So we invented outrageous foods, like mashed moose eye, purée of peacock penis, and juggled the numbers on the calorie chart so you could meet your quota.

Learning to write was easier. Towards the end of October, the occupational therapist showed me how to grip a pencil, stabilize the paper, and rest my elbow on the tray table so my arm would be less spastic. It all went very fast, from squiggling to approximate her squares and circles in a broad and erratic way the first day, to copying them rather neatly the next day. Then I was writing whole words and sentences in a shaky kindergarten scrawl which betrayed my lack of fine motor skills. Everyone was impressed. I was a star.

The OT asked me to write a sentence a day, kind of like homework, but a sentence wasn't enough for me. My first attempt was a nearly illegible letter to Naomi.

At first I wrote on the loose pages the OT left me; then I asked Dorothy Hénaut for a journal of my own. Dorothy had been writing journals for as long as I knew her. I had always insisted that I had no time for that sort of thing, but now I began keeping one in earnest. It was more than an OT exercise. It was a tool for my survival. I was processing the strange and troubling events occurring in my body, recording thoughts I couldn't trust my damaged mind to remember, trying to make coherence out of chaos. Writing in my journal became as necessary a part of my daily routine as brushing my teeth and physical therapy.

Journal: October 23
Michael says my writing is already better than his. Today was very "up" with enormous changes in my movement. But now I am tired because I had company all day with no break. Several of my visitors remarked that *now* I look like the old Bonnie.

Journal: October 24
I had a session with Michele Devroede, my old psychotherapist. Laurence Kirmayer suggested I start seeing her again, since she had helped me during what we now know was a silent stroke, while I was filming the SAGE tour.

I hadn't seen her since we both went on vacation in August. When she walked in, I was so full of words I went into a major panic attack. She said, "It's OK, don't talk." She stood by my bed and held my numb feet for the whole hour. Her hands pressed hard against my soles, and both the numbness and the panic ebbed away. We stayed like that without talking for the whole session. I still remember how grounded I felt. How could she just walk in and devise exactly the right treatment completely out of the blue?

Afterwards she said that the panics could be the upper part of my body saying, "Whoa, wait a moment — there is no support underneath." She advised me to keep a pillow at the end of my bed for my feet to rest against. It's true — my upper body has progressed more quickly and has to wait for my legs to catch up. So the panic is a message — slow down and integrate. My own spirit has to put together all the separate therapies and progresses.

The move to the Institut was almost within my grasp. All my energy was focused towards that goal. So I was taken off guard one morning when Suzi told me I'd be going home for the weekend in a few days. At first I thought I must have misunderstood her. I could go home? Home to my own house? I told all my visitors this great news and how excited I was, but I didn't tell them the other part of it: I was scared to be leaving the hospital, even for a weekend. Was I ready? Would I be all right? Or was Michael pushing things again as he had that first night in the emergency room almost three months ago?

How could I get into our house, which had five big steps up to the front porch? How would I use the downstairs bathroom — a tiny converted closet with no room for a wheelchair? How would I get upstairs to our bedroom? It was all too frightening and too much trouble. I didn't belong there.

Michael, on the other hand, couldn't wait to get me home. He had rented all sorts of hospital equipment — an IV hanger, a commode. I was overwhelmed by the extent of his desire to have me back. The tubes and machines and shitting in my pants were just petty details. I was his wife and he wanted me with him.

I remember that first ride home, in a special ambulance van with a lift for the wheelchair. My equilibrium was so unhinged that each bump in the road felt like a major accident. Every pebble was a cliff, every pothole a ravine. I couldn't tell what was moving: me or the things around me. When we drove down the street, my disordered senses said the buildings were falling sideways. When the attendants opened the van door, it felt like I was falling backwards. When they wheeled me out, it felt like the van was driving away. Michael reassured me that this sense of disorientation was all part of the stroke and would no doubt improve with time. That knowledge was comforting when I was safe in bed, but did nothing to lessen the terror of the experience as it was happening.

When we got to our high front steps, the attendants carried me up in the wheelchair. It was a heavy, awkward load. I worried that I would slip out of the chair or that my helpers would stumble and fall. With each lurch the steps seemed to fly up at me. Michael stood watching at the top of the stairs, his recurring back injury preventing him from grabbing me out of their hands, but not from yelling anxious instructions. I was home.

Once I was inside my family conspired to turn obstacles into adventures. Seth, who had greatly admired Georgio the ICU orderly, danced me from the wheelchair onto the commode. Meena cooked my favourite lemon chicken, stuffed cabbage and beets, and threw them in the blender. One of our neighbours, J.B., was on call to help Seth carry me upstairs at night and down in the morning. J.B. was a rebellious young man at this stage, with a magnificent purple mohawk of great height and stiffness. He came regularly that weekend, bringing a crew of friends who carried me gently with hands interlocked to make a solid seat, my arms around their spiked heads.

My only sorrow that weekend was the much anticipated reunion with our dog Lucy. She greeted me enthusiastically, but when I hugged her head, I felt steel-wool rather than her golden retriever silkiness. It was dysaesthesia, a neurological abnormality that painfully heightened my sense of touch. I was more than disappointed. My fantasy of the roomful of furry puppies had sustained me through so many nightmare hours, but now my own furry puppy was like a wire brush. But it didn't faze Lucy. She was pathologically solicitous of me. She would not leave me for a second, as if some instinct let her know I was needful of love and protection.

All my senses were screwed up, my sense of humour most and best of all. I laughed at anything, and my family laughed with me. We laughed when I dropped and spilled things. We laughed that I sounded like a drunk with marbles in my mouth. My first night home, I fell out of bed with a great crash that woke Naomi, who rushed in to save me and found Michael rolling on the floor with me, laughing too hard to help me up.

We laughed in part for our own protection. Did we sometimes laugh too loud to mask the "tragedy" of my illness? I don't think so. Our family had always been intense and, let's admit it, earnest. We'd done too little laughing per lived minute. We were always planning for the future: the next film, the weekend, college. All of a sudden the future was gone, too fragile to imagine, and there was just the moment. It was hilarious. Such *nachus*.

INTERLUDE: LUCY

Journal: September 23, 1994
Here I am, still in my bathrobe, writing instead of going out into the glorious Fall day. Lucy would not have tolerated such behaviour.

She died yesterday at the age of fourteen, Naomi's runt puppy, after collapsing in the formal gardens of the Empress Hotel. Michael was giving an obstetrics course in Victoria, and his hosts had booked us into the regal old landmark. Lucy acted like she belonged there, charming the stiffly uniformed doorman. She "pulled" my scooter, Gladys, through the wide corridors, under the watchful eyes of the portraits of the wives of Attorneys-General. We all had an evening stroll and came upon the annual Take Back the Night demonstration at the B.C. legislature. I rang Gladys's bell to cheer them on. I went to bed telling Michael how happy and excited I was feeling. "About your book?" he asked. "About every moment," I said.

I had arranged to meet one of my stroke buddies, Bill Livant, in the hotel gardens the next morning. We traded stroke stories while Lucy rolled on the sunny grass. Bill showed me how he invented a balancing exercise he calls "tracking the birds" on his daily beach walks. He points and follows the various birds with his arms and body. It looks like Tai Chi. I told him how I sometimes get down and roll on the grass with Lucy. It's great exercise for our respective hip and spine problems. Bill suggested I join her there on the

Empress lawn, but I was inhibited by the grand setting. Lucy rolled on irreverently, delighting a gaggle of nursery school children, leashed to each other, laughing. But suddenly Lucy got up, staggered and keeled over onto her side. Her legs wouldn't support her. I got down and stroked her. It felt awfully familiar.

I said to Bill, "Something's wrong. Keep comforting Lucy while I scoot to call Michael." Lucy automatically tried to get up when I re-mounted Gladys but her legs wouldn't follow her head. By the time I returned, Lucy's front paws were rigid. Her claws were stuck in the grating under the bench — I tried to free them but her foot wouldn't bend. I had flashes of desperately uncurling my mother's clenched fists, and of my own leg stuck in the metal rails of my hospital bed.

She began to shake with seizures. Michael arrived, anticipating Lucy's death with every step. Kevin, the Empress doorman, brought our van. He was in tears as he helped Michael lift Lucy inside. Michael asked Kevin to come with him to the veterinary hospital. I wanted to go, but I didn't insist. There was no room for Gladys, I didn't know the way, I couldn't help carry Lucy.

After a few hours and frequent phone reports, Michael came back for me. He told me Lucy was on the "ward." I had a stupid picture of dogs in beds, but she was lying at the bottom of one of several stacked rows of kennels. I had to sprawl down in the narrow aisle to reach in and touch her. She tried to raise her head. She was panting. She looked terrible. Next to her, a bigger dog was yelping with seizures.

There were no miracles. Several vets consulted with us. They all felt there was no chance of recovery — she had been rigid for over five hours. It was surely something in her brain

— maybe a tumour but more likely a brain-stem stroke. There was talk of a CAT scan, but for what purpose? There was no veterinary Skip Peerless, no animal rehabilitation institute.

The decision wasn't difficult. We should take her out of her misery as quickly as possible. I leaned over to kiss her between the eyes, once for me and once for Naomi. I said thank you, and she wagged her tail. "Pt alert and smiling."

INSTITUT DE RÉADAPTATION DE MONTRÉAL

≈

Autumn

Journal: October 30, 1987
Day 1 at the Institut was lonely and strange. Everyone
around me is in wheelchairs and I resent being in one, and
fear it may be permanent, as it seems to be for most of the
others. But on the other hand, being around all these sad,
broken people may serve as motivation to work hard and
GET OUT OF HERE!

*Who wrote these journals? When is she going to wise up? I
want to add footnotes to make sure every reader understands
that when I wrote the words: "sad, broken people" in 1987,
it was because I believed wheelchairs meant powerlessness. I
wanted only to return to normal, to be "the old Bonnie" again.
I couldn't conceive of coming to terms with being disabled, let
alone a world where differences could be accepted and accom-
modated as a right, not a burden. I want to place warning signs
with flashing lights around all the frightened stereotypes of
disabled people that litter my journal pages: Danger — Bad
Attitude.*

*What really happened in 1987? Is the truth in the journals
I wrote at the time, or in my present-day perceptions? Sometimes they're so different I can't recognize myself. I never said
that! Never!*

But I have to let the old Bonnie speak for herself. I can't demand that she know what took me so long to learn. And sometimes she still lurks underneath. The journals don't lie even though they sometimes reveal my ignorance and fear. Even though they are shot through with silences, events unconsciously ignored and avoided as I tried to write my life into a happy ending. A triumph over tragedy.

I arrived at my new home by ambulance. Michael wheeled me down the hall to the admissions desk, past necking teenagers with cerebral palsy, amputees, quadriplegic ex-bikers in black leather jackets. I had never seen so many wheelchairs. Michael was giddy, flying, telling me over and over how happy he was. I could see why he liked it: the JGH was old and dark, with hospital-beige walls. Here at the Institut everything was open and light. Bright walls were plastered with Don't Drink and Drive posters (*L'alcool c'est Volant*). But I couldn't match Michael's enthusiasm. The warm colours seemed false, the poster warnings too late for many of the residents.

After a series of admissions formalities, I was interviewed by a psychiatric consultant called in to assess my panic attacks. He talked to me for over an hour, questioning me about my childhood and unresolved feelings about my father. I eventually asked to leave, pleading exhaustion. He reluctantly agreed that I could continue psychotherapy with Michele Devroede, as I wished, instead of becoming his patient. Actually, we weren't called "patients" at the Institut, nor were we "residents" or "clients." In French we were *bénéficiaires*, which sounded awfully like "charity-cases" to me.

Finally Michael took me up to my new room and my new roommate. Paulette was not happy to see me; I could only guess that she'd had the room to herself for a few days before

I was admitted, and liked it. She didn't respond to any of our introductory chatter and curiosity. I didn't realize she could hardly speak. I didn't yet know that she'd been in hospital for over a year, that she never had visitors, that her youngest child had been killed in the car accident which permanently injured her own brain, that her husband had subsequently abandoned her and their two young sons, who were now living with her elderly mother. All I knew was that when she decided to say something, it came out as an unintelligible drawl — I couldn't even tell that it was French. Did I sound like that too?

When she left for supper in the cafeteria, she went from fierce scowls to extravagant, sky-lighting smiles, which scared me just as much. How could an adult human being have become so like a child? She's brain-damaged, I told myself. Like me.

I was crying for the first time since I had the stroke. Maybe I had been afraid to cry before, scared that once I started I'd never stop. I didn't even know I was crying until I tasted the salt on my lips. I couldn't feel the tears running down my face. Michael wiped my cheek. I think I yelled at him then, asking why he was so happy when I was still in a wheelchair, still in an institution. He said, "I did all my crying before, when it looked like you might die. Now all I see is your progress."

After I was thoroughly comforted, Michael left for dinner. Mine was brought to my room by a six-foot nurse's aide in a red dustmop wig, rosy cheeks, striped socks, and a white apron: Jimmy Deakin as Raggedy Ann, on his way to the *bénéficiaires'* Halloween party. Jimmy explained that since I was new, I would not have to go down to the cafeteria but could eat in my room for a few days. My special puréed dinner had not been ordered yet, so I was to eat regular food — steak and *frites*. Whoopie! After Jimmy left, I wolfed it down, choking on the gristly meat. I would cough up the culprit and regurgitate it whole. Then I would chew it more slowly for the juices, and spit out the bolus. It was thoroughly disgusting, but I was alone so why not? I was enjoying myself until I suddenly got scared that the meat would get irretrievably lodged in my throat, and I would choke and die alone in my room, like someone in a grim tabloid article. How could Michael have left me alone in this place? Luckily, Naomi, Meena and Anne Usher arrived before that dire fate overtook me, and I was suddenly as up as I had been down before. Anne reported that the halls were full of people in costumes, and persuaded me to go down to the cafeteria with her for the Halloween party.

The party seemed to be run entirely by the *bénéficiaires*. The room was loud and joyous and thick with smoke, sending my one unparalyzed vocal chord into spasms. I had never seen such an array of disabilities — the neurological ward at the JGH was mostly older patients with strokes and Parkinson's — and here were all these weird people dressed up even more weird for Halloween! There were paralyzed princesses, peg-leg pirates, beggars and monsters of all description. There was a beautiful Cleopatra borne in on her litter by three or four dashing paraplegics. She won the prize for best costume. I learned the next day that she was always horizontal. Still later I learned that she used to play flute.

Jimmy Deakin put me to bed that night in what became a night-time ritual. He brought me milk and cookies and chatted about his kids and mine while I ate. He helped me go to the bathroom and brush my teeth, then positioned me for the night. He knew just how to arrange the pillows for ultimate comfort and support. I didn't miss the JGH at all.

Over the next week I was seen and assessed by all the departments at the Institut. The neuropsychology tests were endless and sometimes humiliating: memory, problem-solving, pattern-finding, picture-drawing, deductive reasoning, abstract conceptualization, what's-wrong-with-this-picture? I kept feeling as if I was doing terribly, that I had lost my ability to think logically, to recall, to discern. The worst tests were the ones where you were supposed to figure out sequencing patterns of numbers, which I was never terrific at. I see now that according to the consultation report, I didn't do badly, though they didn't tell me then. I had a nagging feeling for a long time that yes, I was functional, good enough for them, but I had lost a great deal of my intellectual acuity. I wasn't sure I was "all there." I didn't know what might be missing. My thinking was slow. I reversed syllables, fractured idioms. "The ball's in your park," I'd say. "People who live in glass houses shouldn't throw up." I often couldn't find the name for something and would have to describe its attributes: "That thing with the long handle you use for sweeping the floor."

This new relationship to language wasn't entirely negative; I became sensitive to hidden meanings, the literal ones, buried in familiarity. It was fun making these new discoveries. Discover. Re-member. In-valid. As in the work of Mary Daly, the feminist theologian, words fell apart, revealing their insides. But these gains could not be measured on their tests. Only the losses showed.

Michael: Some of the effects you experienced — difficulty concentrating, inability to deal with more than one thing at a time, trouble with choices and decisions, scrambling words — are in a sense "typical" of people with stroke. Part of stroke is extreme fatigue; your terrible illness, your struggle to stay alive and recover, made you completely exhausted. The same is true of personality changes: you had extreme, exaggerated responses; you were inappropriately accepting or frighteningly demanding; you loved or hated. There were abrupt mood swings; you laughed too loud or cried without provocation, were often irritable and totally disinhibited. These characteristics all increased with fatigue.

Journal: November 6
My funk of the last few days was relieved by several factors:

1) One of the doctors assured me that most people get depressed at this stage of rehab — after all the life-and-death drama is over and the long slog to recovery lies ahead.

2) I woke up this morning to blood on the plastic sheets — my first period since the stroke! I had been looking forward to menopause and the end of my menstrual cycles, but now I celebrate the return of normalcy — even PMS!

3) Joe Carlton came to visit. He repeated his absolute faith that I will keep improving, and reminded me that we have a tennis date. Seeing Joe again made me realize: I HAVEN'T HAD A SINGLE PANIC ATTACK SINCE I GOT TO THE INSTITUT! When I last saw him, they still ruled my life, and now I take their absence for granted.

So I'm feeling joyous again, though TIRED in the extreme. What a yo-yo I am! The smallest thing can either send me flying, or shoot me down. The OT intern helped me lease a lightweight wheelchair yesterday and when they asked if we wanted to buy instead, she said: "No, it's temporary!"

Later that week, as I pushed my way to yet another test, I spotted André, a man who had crewed for a day on *Mile Zero*, with one of the Institut administrators. I'd known André for years. Michael had helped his partner with the delivery of their baby. I greeted him spontaneously. To my dismay, he did not recognize me. I had to introduce myself by name.

André recovered from his embarrassment with a quick brainstorm. He was here as Location Manager for a made-for-Quebec-TV-movie to be shot next week at the Institut. Could I show the actor (heart-throb Michel Coté) something about using a wheelchair? The story-line was about what happens to his love affair (with the talented Marie Tifo) after a car accident disables him. No, I'm sorry, I couldn't. Well, would I come down to the shoot as an extra? It would be fun for me, just like old times to be on the set.

Hadn't he noticed that I was no longer Bonnie Klein? Did he want the whole world to see me as part of a freak show? I could hardly hold myself in a sitting position in the wheelchair. My head hung crookedly. The right side of my face drooped down: mouth, chin, eyebrows. My eyes were usually closed. I looked, acted and felt like a Stroke Victim, the kind of person you try not to stare at. And that was in a still position, doing nothing. As soon as I added any movement, my strangeness was magnified. If I got excited, confused or stressed, I would cough uncontrollably, spewing spittle. My legs bounced around of their own volition as if they had nothing to do with me. I hadn't yet learned how to stop their mortifying movement with pressure from my hands. Lesley Levy urged me to remember that I was still the same person I'd always been, but I couldn't bring myself to believe her.

How could I expose what I had become to a camera?

But André was persistent and sent messages to my room about the call-schedule for the shoot. I avoided it most of the week, worn down by the endless batteries of tests. In the end, my curiosity won out. I went downstairs to occupational therapy ("*ergo*" in Institut-French) on the final day of the shoot. They were filming an emotional scene with the actor re-learning to drive in the simulated *ergo* half-car. The filmmakers greeted me with what felt like sincere delight. Then I was directed for the action: the camera would start with a close-up of me, and pull back as I wheeled up a ramp to reveal the star crying in the funny car. It crossed my mind that this cameo appearance was like a Hollywood in-joke: name-that-crip. But I gritted my teeth and did my bit — several takes while the camera operator timed his zoom to my slow-motion ascent.

After my week of tests, real life finally began. I was given an *horaire* or schedule, like at school. Every day I had an hour of *ergo*, an hour of *ortho* (speech therapy), plus an hour of speech lab (supervised by a computer which graphed my voice as I spoke, feeding it back to me while I struggled to make the sound look right). Practical details like eating, going to the bathroom, or wheeling down the long corridors to my next appointment took up most my time in between formal sessions. It wasn't summer camp, it was boot camp. Luckily, I would have a furlough at home every weekend.

Ergo was first thing after breakfast. The *ergo* intern taught me how to dress and bathe myself, all in carefully thought-out stages. I learned to put on my bra by hooking it in front and turning it around, to pull up my pants while lying on the bed, to put on my sneakers and socks. Laces were beyond me. Thank God for Velcro!

Brushing my teeth was complicated. I got confused between turning on the water and putting toothpaste on the brush. Unless I doggedly recited the intern's step-by-step instructions, I'd end up putting toothpaste on the faucet and throwing the toothpaste cap down the sink.

My roommate Paulette could shower herself. I couldn't imagine the strength and courage it would take to transfer from the wheelchair to the plastic bench in the tub, especially when wet and slippery. The *ergo* intern taught me the steps involved and the safeguards, till I was ready to try by myself with a nurse's aide standing by *au cas où* (just in case). I had to line up my wheelchair exactly parallel to the plastic bench, lock the brake, remove one of the detachable arms, and transfer from the chair to the bath-bench by wriggling my bum slowly over the "chasm" from chair to bench.

Once there, I had to adjust the water temperature, starting always with cold for safety and remembering that I couldn't feel enough to keep from burning myself. Only then could I begin soaping and shampooing, pushing a lever to switch to the hand-held shower hose to rinse. I invariably soaked the toilet paper roll across the tiled room. Towelling myself dry was another problem. I couldn't tell which was moving, me or the towel. I would as likely move myself off the seat.

My toileting traumas continued at the IRM, where I had graduated to using the regular bathroom (with help) during the day. It was particularly stressful in the morning. They routinely gave me a stool softener, Colace, because sedentary people tend to get constipated. But sometimes my problem was the opposite. My morning bowel movement was stimulated by breakfast tea (I still couldn't swallow coffee). It came with a sudden cramp. The cafeteria was on the ground level and my room (and bathroom) was on the second floor. I had to wheel to the elevator and then wait for it to arrive and be loaded — only four wheelchairs at a time. By the time I got to my floor I was desperate. I would yell from the elevator door that I needed an aide for the bathroom and pray that one — preferably female — got there before I shit my pants. By this time I was well enough to feel humiliated by men helping me onto the toilet, which increased my motivation to manage it by myself.

The manoeuver to the toilet was tricky — especially with flaccid sphincter muscles. There was a floor-to-ceiling pole, like a fireman's pole, in front of the toilet. I'd position and brake the chair, reach for the pole and pull myself up while the aide pulled down my pants — there was no way to get my pants down myself, as I was clinging to the pole with both hands. Then I would pivot around to sit on the toilet.

The aide would usually leave me to do my business in private. When I was finished, I would buzz, and wait on the toilet until rescued. There was a ward of quads down the hall whose needs were much greater than mine, so I sometimes ended up sitting there for quite a while.

Eventually the *ergo* intern taught me how to wiggle my pants off with one hand, an inch at a time, while holding onto the pole with the other. I wore nothing but elasticized waists for years — buttons and zippers were out of the question.

At night the bathroom was inaccessible. Our wheelchairs were parked in the hall after 10 p.m. so the staff could get to us without tripping over them in the dark, but it meant I was stranded. My mattress had a plastic sheet over it for the inevitable bedwetting.

My *ortho* (short for *orthophoniste* or speech therapist), Miriam, was an orthodox Jewish woman (an ortho *ortho*?) with a wig, recently married and now pregnant, who had a sweet smile and childlike voice. Was she patronizing me? Or is this an occupational hazard when you work with people with language problems?

Miriam took me under her ample wing. We worked in English, which was a welcome respite in my French-speaking day, but she was tough. I had the feeling she thought I had lost more than anyone else acknowledged. She noted each mangled word and fed it back until I got it right. She was a stickler about my posture, always nudging me to sit up straight, stop slumping, don't let my mouth hang open. I thought she just didn't want me to look sloppy; I didn't realize at the time that how I sat affected my breathing which in turn affected my vocal production.

Miriam was strict about "homework" which she wrote out in large, clear print. A patient patient, I was conscientious about my practice, and proud. There were strengthening exercises for my tongue: trying to touch the tip to the roof of my mouth and around the insides of my lips and cheeks. At her suggestion, I did these in front of a mirror, which forced me to see how grossly distorted my tongue had become. It was redraw and quavery, so thick it was almost square, making speech and swallowing more awkward.

Miriam had me practise breath control by blowing out candles or reciting increasingly long sentences without stopping for breath. (The pretty little girl threw the striped ball to her friend. The pretty little blond girl threw the red striped ball to her friend.) I would articulate long lists of sounds which were difficult for me (baba, bobo, beebee, booboo; mama, momo, meemee, moomoo).

After *ortho* I was ready to collapse in my room. Alongside my bed was a wall-to-wall window overlooking a large field.

It was the first time in four months that I could see the world, the weather, the changing of the seasons. The far end of the field had the autumn vestiges of a large vegetable garden: corn stalks, tomato vines, sunflowers. I later learned that this was a communal garden — not for the Institut community (and why not? but that's a question I would only ask myself years later) — but for the neighborhood, a tidy jumble of fifties-style duplexes.

I spent hours staring out the window, listening to Peter Gzowski, Bob Kerr, and Jurgen Gothe on the CBC. By my bed I kept my journal, my *Friends' Book of Healing*, and my precious radio and cassette player. And joy! I had a generous window-ledge running the width of the room for all my treasures: audio cassettes, family photographs, books and magazines, asters from Irene Kupferszmidt, my humidifier. Children's art was taped to the clothes locker and, as always, Naomi's poem was by my bed.

Between my double vision and my eyes bouncing around, I had not been able to read for a long time. Now my eyes were calming down, and I tried reading newspapers and favourite magazines. Exhaustion made it impossible to concentrate; I could not keep an idea in my head from the beginning to the end of a single sentence. When I found myself rereading the same sentence more than three times, I knew it was time to wait for a more alert moment.

Over the next months and years, what I wanted to read most of all were accounts of people who had been where I was — and recovered. Michael and Lesley gave me Bernie Siegel's work, *Love, Medicine, & Miracles*, about the patients' role in their own healing. Other wise friends gave me books by Oliver Sacks. *The Man Who Mistook His Wife For A Hat*, which I had ignored for all the months it was on bestseller lists, gave me the first intriguing clue that there might be another way to look at "abnormality": as difference, uniqueness or even gift. I devoured his books. *A Leg To Stand On*, about Sacks' own story of temporary neurological disability, became part of my growing collection of personal narratives of illness survived and transcended, what author Nancy Mairs ironically calls "the literature of personal disaster." I read about Patricia Neal's recovery from a stroke and re-learning of language, Helen Keller, Norman Cousins, May Sarton . . . After years of reading nothing but earnest non-fiction, I attacked fat novels like Isabel Allende's *House of the Spirits*, rediscovering the pleasure of fiction.

Journal: November 10
Yesterday was frustrating — back to the Institut after a wonderful weekend at home, to do the same boring *ortho* exercises and still no physio. If rehab is going to take as long as people anticipate then let's begin. I'm angry at being here, and feel less optimistic than I was. No one will guarantee full recovery. When Michele Devroede came for our session I was crying (again). I told her I was just feeling sorry for myself. She encouraged me to go ahead and feel sorry, it wasn't going to impede my progress.

I was eager to begin physio, which for me was the only thing that counted; it meant learning how to walk. But for the first few weeks I was told I wasn't ready. Considering I had made such "miraculous" and speedy progress in so many domains, including the leap from scribble to legible journal writing in a few days, I secretly believed that it would be the same way with walking. I would get up from the wheelchair, stagger for a few minutes, and walk off needing only a few corrections.

I was pleased when my *ortho*, Miriam, told me that my assigned physio, Michel Danakas, was one of the best in the Institut. But when I finally was allowed to begin physio, Michel merely dropped by from time to time to check up on me; my body was in the hands of a nervous young intern who needed even more reassurance than I did. I had no confidence that she knew what she was doing. And after the exalted Michel Danakas told me I should stop my acupuncture sessions with Bernard, I didn't have much faith in him either. "If you do so many therapies at once, how can we tell which one is working?" he asked. "I don't give a damn which one works," I muttered to myself. "I just want to get better." It seemed like typical professional chauvinism. Bernard said no one thing was responsible for my progress; we were a team, all of us, including me.

The intern spent weeks "assessing" me: measuring every minute angle of movement; testing and timing my reactions to hot and cold, sharp and dull. The testing seemed irritatingly pointless to me, but it was also tiring, and I needed many rest stops when I would just lie still on the mattress, which seemed irritatingly pointless to the intern. At the very end of our time she'd stretch my arms and legs, and do some passive range-of-motion exercises. After a few weeks of this and a few awkward weekends in bed at home, I asked her if she could stretch my groin so it would be possible to have intercourse. She pretended not to hear me. No one ever talked to me about sex: no physio, no doctor, no OT, no psychologist. Michael and I figured it out ourselves, not without pain.

But for all its frustrations, going to physio meant going to the gym — the centrepiece, the place of honour, the nerve-centre of the Institut. It was a huge room with a wall of wide windows running its length and lacquered, blond wood floors scattered with glossy red and blue vinyl-covered mats. The thera-

pists wore bright T-shirts, Hawaiian shorts, psychedelic sneakers and sweats. To my surprise, I was excited by the visual spec-
tacle. The sunlight was fractured by window blinds creating
dancing patterns of light on the figures within. And the figures
themselves were dancing. *Bénéficiaires* and therapists became
partners in the most original of *pas de deux*. Winch-transfers
were breathtaking lifts, and leg-stretches were transformed into
sensual intimacies. The practical techniques of physiotherapy
created endless configurations of body parts, one arm stretching to reach the other's hand, a leg on the other's shoulder.

That was the view from my filmmaker's eye, but my other
eye flinched from this display. I hated seeing the droolers at the
gym (though I also drooled). There was a young couple who
always seemed to be slobbering. I wanted to yell at them,
"Control yourselves, you're grown-ups." They flailed their
limbs around with no control, contorted their mouths to utter
stretched words I couldn't discern, and hooted their laughter,
or was it grief? Everyone at the gym was always joking and
raucous. The patients pulled tricks on the therapists and the
therapists teased the patients and everyone laughed their heads
off. Most of it was grade-school humour about colostomy
bags and impotence. I thought it was sick: what do these people have to laugh about? (In truth I envied their camaraderie.)

Evenings everyone gathered in the lounge at the end of the
corridor to watch television and smoke. I remember wheeling
in there one evening early on and feeling repulsed by the slap-
stick comedy they were blasting. My CBC-classism was offended.
I wasn't even into the hockey games which blur those class
lines for other people, mostly men. I asked myself, why should
I socialize with these people? We have nothing in common.
This is only a passing phase for me: I'm going to be healthy
and "normal" again soon.

I certainly didn't think of myself as a snob. "Some of my best friends were working class." But they were the upwardly mobile exceptions. We knew each other within a middle-class context — the NFB, or Herzl — where middle-class attitudes were the unacknowledged rule. I had never been in the minority before. I wondered if maybe working-class people had a higher percentage of accidents. But one friend laughed when I suggested that. "This is a more accurate representation of Canadian society," she said. "It's your life that's been distorted."

Talking was an effort, and people had a hard time understanding me, between my choking, my breathy voice and my American-accented French. They couldn't even understand my name — "Monique?" "Paula?" I got frustrated and angry. How stupid could they be?

I started resenting the French. When I was well and on top of the world, I had prided myself on being progressive and open. We had immigrated to Quebec because it was known to be particularly welcoming to draft-dodgers. Michael and I made a big effort to learn French and succeeded well beyond most native English Montrealers. He had worked as a volunteer physician, along with other war resisters, in Canada's first (pre-Medicare) free medical clinic, organized by a Francophone welfare and citizens' group. I taught them how to use portable video as an organizing tool, with Dorothy Hénaut urging me on in French. We made a film of the project, with an entirely French crew. I loved learning a new language and was proud of myself. What good immigrants! I found the Québecois culture creative, joyful, and politicized in a way I didn't know in the U.S. or English Canada. So it was shocking to me to discover how hostile and superior I felt in that television lounge, how lonely and isolated.

What was I doing here? What was I trying to prove?

There were organized evening activities like bingo, pool, church choir, and occasional excursions to the movies, but I never went. I told myself I was getting everything I needed from visits and phone calls with my friends and family. The only *bénéficiaire* I ever really talked to in those first weeks was a quadriplegic man named Guy. He befriended me because he befriended everybody. He made evening "rounds" every night on each floor of the Institut, with a personal word for everyone. He was one of the few people who could make Paulette laugh — uproariously. At first I thought he was a staff person, or a chaplain, but I learned that he was a self-appointed ambassador of goodwill. I had trouble understanding his rural accent, so I was never sure whether he was a highway cop who had been injured while pursuing a criminal, or a criminal injured while being pursued by a highway cop. In any case, Guy's vehicle went off an icy road and exploded in flames. He was thrown from the car, his neck broken. He couldn't get over his great good luck in being alive.

I tried the lounge again on the day that the former Quebec premier and nationalist hero René Lévesque was buried. All of Quebec was glued to the television. I watched this moment of history in a room full of broken mourners, feeling my Otherness more than ever.

Michael was surprised by my uncharacteristic unfriendliness. But I wasn't interested in befriending any of these people, it was too threatening. Among my own friends, I was different and special now. Here I wasn't at all special, just another cripple among cripples, a little luckier than some and unluckier than others. I was stripped of all the roles which defined me to myself and gave me status. My doctor-husband was unknown except as a visitor like other visitors. Nobody knew of my films; nobody spoke my language.

I told myself I had no extra energy to spend on anything but rehab work. I sat alone in the cafeteria so I wouldn't have to talk and people wouldn't see me gag, choke, spit out, and spill. I used a paper bib which an orderly tied around my neck. It was always repulsive after I ate. The smoke made my choking worse. Smoking was tolerated even in the non-smoking areas. The rationale for such lenience in a health institution, full of respiratory disorders, was that "handicapped people have so few pleasures." All the staff, from the chief administrator on down, were smokers, and the legislation was cheerfully ignored.

My room was my haven. It was the only place besides the gym and the therapy rooms where there was no smoking allowed. But Paulette was there too, hiding out like me, from what I never knew. She had one tape only: Bob Marley's *Confrontation*. I was excited because Seth played it at home. But soon I felt if I heard "Chant Down Babylon" one more time, I'd go crazy. If it wasn't Bob Marley, it was the French Top 40. I would ask her to please turn the radio off when she left the room, but she'd be gone for hours and leave it blaring. For me to turn it off meant a transfer from the bed to the wheelchair and inching my way around the narrow aisle to her bedside table. I did it once or twice and she was furious that I had touched something of hers. She had so little: a bouquet of plastic flowers, a little Christmas crèche and her radio. She was right to be protective, because one time, in my fumbling, I knocked over her crèche and it shattered. When she came back to the room and saw it, she threw the pieces at me and didn't speak to me for weeks.

Between the tension in my room and choking from the smoke in the cafeteria, it was hard to find a place to visit with friends. They came bearing home-made lunches and tasty take-out dinners to fatten me up, as I had lost about thirty pounds and was desperately skinny. I looked forward to the food, but I was far too tired for conversation. When the dictatorial Michel Danakas sent word that I should limit my visitors to one a night instead of cramming them in over lunch and during my afternoon break, I was relieved rather than angry at his presumption. Weekends became the focus of my social life.

Michael came for me the minute my Friday afternoon speech lab was over, and brought me back to the Institut just before curfew Sunday night. The second weekend he devised a plan to bring me back early Monday morning before the 8 a.m. staff meeting at Herzl that began his week. I thought it was bad for him to begin his week after a night of sleep interrupted by my restlessness, but he thought it was a brilliant idea, and from then on I was three nights home, four nights at the Institut.

Friday nights I was too tired for anything but Meena's *Shabbat* dinner and an early bed. Starting Saturday morning, however, our home became the kind of open house I'd always dreamed of, but had never made time for. Saturday night potluck dinners were a weekly event. Michael and Naomi took over the host role I had previously monopolized. I learned — not without difficulty — to be less perfectionist when they didn't do it *exactly* as I would. Naomi would serve chips to Rabbi Ron's little kids in a breakable family heirloom. Michael had a habit of putting out everything as it arrived, including desserts, which might be followed by cream of broccoli soup. I was shocked to discover that we now had a microwave oven, smuggled from New Jersey by Annie and Philip. We'd never had one before because Rosalie Bertell, from *Speaking Our Peace*, said they emitted cancer-causing radiation. When I objected, Michael told me that since he and Naomi were doing the cooking, they would do it their way.

Seth continued to come home every weekend. I was worried that he couldn't be developing any kind of social life at university, but he was unambivalent about coming. One of our weekend rituals was showing off my new accomplishments to Seth. I wouldn't tell him so I could see if he noticed "Mom's new trick." He was always wildly impressed. Through his eyes I could see my real progress, too often masked behind the everyday grind of exercises at the Institut.

I knew I looked strange. I was desperate not to be an embarrassment, especially to Naomi. I remembered the easy humiliation of my own teenage years. But "normal" was an act I had forgotten. I cursed liberally and discussed my toilet needs; I was what the physicians called "disinhibited." Once I was lying on the sofa when Naomi came in with her current boyfriend. I heard my laughter, loud, deep and rhythmic, at some dumb joke I had made. All the insults of childhood pointed their fingers at me. Grinning idiot. Retard. Spazz. I had never used those words about anyone else; why was I now using them against myself? Was that how Naomi and her boyfriend saw me? Was that who I was? I asked Naomi about it later and she reassured me that she thought I was very funny, and that she was nothing but proud of her mom.

I hadn't seen my own mother for three months. Michael thought that seeing me in the hospital would only confuse and upset her. Naomi and Meena both visited her; I don't think Michael could handle it.

Now that I was out on weekends, a visit was possible. Her nursing home was inaccessible, so Seth and Michael brought her to our house. I was dreading her reaction to finding me in a wheelchair. Naomi helped me fix myself up so I looked as well as possible. But when they brought her into the living room, she just smiled vaguely. All those weeks of worrying about her reaction and she had none. She barely knew me. I didn't feel relief but terrible loneliness. I had thought I'd accepted the Alzheimer's before but this was the moment of truth. It was as if I had no mother. When she left I couldn't stop crying. Seth tried to comfort me, saying, "Perhaps it's a blessing that she's not aware of what you've been going through." To which Michael sadly replied, "Such *nachus*."

Michael lost no time inventing adaptations for life at home. One of my biggest problems was getting someone's attention from room-to-room with my still thin voice. Michael's solution was a walkie-talkie, the children's toy variety. It worked fine, as long as it was turned on, and in the same room as other people. As a fail-safe he bought a green plastic whistle, also from the toy department, which he hung from a turquoise necklace. It was shrill and effective when I remembered to wear it.

I used a rented commode, placed indiscreetly in a corner of the dining room, until I mastered the chair-to-toilet transfer. Then Michael installed a vast array of stainless-steel grab-bars which medicalized the look of our old Victorian bathrooms. Even with the bars, I didn't have enough leg strength to get all the way up or down from the toilet, so we resurrected the big plastic raised toilet-seat from the basement where it had lived since my mother moved to the nursing home.

Because the upstairs bathroom was down a long corridor, I needed a bedpan for the night. Everyone was so matter-of-fact about the commode and bedpan that I never felt humiliated. Michael put a rubber pad under the sheet; he never seemed put off by his incontinent partner. We delighted in the warmth of sharing a bed again.

Michael sometimes joined me in the bathtub, but he didn't always want to get wet or undressed, so I had to learn to do it "all by myself" with Michael (draped in towels for the inevitable splashing) helping me in and out. There was a lot of trial and error — some of it hairy. What worked ultimately was a maneuver we called "The Tripod." Michael would stand on my toes and support me with stiff arms while I lowered myself to the edge of the bathtub, which we made less slippery with a rubber mat. Then, using the new side-bars, I would carefully pivot around and lift one leg at a time over the ledge and into the bath. From there, I could bump down gently and give over my tense muscles to the soothing water.

Getting out was harder. I didn't have the strength to lift myself to a standing position or back to the edge of the tub without leverage, so after many unsuccessful and slippery attempts, we invented Plan B. This one became known as "All Fours." I would manage to squirm myself around in the narrow bathtub until I was kneeling on hands and knees, a position I was learning in the gym. Now I had leverage and support to reach for the hand-grips and pull myself to the edge of the tub, from which I could again swivel over to dry land. The All Fours position was secure and worked well. The only downside was that I felt like a dog. Worse, like a cow, with my middle-aged boobs drooping down.

Lucy and I were close friends, with all the time I spent exercising on the floor. She thought it was a delicious game. I was a sitting duck for her retriever tongue, and I incorporated her licks and smooches into my exercise routines, even though her hair in my mouth (like everything else) made me choke. My weekly comings and goings upset her, and she developed a phobia about suitcases. Whenever she saw a bag in our bedroom or stairs she would lie beside it moping, or follow me around the house, refusing to leave my side.

I had a daily physio routine at home. Michael was scared to let any time go by when I wasn't working. Every doctor who saw me, from Joe Carlton to Skip Peerless, warned that there was a "window of opportunity" for relearning before recovery became less and less possible, a limited time period when the nerves could find new pathways around the damaged areas, after which, progress would cease. Did I have a year? Two years? No one who explained this theory could be more precise.

There was yet another race against time. Michael drew me a graph with a gradual upward curve for recovery, and a downhill curve for the natural process of aging. I had to recover as much as I could before the lines intersected and recovery was overtaken and reversed. It made sense because my deficits were similar to those that come with natural aging, when reflexes slow, balance wavers, muscles weaken, tremors set in. This graphic information created enormous pressure. The window of opportunity was closing like a vice. My old age would be even less mobile, so I'd better get to the highest point from which to begin the downhill slide.

I ask myself in retrospect how much my fierce motivation was for Michael's sake. His graph was not a threat but a picture of his fears, drawn to urge me on in my recovery, which I translated into an image of the burden I might be on him in my old age. I had to get as well as I could for him. The obligation was self-imposed, but the race concept was truer to Michael's nature than mine.

I had another immediate priority. It was on an early November weekend that Sidonie brought over a videotape of her three-hour cut of *Mile Zero*, and my work on the film resumed. I watched it alone, in half-hour segments over several weekends, as I couldn't sit any longer than that. I was eager to begin, but there were moments when I questioned the wisdom of it. Was it too early in my recovery? Was I squandering energy on the film while the window of opportunity slowly closed? Should I be in *ergo* making potholders instead?

The first work session took place in our small living room, with Irene-the-co-producer, Sidonie-the-editor and me-the-director-with-a-stroke. In documentary film, this is where the interesting work begins. Since documentaries exist in the director's head, there is no script. Hopefully, you've captured the "reality" during the shoot; now the film begins to tell you what it's about and your work is to shape and heighten that meaning.

As we watched and talked I was not sure what I could contribute. I didn't know how much mental ability I had lost. The neuropsychologist and the speech therapist at the Institut both led me to believe some loss was inevitable. I spoke very slowly and sometimes forgot what I was saying in mid-sentence. I hated when someone else finished what they thought I was going to say; it undermined what little confidence I had left. I couldn't cope with being asked two things at once, or even sipping water and watching the film at the same time. When Irene spoke too fast or worse, interrupted me, I got frustrated and angry, and lost my train of thought completely. Sidonie has the proverbial saint's patience, but Irene tends to be quick. I couldn't keep up.

I felt guilty to have had a stroke, abandoning Irene and Sidonie with an unfinished film. Since my stroke, Irene was giving much more time to *Mile Zero* than she had originally committed. Sometimes I became irritable, feeling she was over-stepping my role as director. She felt unappreciated; I felt loss of control. During one particularly difficult session, the thought crossed my mind that maybe my work on *Mile Zero* wasn't real. Maybe Sidonie and Irene were humouring me — letting me think that I was contributing to the film because they thought it would help my healing. When I dared to ask Sidonie about it, she reassured me that she would never participate in such a charade — I was still the director, it was still my film.

Journal: November 20, 1987
I returned to the Institut exhausted from my wild weekend. I had worked two half-days on the film. I felt more confident than last week — I *can* work — slower than before, but perhaps better, more focused. When I work, I forget to take my Xanax.

Michel Danakas scolded me for wearing myself out on the film. He says my real work is at the Institut.

Xanax, a tranquillizer, and Ludiomil, an anti-depressant, had originally been prescribed to help with panic attacks back in London, but I was still taking them. I'd always been cautious about any drug which affected the mind. I'd heard too many stories of tranquillizers being casually prescribed to women. Michael respected my fears but assured me that this was an appropriate use of those drugs. When I no longer needed them, my body would help me phase off.

For now, I was desperate. Desperate to avoid a return of the panics, or panicked because I was addicted, I couldn't say. I was prescribed Xanax every four hours. My heart palpitated for the last minutes before each dose. When visiting hours ended at 9 p.m., I started looking at my watch and listening for the meds wagon in the hall. When Jimmy came around with the juice and cookies, I'd ask him how far down the hall the nurse was. She seemed to be dispensing meds later and later, sometimes she hadn't even begun. I couldn't wait another half hour. I pestered Jimmy to tell her I wanted to go to sleep early, so could she please bring my medications right now. I was hooked.

At home on weekends, I took responsibility for remembering my medication. There was little danger of forgetting. By now I usually recognized the signs: chest pains, shakiness, falling apart. Xanax time! When I became very involved with something, like working on *Mile Zero*, I might not notice that I had passed the four-hour interval. When I noticed, I panicked. Quick, the Xanax, quick! Any time I went out of the house, the little bottle was standard equipment. In fact, I had several little bottles, *au cas où*.

Journal: November 30, 1987
American Thanksgiving weekend. This has been my best Thanksgiving ever, despite some ups and downs. In the afternoon, Annie and Philip were in the kitchen preparing the turkey. I'd had my weekly deep muscle massage and was left alone in the living room to rest on the massage table. After awhile, I was stiff and uncomfortable and I called for help to get down. No answer. My whistle was upstairs, as usual. I called and called until I was hoarse and terrified. It seemed like hours. When Philip finally came, my fear became anger: "Why did you have the radio on when you knew I was all alone and you're both hard of hearing?"

Philip felt terrible and I was immediately ashamed.

We had made up by the time the guests arrived: Isabel, Bernard, Sidonie, Terre, and soon after that, Joe Carlton and his wife, Susan, whom I had never met before. I was sitting on the couch and Terre was in my wheelchair, and Susan mistook her for me. Terre strung her along for a few minutes, in our old "Terre Klein and Bonnie Nash" routine. Everyone thought it was hilarious, including Susan, but I was suddenly upset by it. I didn't like seeing Terre in that chair. I didn't want anyone I loved to be in a wheelchair. For Terre, it was just a place to sit, but for me it's a hated symbol. I cling to the words of the *ergo* intern who said it was only temporary, and to the Peerless prediction: if I'm not exactly standing, at least I can get up with support to transfer from one chair to another.

After a few tears that no one but Michael noticed, my mood swung again. Here I was, at home with family and friends, and no nose tube. Thanksgiving!

I wanted to somehow consecrate this occasion, but I knew of no appropriate ritual. I couldn't look for the words in a book, or wait for someone else to say them. If it was going to happen, I would have to create it.

At my request, Michael tapped on a wineglass before dinner and everyone became silent. I spoke spontaneously, without much breath or volume, about the intimate connection between love, healing, and giving thanks. I became aware in the silence that I was speaking holy words — words the old Bonnie might have been embarrassed to speak. But I'm tougher now. If I can forthrightly discuss my bowel movements, I can certainly risk a little holiness in my own dining room.

INTERLUDE: HOLY SHIT!

Journal: March 10, 1995

As a culture we are hung up about secretions and excretions, the stuff of our bodies. There's not even any casual, everyday language for them; the words are stiffly scientific, or baby-talk, euphemisms, curses. This society is set up so that non-disabled people can pretty well pretend they never pee. But when I was sick, that's what my life was about. There were always secretions from my mouth. I coughed up great gobs and spit them into tissues. I was bothered by the wastefulness of throwing the tissue away after one spit, so I would leave them on the table. Seth, usually the ecologically conscious one among us, would come in and wordlessly dispose of them.

I choke a lot too, then and now. Sometimes I have a choking fit in a restaurant. We often ignore it ourselves until people at neighbouring tables start to panic, looking at Michael as if he's a murderer. "Not to worry. She does this all the time."

I no longer fill my sheets with diarrhea, but it sometimes happens that a piece of soiled toilet paper sticks to my bum and my still-numb senses are not aware of it. I used to go on my way, wondering where that lingering smell was coming from, examining the bottoms of my shoes for the culprit. Now I've learned to check, always check, after wiping myself. Then there's pee. Although I've regained control of my bladder under normal circumstances, I still wet my pants during choking spasms, or when I sneeze or laugh uproariously. For a while I hoped it was just temporary and took to carrying a change of underpants in my backpack. Finally I succumbed to those advertisements I'd always loathed and tried maxi-pads, which give me the promised security.

It took a long time and a lot of denial and humiliation to reach this point. Michael was not encouraging. It was a confusing switch, after the matter of fact warmth he showed during my days of total incontinence. When I wrote maxi-pads on the grocery list, he often either "forgot" to buy them or told me that I had "millions of boxes" around the house. He was slower than I to accept the fact that they were now a permanent part of my life. And he — this is hard to write — commented once or twice when the bathroom smelled of urine-soaked pads — I was saving the earth (again) by trying to recycle old bags that may have been full of holes. When I sensed his disgust, I felt disgusting. I've been careful since then to wrap my pads in store-fresh baggies, tie them and even hide them under other items in the wastebasket. I eventually confronted Michael about his uncharacteristic squeamishness, and he's never since forgotten to add either maxi-pads or baggies to the grocery list.

"We demand the right to pee!" writes disability activist Joan Meister. Lack of accessible washrooms limits the lives of many disabled people. It's amazing how many public places will tell you that they're wheelchair accessible and it turns out their toilet is down a flight of stairs. Or the washroom is too narrow to fit a wheelchair. Or there's no grab-bar. Or the grab-bar is installed too high. I have a friend who drinks no liquids all day if she's planning to go out in the evening. I have other friends who just don't go out. Unholy details can determine where we live, work and go to school, not just whether we go to the occasional movie. It's not the shit that's profane, but the exclusion.

We don't have the luxury of politely ignoring our excrement. We have to think about it, talk about it, plan ahead, strategize, write petitions, lobby governments, chain ourselves to buildings, change the world, or else pee our pants.

WINTER

I finally complained at my weekly medical exam that I wasn't getting adequate physio. The next day, as I was absorbed in my stretching exercises, Michel Danakas himself came bounding across the gym floor. He bounced on my mat with an exuberant "Bonjour Bonnie!" I flinched away in panic, burst into startled tears and hit him with my weak fist. Michel knelt beside me. "*Eh bien, qu'est ce qui arrive?* What's happening?" He put his arms around me and I soaked his T-shirt with tears and snot.

I started working with Michel every day. Like Iolanda before him, he was a cheerleader. "C'mon Bonnie, you can do it. *C'est beau, c'est ça*, that's it." He had noted my first fear-reaction and incorporated it into our sessions. He would throw me off-balance and we would end up rolling around and laughing on the mat. He would urge me to resist. "*Pousse! Pousse!* Push! Push!" he'd say, sounding like an overly enthusiastic childbirth coach. This was a "serious" exercise to develop specific muscle groups through resistance to pressure. But with Michel it was also playing.

I bounced from nervous anxiety to giddy laughter to desperate determination. Around the gym I was a known workaholic. Michel was always trying to get me to ease up. My friend Guy would roll by and tease "*Lâche pas*, Bonnie, *lâche pas*." ("Don't slack off, don't let up.") I started each physio session on my own with stretching and strengthening exercises. Michel would keep an eye on me as I worked, and join me on the mat at a certain point. He would stretch me further, just beyond the point where I had imagined the limit, and then move on to various arcane exercises. I can see now that they were for developing reflexes, balance, trunk control: necessary precursors to walking. But back then I was still waiting for the moment when I would rise from my chair and walk away.

I could always look around the gym and see someone struggling with a skill that I had just mastered. I'd also see people who hadn't been at the Institut very long, doing much more than I could. Older stroke patients especially depressed me because they often went from severe paralysis to walking while I was still slithering on the mat. "He's eighty years old and using four-point canes already. What's wrong with me?" Michel would remind me of the difference between a brain-stem stroke and a hemispheric stroke, but in my heart I was comparing my progress to theirs and despairing. Occasionally I spent the whole session crying on the mat while Michel lay next to me, patting my arm.

I wasn't learning to walk. I was learning to use a wheelchair. It seemed like a waste of time to work so hard perfecting a skill that I would soon leave behind. But I had to admit, it was easier to get around. I stopped crashing into walls, and I even enjoyed the speed I could work up when I wasn't too fatigued. But whenever I rolled over a bump, I thought I was tipping backwards. I would freeze in the chair, eyes screwed shut, hands clenched, breath coming in small screams. Michel assured me

the anti-tip wheels in the back would keep the chair from flip-
ping over. "But it's the sensation of falling, not the reality that
scares me," I would say.

I had lost trust in my body, in the ground beneath my feet.
But maybe I'd always been a chicken. I wasn't raised to take
physical risks. My parents sat shiva the first time I went skiing.
Naomi never tires of telling how, after ten years of downhill
skiing, I would get to the top of a chairlift and yell ahead to the
attendant, "Please help me off; it's my first time." I didn't lie
about many things, but this was life-and-death.

Michael had always encouraged me to face down my physical fears, and I had followed him up mountains, down rivers,
and under oceans to justify his faith in me. I had also learned
to listen to the wisdom of my own body. I liberated myself from
downhill skiing in favour of cross-country, and chose yoga over
squash.

Now Michael was encouraging me to face my fear of falling.
"It's not the end of the world," he'd say. "Get Michel to teach
you how to fall safely."

Michel did not agree. He was mortified when I fell. "No fall
is a good thing," he'd say. "Our purpose is to keep you from
falling." I was with him. I fell a lot, though never while learning to use a new piece of equipment. I would often lose my balance from a sudden turn, or misjudge the distance between
two places, or throw my body on the floor in a brain-scram-
bled attempt to swing a door closed.

Michael had the bright idea to hire a private physio to work
with me over the weekends. How could I rest for two whole
days when the window of opportunity was steadily closing?
Michael was not a natural rester: "No pain, no gain."

Michel was appalled. "*Lentement mais surement*! Slowly
but surely." I was convinced. I told Michael — it was probably

a direct quote from Michel — that healing takes place in the resting as much as in the working. He backed off then. He's a bad rester, but a good learner.

At last Michel said I was ready to work on the parallel bars. These were two handrails running the width of the gym, with a mirror at either end. I transferred from my chair by grabbing the bars and pulling myself up with the upper-body strength I was earning daily in the gym. What joy to be upright! I would take halting steps, grasping the rails for dear life. When I dared look up from my feet, the mirror showed me the difference between where I perceived my body to be and where it really was in space. I could correct my position, unlock my knees, untwist my pelvis, relax my shoulders, straighten my head. So much to remember. The scariest part came when I reached the end: I had to let go with one hand and (gasp) trust that I could stay upright while pivoting around till I could grab the opposite railing and switch hands for the return trip. I felt like a performer on the high-wire.

At first Michel stood beside me, helping to support my weight as I stumbled along holding the bars. Then, as my balance improved, I did it "in harness" with a wide leather belt around my waist and a strap for Michel to hold *au cas où*. I had often seen *bénéficiaires* in harness, leading their physios along the corridors or across the lobby. This was the last stage before "real" walking and the glamour of their independence made them seem less like leashed dogs. Soon I'll be off the bars and walking the halls, I told myself.

Finally Michel brought out the *marchette*, the same three-sided walking frame I had been learning to use at the JGH before my second stroke. We started by walking short distances in the gym. I was supposed to take a step, then lift the *marchette* and place it ahead of me for the next step. But what would happen to me during the time that the walker was off the ground? How was I supposed to stay up? What made them think I could do this?

Walking with the *marchette* was an enormous strain: supporting my weight, standing upright, shifting to lift one leg, remembering to bend at the knee, to step down with the heel first. A rote litany. "Look ahead at where you want to go," Michel would remind me. "Don't look at the floor." But how else could I be sure the floor was still there, when I couldn't feel it beneath my feet?

It took many weeks, but I did it: three steps, five steps, halfway across the gym. Michel lavished praise on each nervous victory. "WOW!" he'd say, in about ten syllables. "WOOO-OOW!"

Michel Danakas: I remember going back to the office, sitting down, completely drained. Working one hour with one person can be as tough as working with eight. But then there are seven other people waiting for their time. You were one of the tough ones like that. On a scale of ten, you were around nine. When someone says they want to walk by next month, then I say to myself, oh, oh, watch out. If their expectations are really high, then whatever I do won't be good enough because they don't progress fast enough for their dreams. I felt like I held you only by a small string, and some little thing might cut the string and you would give up.

Journal: December 10, 1987
Michael came to see me in physio but he didn't find me at

first because he was looking at wheelchair level and I was up with the *marchotte*!

I can walk the length of the gym now, using the *marchette*, and I jumped my leg weights from 1/2 lb to 1-1/2 lbs. This week I continued going to the bathroom alone in the daytime. I pulled up my pants with two hands! At night I still wet the green plasticized sheet and buzz for the night nurse when the cold wakes me.

Ergothérapie (occupational therapy in English) was like home economics for absolute beginners, with a functioning kitchen and mock-ups of bed, stairs, bathroom and the half-car that appeared in André's film. Everyone was assigned a partner, and we played games and did projects together. My partner was Denise, who lived across the hall from me. She was more sociable than Paulette; in fact, she never stopped talking. She was a full-time housewife from the suburbs: not my type, I once would have thought, but now we were friends. She'd had delicate spinal surgery to remove a malignant tumour and was praying it would not recur. Michael was not optimistic about her prognosis, but I reminded him that people had not been optimistic about mine.

The *ergo* lab with its large collection of children's games, could have been a place to play as adults (like physio down the hall). Instead, the therapists proceeded with humiliating seriousness. We worked at shuffleboard and ping-pong and navigated obstacle courses. We did pre-kindergarten puzzles with large wooden pieces, carnival games with clown-face targets, and uninspired paint-by-number crafts. Denise devoted herself to a pre-fabricated wooden nativity scene for Christmas, while I made potholders.

But some activities were clearly useful. Michael was taught proper wheelchair handling and transfer mechanics, saving his already strained back. On the mock-up stairs-to-nowhere I learned how to transfer from the wheelchair to the floor and then bump down the stairs by pushing with both hands, wiggling to the edge of the step, and then pushing off until my bum landed on the step below. Going up was much harder because it's anti-gravity.

A high point came when Evelyne, our *ergothérapeute*, asked Denise and me if we would like to prepare a lunch, and invite some guests. We were delighted at the chance to entertain our respective physiotherapists. It took something like two weeks to prepare this extravaganza, including planning, invitation-making, writing shopping lists, the wheelchair excursion to buy groceries at Steinberg's supermarket in the mall across the street, and finally cooking, setting the table, serving and cleaning. If the purpose of the activity was to encourage us to resume our culinary activities, it convinced me that I could either cook or have a life.

Journal: December 13, 1987
Razelle is here for the weekend! She walked into the *ergo* lab yesterday, hugged me and cried: "She's moving!" She stayed for an hour and Denise and I showed off our prowess at bean bag toss. I had the best visit ever with her. Tonight we ate at L'Impromptu, my first outing. I had a moment of self-consciousness wheeling to the bathroom, which passed. The bathroom was wheelchair accessible — with proper grab-bars! — in spite of the small size of the restaurant.

When we came home, it was just starting to snow, but I made it up the steps clinging to the rail and Michael's arm.

Winter looked beautiful until I tried to wheel in the snow. I could no longer roll myself down to the car when Michael arrived to pick me up, but had to wait for him to help me through the slush. An unshovelled walk was as impossible as a curb for my chair, and far too slippery to negotiate with the *marchette*. At home, there was no sidewalk from the driveway to the front door, just a path across the lawn. After the first big snowfall, Michael purchased a thirty-metre strip of indoor-outdoor and rolled out the red carpet for me. It got pretty filthy and forlorn after a Montreal winter, but it served its purpose.

Chanukah came early that year, shortly before the Institut's two-week winter break when almost all the patients went home for the holidays. Seth was supposed to make it back for the first night's celebration. Unfortunately his train got stalled in the snow just outside of Montreal station and he ended up sitting in a tunnel for two hours before the tracks were cleared. On the second night Seth came to the Institut with Naomi and Michael and our Chanukah menorah to light candles with me. One of the Mitzvot of Chanukah is to put the lighted menorah, a symbol of the miracle, in a window so it can be seen by passers-by. I saw it as a gesture of openness and pride about being Jewish in a predominantly non-Jewish culture. Besides, it is very beautiful to watch eight candles burning against the winter night. Do we transport this tradition to a shared room in a Catholic hospital? My husband and children did it without hesitation. We chanted the three blessings and even sang some Chanukah songs. To everyone's surprise, most of all my own, my usually discordant singing voice came out sweet and sure. What miracles a paralyzed vocal chord can accomplish.

The Herzl Chanukah party was on a weeknight, so I got an evening pass from the Institut. It was a chance for me to get dressed up and see people who'd been so important to me when I was at the JGH. For the last ten years, the party had been a potluck at our home, but this year it was at a gigantic Chinese restaurant which claimed to be wheelchair accessible. When we got there, we discovered that "accessible" meant that the waiters would be happy to carry me up the stairs. Michael was furious. I, on the other hand, thought it was a great adventure to be escorted on a freight elevator full of garbage through the bowels of the kitchen, and then carried up the remaining stairs by several strong family practice residents.

As it turns out, I didn't last long. I learned what was to become a pattern (and persists even now): the anticipation of such an event, and the kerfuffle around accessing it, plus the excitement of being in a crowd of people, exhausted me. I didn't even make it past the hors d'oeuvres, let alone the dancing. I couldn't wait to go "home" where Jimmy would tuck me into bed.

Michael had seen an ad for a "honeymoon break" at the Meridien, a hotel on top of one of the giant underground malls which Montreal has made famous, with shopping, restaurants, cinemas and even the metro-transit all available without going outdoors. He thought if I wasn't well enough to go out of town during my winter break, maybe we could pretend by spending a weekend at the Meridien.

Our hotel room was fine, but reality hit outside its comforts. The swimming pool was accessible, but not the bathroom, dressing room, hot tub or sauna. Once in, the water was too cold for my poor circulation and hypersensitivity; it had none of the womb-like warmth of the overheated Institut *piscine* that I had recently begun to use. I got out as fast as I got in — which was not fast at all, given the lack of transfer apparatus.

After the swimming fiasco, we planned an intimate dinner in the hotel restaurant. Michael had to bump the wheelchair down some cosmetically gratuitous steps from one level to another, a guaranteed route to backache since the wheelchair handles were too low even for plain pushing, let alone stairs. Dinner had to be negotiated around too salty, too spicy, too hot, too cold. I choked and spit up the pricey food. After dinner, I was ready for bed. I think we brought a bedpan to this honeymoon. I was too exhausted to even try having sex. After less than twenty-four hours, we were happy to go home.

Two weeks at home was heaven. That was the holiday when I learned to dance. I don't remember how it started, whether it was another of Michael's bright ideas for therapy, or a spontaneous moment that just happened in the privacy of our living room. Maybe Michael noticed my unruly feet tapping to the Preservation Hall Jazz Band, trying to dance my body out of the wheelchair. At any rate, he quickly rolled back the carpet (my feet stuck to rugs), took my hand, and we jitterbugged to Louis Armstrong, Benny Goodman, Ike and Tina Turner. I usually had trouble shifting my weight from one foot to the other, but dancing somehow allowed me to by-pass all that left-brain stuff. The beat went right from the music into my body and my feet were released. My movements were rigid and jerky and Michael had to loosen my knuckles when his arm became white from my deathly grip, but I was dancing. Lucy ran for cover. Naomi, who used to get annoyed by any physical expressions of emotion between Michael and me, got a big kick out of watching from the stairway. Once she even deigned to dance with me herself.

Terre Nash: During Christmas break you brought home the *marchette*. You used it all over the house. You would walk to the kitchen, sit down and rest a while, and then walk to the dining room. I said to you, "Remember the Peerless prediction: 'Standing by Thanksgiving, walking by Christmas.' And look at you now, it's true!" But you got mad. You had thought that walking by Christmas would mean really walking. Using the *marchette* didn't count.

Journal: January 4, 1988

The holidays went too fast. Monday morning was glum — back to boot camp after two weeks at home. Michael slept badly and cried when he brought me back to the Institut. Then he called at noon to remind me that we both get depressed on Monday mornings.

Paulette was discharged before the break and is now an outpatient, with physio three times a week, except so far she hasn't shown up. It seems strange, but I miss her. We maintained a tenuous peace for a while and then Michael managed, with many small courtesies, to win her over so that she sometimes even smiled. I cheered (and envied) her achievements as she conquered the four-point canes and then began walking by herself. In exchange, she kept the radio lower and even turned it off when she left the room. The real breakthrough was when her two small boys came to celebrate her birthday in their Sunday best. My admiration for her lovely children overcame her defence, and she expanded to a beaming grin. We had not bonded as survivors of brain injuries but we bonded as mothers. I hope she comes back for physio — Michel says most outpatients don't.

I'm wondering if I'll be ready to leave by the end of January as promised. Everyone I know who's left could walk on their own and I can hardly last for five minutes on the *marchette*, I'm shaky as hell on my new four-point canes, I can't walk *down* steps without a great deal of fear and support, and I still tire easily though less than before. Michel thinks another three weeks is a lot of time to improve, so I'm still aiming for it, though I'm trying to prepare for the possibility that it might be wise to wait longer. Progress at this point is much less dramatic and visible, so I have to fight the tendency to get discouraged.

My new roommate is twenty-five-year-old Martine, who had a car accident two and a half years ago. She spent four months in a coma, and has been hospitalized ever since. She seems positive and cheerful.

Martine had an indulgent mother and a doting fiancé named Stefan. The story was that she'd had another boyfriend with whom she was driving when she had the car accident that landed her in the hospital. She and Stefan became a number sometime afterwards. One night I recounted this to Michael. He pronounced the relationship "sick"; "pathological." Why? I wondered. Was it sick for an "able-bodied" man to love a brain-injured woman? And if so, what did it say about us?

I was afraid to ask such questions. Many people in the Institut were alone. Some were from far away, separated from their families by too many miles for regular visits. Others were simply abandoned. Most husbands leave their wives (90% according to one unsubstantiated statistic) and almost half of women leave disabled husbands. Even more shocking, many disabled children are deserted. I didn't want to think about it.

Journal: January 15, 1988
I had a bad experience in *ergo* this morning. An old patient of Evelyne's came by to say hello — he walks with one cane

and is still unable to work after two years. I wonder what he does all day. Evelyne offered him as a hopeful model, saying he was like us when he began. All I could see was the cane and the limp, and I got suddenly depressed and tearful. When Evelyne asked why, I said I'd expected to go much further, in fact to play tennis this summer. Evelyne broke into uncontrollable laughter at the idea, it seemed so preposterous. I was devastated. She apologized later, though she said she'd be enormously surprised if I could ever run again. She allowed as how it might be helpful to hold onto an image, however unrealistic. She said she hoped she hadn't been too brutal in making me confront reality.

I spent the rest of the day in my room, without the energy to continue. Part of me refuses to believe her, refuses to give up. The other part says there will be no more heroics, no dramatic recovery, just days and weeks and months of hard work with no defined end-point, no light at the end of the tunnel. What's the point? After the ecstasy of survival, what exactly have I survived for?

INTERLUDE: TALKING BACK

Journal May 26, 1995
Who said revenge is sweet? They're right, it's delicious.

Well it wasn't exactly revenge, it was even better. I was invited to give the Keynote Address to the Annual Meeting of the Canadian Association of Occupational Therapists! The profession has decided to become "client-centred" — the jargon of the nineties — and are admitting they don't know exactly what that means. So they invited me — the ultimate mouthy client — to talk on their theme, "Partners in Practice."

What an opportunity to turn almost eight years' experience to good use! We in the disability rights movement say that *we* are the experts about disability, that we long to de-medicalize rehabilitation and take it into our own hands.

After congratulating their commitment to partnership, I innocently asked whether any of the 600 people in the room besides myself considered themselves disabled? As I suspected there were no hands. I pointed out the inherent power inequality in their hoped-for partnership, the unspoken barrier between helper and helpee, provider and consumer, have and have-not. How hard it must be to treat people with disabilities as equals if they don't have daily, ongoing contact as peers and colleagues.

I told them the Evelyne story. When I said I had expected to play tennis, there was a titter in the room. I acknowleded that it *is* laughable in retrospect, that Evelyne knew much more than I knew. As an experienced OT, she also knew that not being able to play tennis or even to walk wasn't the end of the world. She knew that there is life after disability. But I didn't know that as a person who had just become disabled. And she did not try to bridge that gap. She laughed at me! I never trusted her after that, never bonded to her.

It's arrogant of anyone to impose limits on another person's healing. People with disabilities are always telling stories about "the doctor said I'd never do this or the therapist said I'd never do that." We've all defied odds and predictions.

Why? I think the reason some people "succeed" more than others with similar conditions is a combination of factors: social and economic circumstances, motivation and the support of family, friends and therapists.

I proposed that OTs consider themselves our *allies* — clinically and politically, that rehab professionals fight the handicaps that are imposed on us not by our impairments but by societal attitudes, and help us remove the barriers which restrict our movement in the world. No one ever prepared me to live as a disabled person in a world which is often hostile and excluding. I felt like I was the first person in the world to use a wheelchair.

If society doesn't have a place for us then we can't value ourselves. How can somebody have self-esteem when everything around them is telling them the opposite — that they're not worth the additional expense of a Braille version or a personal care attendant or American Sign Language, that these are frills which affect only a few people?

The disability rights movement is redefining independence. I no longer see independence in terms of how far I can walk, as I did in physio, but as control over my life, measured not by tasks I can do without help but by the quality of my life with the help that is needed. That's a more radical definition than the conventional one, and I think more interesting for therapists than teaching us to play checkers or even to walk, and probably closer to the reason most people become rehab professionals in the first place.

I think my speech touched a nerve — I even saw a few tears. Perhaps it's not naive to hope that "client-centred" will be more than the latest catch phrase, and perhaps someday a partnership of equals can be forged around our common strength and vulnerability.

OUTPATIENT

≈

I left the Institut on Valentine's Day. After more than six months of living in institutions, I was ready. My last days were endless. I hated the unchanging routines, the cafeteria food, the bright posters on cold walls. I hated the sight of sweet Jimmy Deakin wheeling the juice and cookies down the hall at night. I was lonely. It was not my home.

On the other hand I was terrified of being discharged. I felt as if the rehab system was giving up on me. Rehabilitation from a stroke is often declared to be complete after six months, or maybe a year. In a strictly cost-benefit analysis, there were diminishing returns for the medical system as my progress plateaued. The high drama was over, and the rest was less interesting for the health professionals.

I don't remember if we had any sort of homecoming ceremony. When Michael grabbed the scissors and cut off the hospital bracelet, marking me a free and well woman, I would have liked to say the Shehechiyanu, a Jewish prayer of thanksgiving which freely translated means: "Thank God we've lived to see this day!" But we probably just grinned.

Nothing was impossible now. We had handled the commode, the carrying up and down stairs, and now I was so much better. It was going to be easy. Meena was going to come full time, so I wouldn't be alone while Michael was at work and Naomi at her new English CÉGEP. I would continue at the Institut as an outpatient, work on my film, see my friends, be a real wife and mother.

Everything would return to normal.

Journal: February 18, 1988
Suddenly I'm thinking of myself not as ill, but as a well person (with a temporary inconvenience). Is that the difference between hospital and home?

I love being here. It's better than ever, because now instead of constantly sniping at each other, Michael and Naomi are a team, looking out for each other, strategizing for my comfort. On nights when Michael is on call and Naomi has a date, she takes his beeper with her and if he gets called in, she races home so I don't have to be alone. I can just imagine her dancing in some funky club with a doctor's pager clipped to her jeans.

I'd never heard of a Jewish ceremony for leaving the hospital, but renewing tradition is what Reconstructionist Judaism is all about. I spoke to Rabbi Ron who responded with enthusiasm: we would create a special *Shabbat* service. He brought over stacks of material about healing he'd collected from both traditional and contemporary Jewish sources: Hannah Szenes, Mordecai Kaplan, the Psalms, an adapted mourner's kaddish.

Ron and I compiled a supplement for the *Shabbat* service, and called it "A Celebration of Life." Naomi agreed to include her "Dear Mommy" poem and Seth wrote on what he'd learned about me, his dad and his sister as we lived this crisis. I added Marge Piercy, Judy Chicago, Lao Tsu: "A journey of a thousand miles begins with a single step."

We put an announcement in the synagogue bulletin, and invited a few friends from Herzl and the NFB. Seth, an old hand at estimating political crowd size, said there were 150 people there that Saturday morning, including people we hardly knew, who had been following the course of my illness through Rabbi Ron's weekly updates at *Shabbat* services. My stroke had become a community event, reminding people of the fragility of their own lives and dreams.

I sat in the front row, with Michael and the kids and Annie and Phil who drove up from New Jersey with a vanful of homemade goodies for the event. Our family was called up for the first Aliyah, the blessing before the weekly Torah reading. I had been sitting through the service worrying about how I would get up the two shallow steps to the *Bimah*. When the moment came, Michael and Naomi took my arms and I managed it without stumbling. Everyone was silent. We stood at the open Torah scroll, and together we chanted the ancient sweet melody. Ron led the congregation in the Shehechiyanu.

Next came the D'var Torah, the Jewish equivalent of a sermon. Today it was not Rabbi Ron but Michael Klein who gave the D'var. It was the first time Michael, who had not had a Bar Mitzvah ceremony, ever spoke in synagogue. His D'var was a thank-you in the form of personal stories about the many ways people had helped us. He couldn't resist telling the story of Rabbi Ron coming to visit me at the JGH when I was unable to roll over. "Can I do anything to help?" Ron had asked. "Rub my ass!" I replied in my breathy, disinhibited new voice.

In the synagogue, when Ron asked if I wanted to say a few words, my heart was too full to speak.

Journal: February 23
I'm so tired of being tired. Every little activity is big. Like taking a shower. You shower before doing something, right? You shower before breakfast, or before you get dressed and

go somewhere. But no, for me a shower requires going back to bed afterwards to recuperate. I nap throughout the day and still need to go to sleep by 7 p.m. every night.

It's the tiny things that get to me. I can't carry. It's only when you can't that you realize how much you need to. When I use the wheelchair, I can carry things on my lap, but now that I'm up with the *marchette* around the house, I don't have any free hands. We tried to saddle Lucy with a carry-pack but the old dog didn't tolerate this new trick. Michael suggested I use a knapsack, but it throws my balance off. Even carrying a towel around my neck is too much for my tenuous *marchette* skills. Pockets work, or holding things with my teeth, or dropping things down from the stairwell (except it breaks the backs of books). But I can't put a cup of tea in my pocket or throw it down stairs.

Spontaneity is a luxury. I have to plan ahead to remember everything I need, so I don't have to blow that stupid whistle for Meena to come help me. "Please bring me the phone, bring me my box of Kleenex." I try to ask nicely, but I feel so demanding, so . . . colonial. What is this white lady doing, blowing a whistle as if Meena were some dog?

Surely I used to organize myself better. Surely I used to run out the door grabbing my bag knowing my keys, wallet, notebooks, pens, phone lists were all there. Now when I go out, or even downstairs, I have lists that I check and recheck — sweaters, medications, emergency food rations, maxi-pads and extra underpants, my journal — and still I forget things. Planning is hard work. Pressure work. But I'm learning to be patient and recognize what I really need and what I can do without. I can sit and think instead of asking someone to bring me my journal.

Three days a week I went to the Institut for physio, *ergo* and *ortho*. Just getting ready to go was a big deal. I was much too shaky to use public transit by myself, and besides it was totally inaccessible. Montreal had never heard of lift-equipped public buses, and the Metro stations all had narrow escalators or steps. No one had prepared me for the world of Transport Adapté, the parallel transit system for people with disabilities. To qualify, I discovered, I needed a medical certificate saying I was "permanently disabled." I hated that piece of paper. It was a lie. I was getting better.

Transport Adapté had a few buses and special cars for people with electric wheelchairs, but for people like me, with folding manual chairs, they contracted out to private cab companies whose drivers were resentful of the extra time we took. I got the feeling that everyone at Transport Adapté was overworked, exploited and angry. To book a ride, I had to call several days in advance, give them the exact address I was coming from and going to, and the exact times I wanted to be picked up and returned. I had to be ready at the door ten minutes before the reserved time, but they might not get there until twenty minutes after. Or they might be much later. Or my booking might have been lost. You were not allowed to call and check until after the allowable twenty minutes' lateness. The line was always busy. If you weren't waiting at the door when they arrived, they would leave. If I was at the Institut, where the phone was a long walk from the front door, to call or not to call was a big dilemma. If the driver showed up while I was *en route* to the phone or waiting on hold, then I'd miss the ride. Such is the drama of parallel transport. It was much easier to stay at home and, except for my outpatient appointments, that's mostly what I did.

The Institut was not set up for outpatients. They had a full roster of inpatients whose needs were urgent. We were a sideline, fit into the cracks of their regular program. When I'd been a real patient, I lay down in my room after lunch every day before I went to lab or gym. Now I ended up alone in a staff lounge feeling like a trespasser, eating my bag lunch and napping on the plastic sofa. By the end of the day I would be shaking with exhaustion, ready to go home and collapse if only the Transport Adapté would come.

On days when I wasn't at the Institut, I would practise walking on four-point canes. Meena would help me with my coat and boots, leash up Lucy, and off we'd go. I'd count my progress by house numbers and landmarks: one driveway down, then two, then all the way to the fire hydrant. I was so precariously upright that it seemed a wind or a passing car could knock me over. The slant of the sidewalk felt like a steep ridge on which I was balancing.

For longer jaunts, Meena would push me in the wheelchair. She took me shopping on Rue Sherbrooke which was just around the corner. This was the neighbourhood where I had lived for years, where I had frequented the old greystone shops without ever really noticing the steep granite step at each doorway.

Meena Williams: I know you didn't feel too pleasant sometimes, always needing help. I don't blame you. It's hard to be in someone else's hands like that. Often you were nervous. It was good when Michael put that Mickey Mouse bell on your wheelchair, because you could ring it when you thought you might bump into someone. You had some control. But any unexpected noise, or a car that suddenly appeared would upset you. "Wait, wait, that guy's pulling out!" You had to depend on my eyes, my hands. And you felt every hump in the road. Sometimes you'd say, "Why didn't you steer around that?" But that's just the way the roads are. Especially in the snow. It was hard. This climate was not meant for wheelchairs.

When I became steady enough on four-point canes, I would carry them across my lap in the chair, and with much courage and Meena's help, I would ascend the few steps for a haircut at the local beauty parlour. This was the same place where I'd had my hair cut for years, rushing in at 5 o'clock after a day of work. Now a hair appointment was a major activity, only to be undertaken on a good day, followed by an afternoon in bed. I felt awkward; everyone stared at me, distracted from their chit-chat and *Chatelaine*. As my hair was cut, I studied my face in the mirror. Had I changed? I was thinner, paler, but still recognizably me. I looked normal, even pretty. But then I stuck out my tongue and there was the Truth — thick and distorted, like a slab of raw liver — a monster tongue in a woman's mouth.

By this time a ramp had been installed at my mother's nursing home, so I went to visit her twice a week. But no matter how often I went, I always felt guilty for not going more. The first time, my mother got agitated as soon as she saw me. "Are you wondering why Bonnie's in a wheelchair?" Michael asked. She nodded, crying. Michael took her hand. "Bonnie was sick but she's better now," he explained, and that was the end of it. She always responded to Michael. I don't know if it was a faint echo of their old relationship, or just his deep male voice that she warmed to (as I had to Rick's). He could win a smile from her even on days when all I got was a blank stare.

I hated seeing my mother in that place. I hated the combination of love, pity and recognition that rose in me each time I entered her tiny room. I had been there. I too had tried desperately to talk, only to be misunderstood or ignored. I too had been tied into my wheelchair and pushed from place to place. I too had waited in a bed of excrement for an orderly to come. "The difference is that you're getting better. And she can only get worse," Michael said. It was a cruel difference.

Journal March 2, 1988
My doctor at the Institut said my main obstacles now were proprioception (not knowing where my body is in space) and coordination, problems that aren't easily addressed by therapy. He feels I will still make progress over the next months, though slower, and that we won't know till next autumn to what extent I am "functional."

I came home depressed.

When Michael first suggested we go to the Caribbean for a swimming holiday, it seemed impossible. Our idea of a vacation has always been camping in some out of the way place with strenuous hikes and unusual bathroom facilities. We looked down our noses at tourist traps that promised all the comforts of home. Why not just stay home then? But Michael was sure we could find both accessibility and adventure. We ended up booking a one-week package at a resort hotel in Guadeloupe.

At the airport everyone ignored me, asking Michael whether "she" could walk onto the plane, or if "she" needed the narrow Washington chair to board. My body got numb from sitting so long in the cramped airplane seat, but the narrow bathrooms turned out to be perfect; I could balance using the close walls and grab bars. I wondered how people who couldn't get out of their wheelchairs managed to go to the toilet.

I remember the hot wind on my face as we deplaned, the smell of ocean and flowers. I wanted to throw off my shoes and run barefoot on the beach. Instead, I sat on the hotel bed and cried. I didn't even know how I would get down to the water. It was too far in the walker and the chair couldn't wheel on sand. My body couldn't tolerate the heat any more than it could the cold in Montreal. Michael cried with me that first morning and then we made love in the bland resort room. I decided this was going to be a good vacation after all.

Journal: March 21
This is a vacation of small adventures that are more exciting than all the mountains we once climbed. We found an accessible beach not far from the hotel where I can walk right into the ocean with the *marchette*. Michael has been using all his old swim-teacher tricks to help me in the hotel pool. It's scary and hilarious all at once. I can't kick. I tried and tried, holding onto Michael's waist at the shallow end, but my feet won't move in any orderly fashion. I was holding on so tightly that I pulled his swimming trunks down. We laughed so hard I almost drowned. None of the other guests seemed to find it funny at all.

The other guests were mostly European tourists with bronzed muscles and designer swimwear. They would congregate on the beach or in the dining room, striking up flirtations and friendships. Michael and I sat alone. No one asked our names. No one said hello if we passed in the courtyard. They averted their eyes and tried not to brush up against me. My body was pale

and emaciated, my muscles still slack from months of paralysis.
I felt like I was polluting their paradise. I was their worst nightmare; a reminder of the mortality of their gym-toned flesh.

Journal: March 24
Today we were crazy! Today I went snorkelling. I think I
agreed to try it out of a silly determination to act as if I could
do anything. And apart from not being able to kick, not
having enough breath to clear the snorkel-tube, and having
to be lifted in and out of the boat, it was great.

Everything I've always loved about snorkelling was still
there: the kaleidoscope light, the day-glo fish. The water allows
me to love my body and to trust it. I can't walk on land, but I
can walk in the accommodating water. My almost constant
pain eases with no gravity to pull me down. When I'm swimming, my movements are fluid, smooth. I feel free and strong.
And I bring that confidence to ground when I emerge.

On our last day, we rented a jeep and drove across the island
to an isolated area of rocky beaches. We found a flat spot overlooking the ocean and Michael wheeled me across the rock to
where I could see the sunset. I asked him to leave me there for
a while. He was a little puzzled but quite willing to go off and
play mountain goat. I listened as his footsteps faded and then
there was nothing but the soft sound of the waves. I watched
the clouds redden. A heron flapped by. It was the first time in
eight months that I had been alone.

Journal: April 2
My post-vacation re-entry was at a new level of wellness.
I went to the Institut without the wheelchair — only four-
point canes!

Wednesday afternoon I worked on *Mile Zero* at the NFB. Being there was a bit overwhelming. I couldn't sleep the night before or for two nights after. I snuck into the building with Sidonie signaling when the corridors were clear so I could avoid gawkers. We had a fine work session and I realized once again how much I like making films. My earlier insecurity is gone now — I know I'm still good at it. I love persisting until it's just right — even when it exhausts me.

At that point, we had *Mile Zero* work sessions once or twice a week, and in between Sidonie called with questions and progress reports. The film was starting to take shape. It opened with close-ups of individual teenagers talking about their fears for the future. What emerged was not their despair but their passionate love of life. I cried every time we replayed it. The love of life, the fragility of the planet: these abstractions were fierce and immediate to me. Life was sweet and full and precious in a way I had never known before.

By June the final edit was nearly complete and I took time off to go to California with Michael. Our trip was first planned as a week of visiting family; my big chance to "meet" my new sister-in-law Lyn, whose voice and gentle massages I remembered through the haze of my second stroke. But now I had another serendipitous motivation. While I was still at the Institut, a friend had sent me an article about Emilie Conrad Da'oud, a dancer in L.A. who was reported to work "miracles" with severely paralyzed people. More recently, I'd received a letter from Susan Griffin, a feminist poet and philosopher, whom I'd filmed for *Not a Love Story*. Susan had become profoundly ill with what was finally diagnosed as Chronic Fatigue Immune Dysfunction Syndrome, and was greatly helped by Emilie Conrad Da'oud. Well, it was clear the goddess was sending me a message in stereo about this Emilie. I wrote and asked if she would meet me when we came to L.A. She had no workshops scheduled for that time, but she agreed to see me privately for a very modest fee.

Emilie came to our motel for the first appointment. I didn't know what to expect. She sounded so "New Agey" in the article I'd read, talking about cellular knowledge and micro-movements and alternatives to the central nervous system. This was not the sort of thing I would do in my right mind, but then I hadn't been in my right mind since last August. Our approach to stroke treatment had been to try anything and everything; we called it the "no stone unturned" method.

Emilie was no stone. She was a bit less exotic than her photographs, and she spoke New Age with a very familiar Long Island accent, but she was also darkly, dancerly beautiful, and exuded a passionate confidence. I liked her right away.

Our work started flat on the floor of the tiny motel room, in silence. We concentrated on my breath. She asked me to pay attention to any natural movement that occurred, even a twinge in a finger or a jerk in my thigh, and to exaggerate it and follow it through. In a short amount of time, I was moving my limbs in unaccustomed ways, swaying and writhing in all directions in movements which Emilie called "primal" because they imitate the evolution of the species and each individual. There were no formal directions, just the natural movement of my body, directed from the inside out. There was no right or wrong, not even a better or worse. I was self-conscious at first. I wasn't used to this formlessness. In physio, I told my body what it should do; here I followed its impulses. When I relaxed into the experience, I discovered my body wanted to do many of the same movements I was struggling with in physio: the reaches, the bridging, the balancing. I felt my body wanting to stretch itself, to push and test itself, by its own volition. But unlike physio, the movements were smooth and varied, no sharp angles but big curves in many dimensions.

"You're a dancer," Emilie said. How outrageous! It was wild, sensuous and pleasureful. I felt totally alive.

In the next session Emilie added words, or rather sounds, because their meanings were beside the point: JACQUES, JACQUES, SATCHADANANDA (or was it CHICHINITZA?) Making these sounds caused my body to move in strange ways. I became aware that all the parts were connected; my speaking, my breathing and my movement — which had been fragmented into *ortho*, *ergo* and physio — were all related through my central nervous system! It seems so obvious now, but back then, I had lost all sense of my body's integrity.

I'd invited Michael to this session, not sure how he would respond. His first, knee-jerk (read: medical) reaction to "someone like" Emilie would normally be sceptical. He was not too hung up on credentials but he was suspicious of claims of miracle cures, and made corny jokes about "ass-holistic therapy." But as usual, he surprised me. Emilie, for her part, was warm and respectful of Michael, not a knee-jerk doctor-hater. I think she appreciated validation from a socially sanctioned expert.

For our final session, Emilie invited us to her home. Located in an area of boring California tract houses, hers had been transformed. I lay on a batik-covered daybed, and Michael, Lyn and Emilie sprawled around on giant tapestry cushions.

Emilie started by showing us some videos about her work. Watching them, I was struck by the utter sexiness of her body moving to its own inner direction. I was amazed, and envious, at the suppleness of her torso, how she could move each individual rib. She laughed at my awe and taught me what she called a tidal movement that undulated through my body like a soft wave. "Movement isn't something we *do*," she said, "it's something we *are*." Later that night, I had my first orgasm since my stroke.

The brief weekend with Emilie restored my confidence in my body and my feminist respect for its wisdom, which I had lost in the passive helplessness taught by my months of hospital and rehabilitation. I was a dancer too! I could play as well as work with my body; I could have fun, pleasure, beautiful music. I could take control of my healing: no therapist knew my body as well as I did.

Journal: June 2
I feel as if I've begun an entirely new chapter in my rehabilitation, one which I'll be writing myself. I'm a little nervous about returning to the Institut as an outpatient. How can I integrate these seemingly contradictory approaches, one from the inside out and the other from the outside in? How can I choose what's more important: my gait or my dancing cells? Do I have to choose? What would Michel Danakas think if I told him about wriggling formlessly and aimlessly on the floor instead of doing ten repetitions of the genuflection on my right leg with control?

For the time being, I'll try to lead a double life.

Journal: June 3
First day back at the Institut, I was struck by how many of the same *bénéficiaires* were still there, though I was only gone two and a half weeks. It seemed like so much more.

In physio I practised with ordinary canes. They feel so spindly and thin — how can they support me? It was tiring, but nothing like the first time with the walker or the four-point canes. I can do this! I was so thrilled I cried, and so did Michel!

But Evelyne, despite her pleasant welcome is de-motivatingly negative. She said that Denise will probably walk without canes, whereas I — if I'm lucky — might get down to one cane. No, I said angrily, I will do without them too. Who gave her the right to dismiss my dreams? Does she think that's her job — to stamp out "false hope"? What a difference, after Emilie's repeated encouragement that I will recover completely. I'm not going back to OT — why should I?

Journal: June 10
We got a letter this morning from Skip Peerless. He was astounded by the snorkelling pictures Michael sent. *And* he said he thinks I will still be recovering twelve to eighteen months from now! That's good news, because lately I've had trouble imagining how I will go from walking as I do now — with fatiguing instability and dependence on canes — to walking unaided. If the time-frame for the transition is stretched, then it appears more feasible. Like the kids in *Mile Zero* say, you've got to believe change is possible before you can make it happen.

Journal: June 11
"In the face of uncertainty, there is nothing wrong with hope." — C. Carl Simonton

Journal: June 17
Michael turned fifty today — a reminder of that race against time. Last night I dreamt I was at the Montreal Film Festival, on a scaffold high up outside a tall building, delivering some urgent message. I woke up and took a few steps without canes. Michael was ecstatic, but when I got to the Institut and

showed Michel, he said it was "not functional walking" and probably bad for my body because I was so tense and rigid.

In July, Miriam finally had her baby and went on maternity leave. My new therapist was Judith Blumberger, the head of *orthothérapie*. We had nodded to each other in the hallways for months, but never spoken. She seemed nice enough, but *ortho*, with its endless tongue exercises and rote recitations, was one of the most tedious hours of my day.

Judith Blumberger: When we first started, you were still the Perfect Patient — doing what you were told and never asking questions. You had these word lists, twenty-five or thirty monosyllabic words. You'd probably been doing the same ones for months — ploughing through, from beginning to end, every word on the list. The first thing that struck me was that twenty-five words was too much. I told you to pick a few of them. You just sat there and stared at me.

"What do you mean?" you asked. "Which ones should I pick?"

"Pick any ones you like," I said.

"But which ones?" you said.

I ended up choosing them because you couldn't. Then I tried to get you to say which ones were hard. You didn't know. You had been taught to say this list, but no one had taught you to pay attention to how it felt. You left that session with six words. I told you to start by *visualizing* yourself saying them well, rather than just sitting down and rattling them off.

I think you liked the visualizing thing, because at our second session you told me about Emilie and California.

I got the impression that this wasn't something you talked about at the Institut.

At that same session, you mentioned that you had a lot of pain in your neck. I asked you to move your jaw and your tongue; sure enough, your range of movement was quite restricted. So I thought, "Well, she has neck pains and limited movement, she likes visualization and she's been to California for therapy with a dancer. Maybe she won't think I'm too outrageous to propose Feldenkrais."

Feldenkrais is an approach to movement which focuses on inner awareness, visualization and intention. What we did was to forget about speech exercises and work on the very basic systems. We followed your breath right down your spine to your pelvis. By doing subtle exercises for your whole body, you changed your voice, because speech involves your whole body.

You showed immediate gain. You were breathing better, your posture was better and of course you were vocalizing better.

Judith used the word "elegance." She didn't treat my body like an awkward enemy I had to fight into submission. She didn't scold my thick tongue. A weight lifted from my chest. I breathed deeper, stood taller, walked like a dancer on my flimsy new canes.

Journal: August 8, 1988
This past weekend was the one-year anniversary of the "insult," as one doctor called it. I was thinking in bed how happy I am. People often remark how awful this year must have been, and in fact it was. But my overwhelming emotion is how exciting each day is, how interesting and wondrous

the human body. I want to live it and pass through it, to go forward, not around. I don't begrudge the time; there's nothing else I'd rather be doing. Activities yield such immediate results, the feedback is so direct and positive, once your time frame is adjusted to the millimetres of progress. This is not to say I don't have moments of extreme frustration and impatience, perhaps more lately as I'm closer to "normal" and can perceive how far I've yet to go. Memory is both a joy and a torment. I can so easily imagine myself as the mobile person I was. A glimpse of a woman playing tennis, a photo of me swimming in a Vermont quarry, triggers instant tears. But even in the midst of a hurricane of grief, I know it will pass.

We spent the weekend in the country with Muriel Duckworth, exactly one year after our missed Hiroshima Day date. It was a perfect celebration. I felt overlapping emotions of extreme sadness — seeing familiar places and friends with whom I swam and danced, just a year ago — and extreme joy.

I even played tennis, holding onto the net with one hand with my wheelchair parked beside me, *au cas où*. It wasn't the same game that first taught me to enjoy my body — I missed the sweat, the swearing, the adrenaline of competition, the glee of winning. But my first hit was thrilling — I had no idea if I was anywhere near the ball till I heard that grand sound of connecting — Wow! I have more fun with the limited things I can do than I ever did before.

In the evenings back at home, Michael, Naomi and I started going to a local outdoor pool where I added swimming to my exercise regime, increasing the number of laps I could do daily. I did barre exercises in the water, stretching my calves and thighs. Michael sometimes stretched me, which was fun but embarrassing, as I stood with my foot on his shoulder, making involuntary noises as my muscles cramped and released. (What is that man doing to her?) Best of all — though I only did it on overcast days when the pool wasn't too crowded — was dancing. I transferred what I had learned on dry land with Emilie to the water where, released from gravity, my movements became liquid. I moved free-form, without strokes, sinking and surfacing, rolling and spreading my arms. I tried not to care what it looked like because it felt so good.

After swimming we would saunter home, Naomi pushing my chair, watching the sunset and the summer night come in. I loved those walks together, but Naomi fretted about the inevitable storms to come. "I can't imagine going through another winter where you can hardly even get outside. You should go away somewhere warm and not come back till spring," she said. I thought it was a brilliant idea, but Michael brought me abruptly back to reality. "What are you talking about?" he said. "I'd have to quit my job! Nobody can take a three-month vacation."

"I'll just have to learn to walk then," I said.

Why did I decide I had to go to the Degas mega-exhibit in Ottawa? And why did I decide to go on the day after I cold-turkeyed off my Xanax?

Even though I don't like mega-shows, I do like Degas. The National Gallery had just opened and I was interested to see it. But it was also this itching worry about being left behind. It was as if everyone in the world was going to see this show and I didn't want to miss out just because I couldn't walk.

Seth offered to take me, which was the best reason to go. He and Michael had been on a canoe-camping trip the weekend before, and it hurt that I couldn't go with them. I wanted my own special time with Seth. I wanted to show my son I still had spunk and spirit.

This was one of those hyped-up art events where you have to make reservations and go at a set time. We were booked for 1:15, and Ottawa was a two-hour drive. If we left at ten, we'd have plenty of time. But of course I didn't manage to get myself together until ten-thirty, and then we had trouble finding parking. By the time Seth pushed me to the museum, we were late and I hadn't had any lunch.

I've always been irritable when hungry, but like everything since the stroke, it had become extreme. First would come the headaches, then the shakes, weakness and confusion. It was one of those things that I needed to plan ahead to avoid, because once I was in that state, I couldn't figure out what to do about it.

Seth asked me what I wanted to do — lunch or the exhibit — a big mistake. Another post-stroke symptom is difficulty with decision-making. When I'm calm, well-fed and unpressured, choosing between two options is difficult. When I'm stressed out and hungry, it becomes a major crisis. I fell apart. I knew I couldn't miss the exhibit, because that's why we were in Ottawa. And I couldn't skip lunch, because I was already in a hunger panic, and it would only get worse.

The foyer was crowded and noisy. Down at wheelchair height I felt lost and claustrophobic. The cramps and chest constrictions of Xanax withdrawal didn't help. A museum guard was standing nearby, taking tickets and giving directions. I pulled on his pantleg to get his attention. I tried to ask him if we could still get in to see the show if we went to the cafeteria first, but I was in too much of a state to ask clearly. I stuttered and babbled, then broke down and cried.

Poor Seth. Here he was, a young man out in public with a mother crying about her lunch. Luckily, the guard seemed perfectly used to such goings-on and once he managed to figure out what I was sobbing about, he gave us his word he would let us in however late we were. Seth rushed me to the cafeteria, applied food, and the storm left as suddenly as it had arrived. (All I remember about the exhibit is that I loved it. It gave me a great new insight into Degas' work, which I have now, of course, entirely forgotten.)

Journal: October 20
En route to London, Ontario, with a video copy of *Mile Zero* — completed last week — in my suitcase. I'm going for a follow-up exam and a pilgrimage: to say thank you, here's the human being who was hardly present the last time around, and to flush out memories so I can put them behind me. My memories of London come in vivid waves of smell and sound, but few visuals. I want to *see* what the hospital looks like, and Peerless and Rick. I remember their voices well.

First stop: Mickey and Linda's, where we'll be staying for the next two days. I couldn't believe I'd never been in their house before — Mickey-and-Linda stories are so much a part of our London mythology.

Next stop: the Magnetic Resonance Imaging Unit — over a year since my last MRI. Last time I was on a respirator. I remember the horrible knocking sound, how claustrophobic it was, and how long I had to stay still. This time it was a piece of cake. I saw myself in the chrome of the machine as I was strapped to the table, eyes bright (and made up) "alert and smiling." Afterwards, Michael rushed out to see the

pictures while I got dressed. He said he was relieved. Interpretation from Peerless tomorrow.

Journal: Oct. 21
I heard Peerless' voice in the hall and recognized it. He was
younger than I remembered — an unassuming, low-key man
in his forties. After the now familiar neurological test, I
asked him for another "prediction" of my progress. He said
he never imagined I'd be so far by now — so much for predictions. Unlike some neuroscientists, he doesn't think the
healing is finished in a year with the rest relearning. He
believes structural reconstitution of my nervous system is
still happening. That was music to my ears!

I still have what appears on the MRI as a small black hole
in my head — a fluid-filled space where the malformation
had been — but it's apparently not a concern.

We went from Peerless' office to the ICU. I had told
Michael that I remembered no one but Rick and Mary, but
I was amazed at how many people recognized me (with a
double take). They were excited to see me; they said their
patients rarely return voluntarily to the scene of their nightmares. Memories came flooding back — the sound of the
respirator, the "Blue Chair," the cry of "x-ray," the RT
(respiratory therapist) whom I associated with E.T.

The first thing Rick said to me was "I can't believe I've
never heard your voice."

"This isn't my original voice," I said. "It's the sexy voice I
always wished I had."

I wanted to tell him how much his care had meant to me:
the cheery monologues; the effort to always tell me what was
going on so I wouldn't be panicked; the positiveness of my
"sexual" interest that told me I was alive. But everyone else

was crowding around and I didn't get the chance to talk to him further.

Eventually, the excitement did me in and Michael took me back to the house where I napped before the Big Event: the "world première" of *Mile Zero*, played on video in Linda and Mickey's living room, and attended by Rick, Peerless, Adrian and several other members of "my" hospital team. Irene and Sidonie sent a telegram of congratulations and Linda produced bottles of champagne.

I was a little nervous, watching everyone watch *Mile Zero*. These were the people who had kept me alive to make this film. I wanted them to like it. I wanted them to laugh in the right places. I wanted to make them proud.

And I think they were. They laughed and listened and clapped loudly at the end. For me, this was the real première.

When I returned to Montreal, plans for official premières in Halifax, Toronto, Montreal and Vancouver were already in gear. My friend Gerry Rogers was hired to coordinate and publicize these events. They were all timed to happen close together, to give a national feeling about launching the film. At least one of the SAGE tour-members would go to every première to do media interviews and answer questions after the screening. All four of them plus Irene, Sidonie and I would attend in Toronto and Montreal.

I think it was someone from the NFB marketing department who first suggested that I do media interviews. They said that because the tour itself had received a lot of coverage, the press would regard the film as "old news." Besides, the Cold War had inconveniently ended while we were finishing the film. They said we needed a new angle or *Mile Zero* would get no publicity. My mid-film stroke would be the perfect hook to grab media attention.

I was appalled. But Gerry took me aside and advised me to consider it seriously. Several reporters had already refused interviews, saying they had "done" the SAGE kids. Without an extra push, *Mile Zero* would die a quiet death and disappear into the NFB archives. Gerry insisted that talking about the film and my stroke didn't have to be exploitative. She reminded me of all the times Sidonie and I had sat around the Institut, musing on the parallels between healing, peace and filmmaking. She quoted me back to myself: "When I'm overwhelmed with how far I have to go, I think about high school kids deciding to stop nuclear war." "Rehab is like filmmaking — you have to try things and risk falling on your face."

I told her that her memory was too damn good, and I promised to think about it. But all I could think of was the long list of reasons not to do it:

– My energy is still limited.

– My voice is still weak.

– I don't want to choke for five minutes on live radio.

– I don't want to distract from the film or steal attention from the kids.

– I don't want people to feel sorry for me, to think this is another sob story.

– I don't want people to say it's a good film because it was made by a cripple.

– I don't want other filmmakers to be jealous.

Jealous? Who could be jealous of a stroke? But I could hear the voices in my mind: "That Bonnie Klein. She even manages to get mileage out of being sick. She uses her stroke to get attention and promote her career."

I couldn't do it. The answer was no.

Gérald Godin changed my mind.

Godin was a popular poet, and a Member of the Quebec National Assembly. He had been the Minister of Culture for the first Parti Québecois government under René Lévesque. I didn't know him personally, but I had once filmed his partner, Pauline Julien, a passionate singer-songwriter.

Dorothy Hénaut was working on a film featuring Julien and Godin, called *A Song for Quebec*, and she asked Godin to come meet me.

He was a wiry, fervent man. The effects of a brain tumour, discovered and removed a year before, were evident in his slow speech and halting gait. Like me he made disinhibited jokes and laughed too loudly. He had a wicked sense of humour, both in person and in his poetry:

— What! You don't remember my phone number?
— Listen, *mon vieux*, you know
they removed a tumour from my brain
the size of a tangerine
well,
your phone number was in it

Although Godin was a politician, and certainly not supposed to have a hole in his head, he decided not to give up his seat in the National Assembly. He continued to speak and vote and represent his downtown Mercier riding, and in the next election he received an even stronger majority than before.

He urged me to be public about my stroke. Being visible as a brain-injured person is a good thing, he said, because it breaks the great taboo attached to brain damage. He said it's important for people who are afraid of us to actually see us, but it's even more important for us to see ourselves. It's important that

we get over the shame. He made me laugh, both at my extravagant new peculiarities, and at the people who turned away,
embarrassed, or presumed to judge me for them.

I thought, OK, if Gérald Godin can speak in the National
Assembly, I can talk to a few paltry reporters. He had given me
this challenge, and it wasn't to be ignored.

I was supposed to arrive in Toronto a few days early so I would
be able to rest up between the press interviews and the launch.
Unfortunately, Michael couldn't come until the day of the
launch, but before I could panic, Naomi offered to go with me.

Gerry had booked us into a downtown high rise hotel. The
"handicapped suite" she had reserved was on the lowest floor,
but that turned out to be the seventh, as the first six were taken
up by ballrooms and convention halls. Newspaper reports of
disabled people burned alive in nursing home fires filled my
mind, but there was nothing I could do but cope with my fear,
hope for the best, and thank God Naomi was with me.

Journal: November 25, 1988
Yesterday was hectic but fun. Naomi and I met Judy Steed
from *The Globe and Mail* at 10 a.m., and talked through
lunch at the Queen Mother restaurant. She'd already seen a
preview copy of *Mile Zero* and interviewed Alison and Seth,
so I felt comfortable talking to her about the details of my
stroke. I can't wait to see what she writes.

When Naomi said she was thinking of becoming a journalist, Judy invited her to come to *The Globe and Mail* the
next day. She also encouraged *me* to write a book about the
stroke. She advised me to start by making lots of tapes, inter-
viewing Michael, our children, friends, doctors, etc. Then
someone could transcribe the whole thing, plus my journals.

But the next stage — selecting, shaping, editing — I don't want to face by myself.

I wrote my speech, and rewrote it, and rewrote it. Michael arrived, and I kept him and Naomi up half the night listening to revisions. I had spoken before film audiences dozens of times, but this was different.

When the moment actually came, I was ready. First Irene spoke about the process of making the film together; then Michael helped me onto the stage. I can't remember how I got up the stairs — maybe they had set up a makeshift ramp. It was my decision to have the première at this inaccessible venue. The fully accessible educational institution that was our other option seemed boring compared to the glamorous and elevator-less Bloor Cinema with its splashy marquee and washrooms one floor up. I decided I'd be fine as long as I drank nothing all afternoon. I didn't think about other wheelchair users who might come, and (of course) there were none.

Journal: November 29

The Toronto opening is over. There was a standing ovation before I spoke, which made it hard to get the words out. I hadn't thought they would stand and clap like that.

The film took on other dimensions with a responsive audience cheering and laughing at unexpected places. The discussion period was full of excitement, with the SAGE kids fielding the questions. Seth was at his relaxed best, full of impassioned analysis and humour. "If we were to take all the money devoted to nuclear weapons, we could find a cure for acne."

After all these months of worrying that *Mile Zero* was taking away from my rehabilitation, I now see that it *was* rehab — occupational therapy as it was no doubt meant to be. It was real, useful work: it required all my previous skills and experience, plus many new adaptations; it connected me to the larger world outside my body; it forced me to "come out" and be seen in public; and it brought me validation as a productive person. I have regained a sense of my self.

INTERLUDE: ROSALIE SORRELS

Journal: July 17, 1993
The Vancouver Folk Music Festival is my idea of heaven: a view of mountains, ocean, sky; a wide expanse of green liberally sprinkled with wheelchairs and guide dogs; accessible toilets; ASL interpretation; and music from around the world. Seth drops by the patch of shade where I have parked myself and Gladys, full of the workshop he just attended. He is particularly moved by U.S. folk singer Rosalie Sorrels. The Festival Program notes that she had a brain aneurysm and "almost had her last gig in the choir of angels."

"You have to interview her for your radio show," Seth says.

I slip a note to the tent manager asking if Rosalie would speak with me about brains. Yes, she would.

Rosalie Sorrels looks weathered by a hard life; a down-to-earth folk musician of bars and back alleys, not coffee house cappuccinos. She walks only a bit tentatively. We trade stories, stunned at how similar our experiences were, and how different.

Rosalie Sorrels: Suddenly, one day, walking into my cabin in Idaho, I felt as if someone had hit me in the back of the head with an axe. There was no warning. I said, "Holy shit!" — those would have been my last words if I had died. I went down like a stone. My daughter tells me I got right back up and said, "There's something wrong with my head, you have to get me to town." She said, "I'll call an ambulance." I said, "I'll kill you if you call an ambulance; we can't afford an ambulance."

I live in the United States, you understand, where you don't have health insurance unless you're rich. So my daughter got some people who live nearby and they took me to a doc-in-the-box. He said, "She's having a migraine. Give her an aspirin and take her home." Now if you give someone an aspirin when they're having a hemorrhage it makes their blood go thinner which could have killed me.

My daughter took me to another doctor and he said that's not a migraine — she needs a CAT scan. And I jumped out of this dying stupor, shot right up and said, "How much will that cost?"

They found an aneurysm — and a surgeon. He was very good. He shaved every lick of my hair off, opened up my head and fixed me — there's one chance to do it; take a tiny little Teflon clip and pinch that flaw shut, and then somehow make it so it will repair itself. I have no idea why I lived through all that but I'm terribly pleased.

The bill was very large, and the people I owed it to were very unpleasant. Friends across the country had benefit concerts and raised about half of it. Then the hospital put me with a collection agency and sued me. The only way you can live through that is to not own anything. Luckily for me, I own my dog and my guitar and that's it. So they settled for $800 instead of the many thousands they were suing me for, because that seemed to be my net worth at the time.

When I got out of that hospital I couldn't walk. No one from the hospital looked at me again because I didn't have any money. I was very mad. I got a walker and I taught myself to walk. I went out every day and walked as far as I could and then I came back, which was twice as far as I could go! And pretty soon I'd feel like I was strong and I'd put the walker down and I would fall. And I'd pull myself back up and start again.

I'm sixty years old, you know, these parts don't last for ever. But I can't afford to get sick. In the States, whenever you talk about there ought to be health insurance, people start saying well who's going to pay for it? I know that's not the case in many other places. Once a person is alive in the world, it's the responsibility of everybody to help see that they get through it. I mean we're all a family after all; the world is a family and you take care of your family. You don't ask who's going to pay for it; you all get busy and figure it out.

I was moved by this tough woman's vision of the human family. And struck by the contrast in the medical care we received. In Canada, I was hospitalized for over six months and in formal rehabilitation for another year and a half. My only personal costs were for all my long-distance phone calls and $46 for a few days of TV in my room. The real cost to

Canada's universal Medicare system (which we are not even told) — for those months of intensive care, the air ambulances, the surgery, the rehabilitation institute, the outpatient care — was more than $150,000 Canadian, around $120,000 U.S. (at that time). We were able to supplement the basic coverage with private medical insurance through Michael's employment. This covered certain equipment, Gladys, for instance, and medically recognized therapies like massage.

Neither Medicare nor private insurance covered any of the complementary therapies — like acupuncture, cranial massage, or chiropractic — not to mention Feldenkrais or Alexander training which, after the first year, were by far the most helpful. But all this time I was receiving a disability pension from the NFB. I was just plain lucky to be among the last filmmakers hired as staff, with full union benefits. My friends who started working at the NFB as freelancers a few months later than I — Terre, Gerry, Sidonie — would not have been covered. In another country, another time, with a less affluent or less supportive family, I could have been left at any of the stages through which I passed in my recuperation.

I shudder that Rosalie was sent home from brain surgery to teach herself to walk while I received so much professional rehabilitation. She reminds me that the nightmare of being sick or disabled in most places in the world is to fall into irrevocable poverty.

COSTA RICA

≈

After telling Naomi that it was impossible to go off somewhere warm for the winter, Michael set about to make it happen. He was attempting to negotiate his sabbatical in three-month installments, when McGill University was contacted by the Ministry of Health in San José, Costa Rica, looking for someone to help train teachers of family medicine. The job would run from January to March — perfect!

I was ready to go. *Mile Zero* was launched and flying on its own. Naomi was graduating with honours from her new CÉGEP. Meena was going to work for a friend whose husband was home with Alzheimer's. Michel Danakas assured me that three months' vacation from my outpatient routine would only do me good. "Promise me you won't look for a physiotherapist there," he said. "You need a mental health holiday."

My big worry was leaving my mother. Her health was fading dramatically, with repeated infections and pneumonias. By December she was totally unresponsive, no smile, no recognition. I told myself I had to accept that she was dying. I tried to awaken her with hugs and stories of my childhood, but it only made her more tired. I started bringing my journal and just sitting with her quietly.

One night I woke up writing her eulogy. The next day I went through all the steps of planning for her funeral, coolly typing

out instructions until suddenly I realized what I was doing and
cried.

In this uncertain state, Michael, Naomi and I left Montreal.
After two weeks vacation in Costa Rica, Naomi would fly home
to wait tables at a yuppie dessert bar and apply to university,
my typed list of funeral arrangements tucked in her suitcase.

Journal: January 3, 1989, Tamarindo
For the next two weeks we'll be here by the Pacific, and then
we move inland to San José and real life. But right now is
forever.

Last night I saw the sun set over the water, with a red
afterglow reflecting on the sand, and Michael riding the
waves, playing like a boy. How many times have I watched
him do this? Today I swam in the ocean, going from hysteria
at the smallest wave to what Michael called "inappropriate
euphoria," floating over waves and trying to dive into them. I
can almost kick, or at any rate I'm dragging my legs less and
pulling better with my arms. I'm walking with canes on the
packed sand, including bumpy patches and inclines. I'm still
choking, but less. I'm staying up later at night. I hardly bite
my tongue at all.

Journal: January 11
Last night Michael and Naomi went to spy on egg-laying
leatherback turtles, a long inaccessible walk to a secluded
beach. Michael felt bad to go without me, especially as I had
a momentary cry at dinner because the restaurant had a giant
step at the front and everyone stared as he and Naomi hauled
me up by the armpits. After, Michael asked, "Are you scared?"

"Of what?" I answered.

But we both knew: scared of not getting better. I told him I'm not scared   I can't afford to be. And if *he's* scared, I don't want to know about it.

This morning I'm sitting on the beach, writing. Naomi and Michael have gone walking again and I feel trapped in the wheelchair, unable to negotiate a move away from the sun in this soft sand. I'm pleased that they know how to meet their own needs, including the need to get away from me. But I can't help resenting their ability to forget me, to walk as far as the beach beckons, to explore without constraints. The anguish is profound when I let it surface. It's always there and releases at the slightest invitation. Joy is equally there: it's not just a cover-up to keep the pain down. That's the emotional roller coaster of my days, my hours.

I've been left on the beach for what seems like well over an hour now. I'm frying in the sun. I haven't stretched. I'm afraid to stand because I fell once in the restaurant already this morning. I don't want to end up on the ground with sand blowing in my face. There are people around who would surely help me, but I'm feeling timid, ashamed to always be asking for help. Besides I don't feel like being "handled" by strangers.

My sun hat has blown off and I can't reach it to keep it from blowing further. I signal for help to a man standing nearby. His wife, further down the beach, clearly sees me but can't get his attention so she gives up and ignores me. At least I have suntan lotion and my journal. At least I don't have to go to the toilet.

Michael and I were in bed when Naomi knocked. "A turtle is laying her eggs on the beach in front of the hotel!" The big joke was that the night before, Michael and Naomi had paid to see this. Of course I thought the turtle had come here for me, breaking all the rules of nature, right under a bright lamp. She dug with great concentration, her rear flippers very powerful. She was small, three feet in diameter, and people speculated it was her youth that led her to this public beach. Some Tico children watched silently. One slightly drunk American tourist was frustrated because he was told not to take photos until the turtle stopped digging and started laying. Apparently she enters a trance, but before then can become disoriented.

When she felt the hole was big enough — God knows how she can judge but she turned out to be precisely right — she began laying. A Tico man, who seemed to be the spontaneous leader, motioned to the children to approach. I was going to leave at that point, satisfied with the awesome digging and nervous to be down at wheelchair height in the looming press of adults, but he beckoned me to the front and people made way. Only the drunk American crowded me too closely, invading the boundary of space which is different for a chair than for someone standing.

At first it looked like she was dropping turds, but then I got a clear view of glistening, pearl-like ping-pong balls. She humped and flexed, laying what seemed like thirty-five or more eggs in half an hour.

When she was finally finished, she began throwing sand to cover the nest. It seemed precariously close to the surface, since people poach the eggs, but she packed it down with her flippers making a loud thump. From time to time she stretched out her neck and uttered a hoarse wail. Satisfaction? Warning? When the nest was perfectly covered, she started walking off in the wrong direction — towards the light and not the sea. We held our collective breath for fear she would not make it back. Then she turned around and made a majestic exit — or entrance, depending on your point of view. We walked with her to the water's edge, till my chair stuck in the wet sand.

Journal: January 17, San José
This is my BIG FIRST DAY ALONE! Another marker in my climb to "normalcy" and I've been looking forward to it. Michael left at 6 a.m. to begin his first day of work. It's my first day of work too; starting the book I decided to write about my stroke and recovery. I was planning to use the solitude to recover some memories of my second stroke: the optimism of our anniversary, followed by the fast slide into total paralysis. I have no real memories of that time, only other people's stories. My plan is to interview everyone — family, friends, health-care providers — and integrate their memories into the book. I need to find my own as well; the lost months are like a weight in my chest, and now that I've set myself up to dig for whatever remains, I'm afraid to start. I don't want to relive that terror, not here alone. Maybe I need to start more slowly, one tentative toe at a time instead of diving right in.

On Saturday, we went to a party for the Costa Rican family practice residents Michael is training, at the country cottage of one of the doctors. I'd been looking forward to meeting people who didn't know me before. No comparisons, no "She used to be a filmmaker" or "You must miss tennis." Just what *is*, now.

Michael lugged my chair from the car and I managed the front steps on canes. I could see that some people were shocked. They didn't expect what they saw. They all knew

Michael, of course, but they didn't know anything about me. They had no idea what was wrong with me or if I'd been like this all my life. A few of the young residents came up immediately and introduced themselves. There were several children who seemed afraid of my chair at first, but they melted when I rang the Mickey Mouse bell. The others kept their distance, sipping drinks, playing soccer and dancing. One woman told Michael the next day that she thought he and I were like brother and sister. My paranoid translation was, "What's a handsome man like you doing with a crippled wife?" But maybe it was a compliment in terms of our similarity, our compatibility. Or maybe all Jews look alike.

At first I came on like a house on fire, shaking everyone's hand, trying to help them deal with me. Then I got tired; big parties are still hard. I have to strain my voice to be heard over other speakers and music. I invariably choke if I try to talk instead of concentrating on swallowing. Sitting in a wheelchair in a crowded room, I'm a captive audience and some people take advantage of that, thinking they're doing me a favour by hanging around with me.

After a while, Michael asked me to dance. It was my first time dancing in public. I imagine we were quite a sight, but I didn't care. It's the miracle of disinhibition, as Gerald Godin would say.

Exhilarated, I asked one of the residents to dance. He showed me a new step that took a lot of fine foot control, and I was laughing and clutching his shirt. Then one of Michael's teaching colleagues asked me to dance. I was totally wiped out, but it was great!

Michael was across the room by then, talking with a group of government officials and hospital administrators. He wheeled me over but once I was there, the administrators would only talk to Michael. They were up on a step and I was down in the wheelchair, but they didn't move any closer. They totally ignored me. They were even talking *about* me, in the third person, as if I wasn't there. At one point, I moved my chair right in front of them. I was obviously saying "I want to be part of this group and get to know you guys." But they continued their conversation, eyes averted. Even now, four days later I can hardly write about it. When I left they didn't say goodbye.

By the time Michael came to bed I was a quivering mess and I blurted out all that I was feeling. "Why should you be burdened with me?" I asked. "This isn't what you bargained for when we got married!" He replied that I was exactly the same person he had married and that it was the best decision of his life. I needed to hear those words, and to be held tightly and told he wasn't tempted by those nubile and athletic young women playing soccer and dancing so effortlessly at the party.

Journal: February 8, San José
Yesterday we discovered a woman who does both massage and acupuncture, so today I awoke revived and energetic. I took down the laundry from the clothesline, holding onto the wobbly rope with one hand, removing the clothes pin with the other, and valiantly attempting to catch each falling item before it hit the dirt. I've come to see the pleasure as well as the boredom in housework. I linger over tasks I used to do as fast as I could, while my mind was working on something "important." Nowadays, cleaning a papaya or cutting strawberries is an activity unto itself with its own aesthetic. I've had to learn to accept how long everything takes. Even now, when I fight it or forget it, my body rebels; I scramble my

words, stumble and fall. I have to listen to what my body is telling me. It's not negotiable.

Journal: February 10, San José

Seth is coming tomorrow for two whole weeks. And the day after Seth arrives Michael is going back to Montreal for three weeks. My excitement at seeing Seth is almost drowned out by my fear of spending a week all by myself in the new apartment we will be moving to. I met the landlord for half an hour, but I don't know anyone else in the neighbourhood.

I've been trying to see it as a challenge, another step on the road back to normalcy. But today I've been alone since Michael went to work at eight, and I've been watching the clock since noon. How will I last a whole week without human contact and specifically without Michael?

I'll be fine. It will be good for me. There's a shared garden at the new apartment, that I can get to just by opening our door — no steps! I can sit out there and read or write in my journal. Hell, it's only from a Saturday to a Thursday. I'll be OK. And the landlord's next door. This is silly.

I'll have to be very disciplined about doing my physio routine while Michael's gone. I rely on him, not just for taking me to the pool, but for his enthusiasm that carries me through the days and weeks when there's no visible progress, and for his crazy improvised exercises which are much more play than work. He's less timid than I am about taking up space in public. At the pool this week, I caught a retired American staring at me. I read in such glances people's own fear of disability, more likely at her age than mine. They must think Michael a saint, watching him boost me in and out of the pool, coach my swimming, invent challenges and variations so I keep strengthening. Sunday we had the pool to ourselves with no one to observe me, and I felt so free. I like to think that I've learned how to block out the stares and the obvious efforts not to stare, but I realize only in their absence how untrue that is.

I'm having trouble with my total dependence on Michael. He is so tactful, fun and uncomplaining. But on the rare and absolutely forgivable moments when he indicates fatigue or — rarer still — irritability, I break up. And then he feels terrible. The other day I had to cross over some freshly-watered lawn to get to the apartment. I couldn't take my sneakers off or scrape them while standing, so I tracked mud through the room to get to a chair. Michael's uncensored horror made me feel like a naughty child.

He's been having back trouble again — we're not sure why. Maybe it's from long commutes in crazy traffic, or from schlepping our belongings from one temporary residence to the next. More likely it's from pushing my wheelchair. Maybe I should have gotten an electric one back in Montreal. But I don't want to buy an expensive machine that makes not walking easier. It feels too much like giving up. Besides, it wouldn't help here in San José where there are no curb-cuts.

I wish I could help Michael. I wish I could tell him to go to bed and let me do the shopping, take the car for a tune-up, make dinner. I keep replaying our conversation about aging. Whenever Michael's back acts up like this, I know he's thinking about the future, worrying about not being in shape to help me.

I *have* to get better.

Journal: February 13, Cahuita
I lay in bed this morning, torturing myself with unanswerable questions. If Michael died or left me, how would I survive?

Old age could be pretty horrible. Why do I get in a knot about these what-if scenarios? I have recurring nightmares that a tumour is forming anew in the water-filled space we saw as a black hole in last October's MRI; or that there is a parallel malformation on the other side, which somehow no one noticed. I must not let myself dwell on these things. I don't know how I'll be doing next month, let alone in twenty years. Life is out of our control, no matter what illusions we carry.

The last day before Michael left was tense. He said I nagged at him. I guess I did. I got frustrated when he kept monkeying with the computer when I felt we should be leaving for the airport to pick up Seth. I felt like a non-person; Michael was totally in control of when we would go. I ask myself if it would have been different if I were not disabled. I honestly don't know.

Tape: February 14
Bonnie: This is CR tape No. 6. We're in Cahuita, a tropical rainforest in Costa Rica, and the date is February 14. Happy Valentine's Day!
Seth: It's the anniversary of the day you came home from the Institut.
Bonnie: Yes. I should be exhilarated. But instead I'm crying.
Seth: Do you want to turn off the tape?
Bonnie: No, let's just keep going. What was I crying about? Oh right — the Institut. I cry about everything these days. You probably noticed how irritable I was with Michael before he left.
Seth: Well...yes.
Bonnie: I guess it was hard to miss. I phoned him in

Montreal last night to apologize for making his departure so awful. I said it was probably in anticipation of
his absence, and especially being alone here after you
go. But Michael wondered if I was also nervous about
seeing you. I could tell from the way my stomach
clenched up that it was true. Because for a long time,
whenever you came home for the weekend, you were
always so excited about the progress I'd made since you
last saw me, even if it was just the week before. And
this time it had been six whole weeks! I wanted to show
you lots of progress, but instead I realized how little
has changed.

Seth: Six weeks is a short time.

Bonnie: But if the progress is so minimal in six weeks,
it's a marker of how much slower it's going to be from
now on. . . . How come you always laugh when people
are crying?

Seth: Nervousness?

Bonnie: I'm sorry to spill it all out on you.

Seth: No, it's OK. It doesn't really surprise me to hear
you talk this way.

Bonnie: What did you expect to find? Did you expect
me to be further along?

Seth: No. I thought it would be pretty much the same.

Bonnie: When you picture me — when you just imagine
me or think of Mom, do you picture me as I am now or
as I was before the stroke?

Seth: I guess it varies. But usually when I imagine you,
it's neither. When I imagine you, it's not doing stuff, it's
sitting and talking. So there's nothing to say it was
before or after.

Bonnie: You think of me as talking, not doing?

Seth: No, it's just that those quiet talking times have been important, ever since I was a little kid and I'd crawl into bed with you and Dad and tell you everything I was thinking about. And we still do it. Just before you left for Costa Rica, we were all lying around, and I was telling you how hard the tour year was, and how much better I felt this year.

Bonnie: And you were surprised when I said this year had been the best one of my life too.

Journal: February 19, San José

Our new apartment was a mess of suitcases and odd cardboard boxes when Seth and I came back from Cahuita. But before he left for Montreal, Seth unpacked everything and stocked all the cupboards with groceries. At first he was nervous about leaving me, but by last night he said he was feeling much more secure. Which made me feel secure too.

This morning was the first time in a year and a half that I've slept in an empty house and woken up alone. Today I have no plans to do anything with anybody. I've been dreading this moment for weeks, but now that it's arrived, I'm thrilled.

I made coffee and cereal with fresh bananas and strawberries, and then I wheeled outside into the amazing accessible garden, and sat under the bougainvillea tree, with the wind in the branches and the hollow thump of a basketball next door. All I missed was *The Sunday Times*.

This is the first place I've stayed in since I've been sick where I can go out the door by myself and sit outside. There are a couple of stone benches, but they have no backs, so I just spread out a towel on the ground. I have this wonderful ability now to get up and down from a flat place using my chair for support. I remember how frustrated I was in Guadeloupe, not to be able to stretch out on the sand without making a big deal of it and getting someone to help me. And now I pop up and down almost easily. I remember asking Michael, "Will there ever be a time when I don't hurt? When my body feels normal?" Now I have times when I don't hurt, and times when I can more or less forget about my body.

I wasn't ready to remember the painful details of the stroke before. But Costa Rica has given me the time and perhaps the distance I needed, and now every day new memories startle into consciousness. Lying on a stretcher in the JGH hallway, waiting for some test. Razelle crying. The smell of Ensure. Naomi arguing with the Hun. I write them down as they come. Write an hour, cry an hour: that's my routine.

The neighbourhood is moving into evening. A flock of parrots squawks by and I have a perfect view of their symmetrical colours. The monkeys' happy hour is in shrieking progress. I hear doors opening, people calling to each other. Our landlord, Eduardo, has come outside and is uncoiling the hose to water the garden. I greet him in my dreadful Spanish and he laughs and says hello back in his dreadful English.

The sun is going down now and I'm thinking about dinner. I know from experience that I have to take care of my hunger before it makes me crazy, but I don't want to miss the sunset. So, a conflict between two loves — how to resolve it? I think I can have both if I walk to the kitchen and fix myself something I can carry back out to the garden, but I don't have any pockets, so how will I carry it? I could put peanut butter on bread and carry it in my mouth but I might choke. I could wrap it around one cane handle so I can kind of hold it and walk at the same time. But which way should I wrap it — so the peanut butter squishes on the cane or my hand? Or I can carry it in my knapsack. That's what I'll do. Perfect solution. Here I go.

OK, here's the denouement we've all been waiting for. I peeled a hard boiled egg, sliced a tomato, buttered some bread, made up a sandwich, all leaning on the counter. Made a big mess. Then wrapped it up in a napkin, tucked it into a plastic bag, put it into my knapsack and trundled out to catch the last five minutes of light. And a hard-boiled egg sandwich never tasted better.

Journal: February 21, San José
I'm amazed at how well I'm doing, doing nothing. The days simply unfold. Even days which are empty of plans are full of surprises. I think I'm learning how to live.

Today I got smart and dragged my exercise mat into the garden. I was able to hear the birds and the basketball and smell the orange blossoms. I felt completely relaxed, not rushing through my exercises but exploring them. I'm beginning to combine what I remember of yoga with Emilie's unstructured movement, Judith's Feldenkrais and Michel's physio, in a routine that's no longer Emilie's or Judith's or Michel's, but mine, improvised to suit my body from the inside out.

Yesterday I was looking through the gate at the garden: the gardenia, the wild orchids, the purple azalea. Front and centre was my black wheelchair; this unnatural machine, hard and shiny, plastic and steel, spoiling the landscape. I hate it. I realized I've been feeling like I too spoil the land-scape, making people uncomfortable just by being there. But today on the mat I reclaimed my right to be a part of nature. Too bad if people can see me through the gate. It's good for them to see me and see how hard I work. It's not ugly, it's life.

Journal: March 1, San José
Michael's return Thursday evening was disappointing. He immediately got busy trying to fix the computer instead of making love. I felt ugly and unsexy, even though he claimed that the problem was his and not mine. On Friday we found a swimming pool not too far from the new apartment, and then discovered I couldn't access the water because the ladder was made of slippery steel tubes and the water level was too low for me to dive from the side. And it was freezing.

This evening when Michael and I danced, I was weepy. Because he had been outside playing basketball — *my* girl-hood sport — while I was curled up in bed. And because what I do is hardly dancing, and dancing was one of the fun things we did together, starting the day we met, twenty-two years ago. I want to kick up my heels and THEY WON'T GO, dammit!

Journal: March 6, San José
Michael got sick yesterday. He woke in the middle of the night and went to the bathroom, and the next thing I knew he kind of crawled back across the floor and collapsed. I didn't know what to do. I couldn't even help him get up onto the bed. I pulled the covers over him and he kind of whim-pered himself to sleep. He was better in a few hours. We figured it was some kind of food poisoning; still, it was a flash of his mortality.

Ever since that incident, we've been close and loving. I guess it startled us into remembering what's important.

Journal: March 10, San José

This morning Michael and I lay in bed and talked for hours.
In the end, he decided he has to resign as Chief of Family
Medicine and Director of the Herzl Family Practice Centre.
He's worn out from over fourteen years of fighting the same
political battles at the JGH where expensive specialty medicine is valued more than the kind of integrated care which
Michael practises and teaches. He will still do childbirth
research and look after patients — the part of his work
which he enjoys the most. But not being Director will give
him the time and space to see what he wants to do next. We
talked about the possibility of moving to a more disability-
friendly city with better weather and accessible transit.
Michael, who is so committed to his work, has consistently
put it second to my recovery. He continues to surprise me —
I think he surprises himself. I told him it doesn't make sense
to leave our friends and all that has defined our lives for so
many years in order to accommodate a wheelchair that I'll
eventually leave behind.

While Michael was settling into this tough decision about his
own work, I played filmmaker for the first time since we've
been in Costa Rica, showing *Speaking Our Peace* at the
Friends' Peace Centre. The audience was appreciative and full
of questions, and my voice stayed strong, with only a few
choking spells.

Michael had toyed with letting one of his colleagues drive
me to the screening, because his back hurt and he's seen
Speaking Our Peace so many times. In the end he decided
to go. I asked why. He replied, "I'm pathologically attached
to you."

It was strange seeing myself in the film. Michael said he had forgotten my old voice. He thinks of the new one as my real voice. Watching the film, I remembered being at the women's peace camp at Greenham Common, surrounded by police with guns and dogs; then at the Eldorado nuclear facility, under police surveillance for asking questions about nuclear contamination. And in the Soviet Union, the film authorities, who were linked to the KGB, were incensed about an interview I'd taped, in Hebrew, with a Jewish refusenik. They called me in, alone, on the eve of our departure, and physically erased the tape. I was the only one, in this room of Soviet film apparatchiks, who understood the disappearing words. It was the worst moment of my filmmaking life, to hear a voice silenced as I stood by, powerless.

People have been reassuring me that I'll be able to make films again. No one is more surprised than I to find out that I can live quite well without that role. At the same time I do remember how satisfying it is. So, while I cavalierly say "I don't need to make films any more," last night I experienced it as a loss.

Journal: March 23, Samara
In a little more than a week we'll be in Montreal. Michael's work is finished, so we're spending our last Costa Rican days here on the Pacific coast. Yesterday morning I swam in the surf, feeling the tide pull me out and in. I was knocked down by a wave and I laughed so hard I could barely get back up.

I've made dramatic progress in the last few weeks, after several months of invisible build up. I feel it as sure-footedness, more trust that my legs will hold me, that the ground won't shift as I step. I can walk without total concentration, with

fewer of those missteps which make every move tentative.
I'm standing straighter and, when I remind myself, I can look
ahead as I walk instead of at my feet! It all comes together
only when I'm perfectly rested and relaxed, but it's enough to
see that it can and *will* come together in time. Michel
Danakas was right. I've become "de-institutionalized."

Journal: March 25, Samara
We called Montreal this morning. We hadn't talked to Naomi
in almost a week, because the hotel we'd reserved turned out
to be inaccessible, and the place where we've been staying
has no telephone. Sure enough, Mom is in the hospital again
with pneumonia. Naomi feels they caught it early enough
and it's under control for the moment, but she is worried. I
couldn't have come to Costa Rica if Naomi were not watching over Mom. I wonder if she knows what an enormous,
unspeakable gift she has given me.

My feelings unfold slowly with the news. Horror that
my mother's body is not letting her die when she has been
waiting so long. Guilt that I have prolonged the wait for my
own convenience, for if I were there I think we would
simply withhold the treatment that keeps forcing her back.
It's a bitter irony that I've been writing about how much it
means to have a loved one beside you touching you, and I
haven't been there for my own mother. Now I can only pray
that she does hold on long enough so that I can say what
she may need to hear. I don't know exactly what words to
use, but I'm sure they'll come if I'm fortunate enough to be
with her again. Maybe she needs to hear that she loved us
and took good care of us, as we love her and are taking
care of her now. Maybe she needs to know it's OK to let go
and die.

Journal: March 31, San José Airport
Sitting on the Lacsa flight, about to depart for Miami I'm
ready to leave now, and anxious to see my mother.

We made this trip in reverse, exactly three months ago.
This time I'm in control. I hate to think I'm becoming at
home in a wheelchair, but I am. I'm wheeling myself short
distances, which exhausted me too much before. I can wheel
away when someone comes too close or I'm in the way. I
noticed that the airport personnel addressed me directly
instead of asking Michael, "Can she walk or does she have
to be carried?" I don't know if it's because I look that much
more alive, or because I'm assertive instead of wishing I were
invisible, or because I'm wheeling myself, but I appreciate
the difference.

Journal: April 2, Montreal
Mom looked shrunken and pale, but didn't seem uncomfortable. The room reeked of Ensure. When I tried to unclench
her fist to hold her hand, she reacted with what seemed like
crying. Michael said "That hurts her now," but I interpreted
her reaction as anger at me for having gone away. After that,
she was unresponsive, except for a feeble smile when Michael
joked with her. I begged for some sign that she knew who I
was. I heard myself "explain" my long absence, how much
good it had done me, etc. But to empty eyes. I finally pressed
her — "Are you angry with me because I left you?" —
realizing how much, how selfishly and absurdly, I wanted to
be forgiven by my mother, as she has always forgiven me.

Journal: April 10
On Sunday the nurse called to say my mother appeared to be
going downhill fast, and we all rushed to the hospital. She

was breathing heavily, and her hands were blue. Her eyes were unfocused, as they'd been most of the week. She still seemed peaceful. We held her hands and stroked her head. When I told her that Naomi was there, she made her only volitional move — she turned her head to look, focused clearly, and reached out her hand for Naomi's. I was pleased that her last gesture before she died was towards her grand-daughter who had stood vigil in my place.

THE LONG HAUL

≈

≈

SPRING, 1989

Spring, one and a half years PS (post-stroke). How do I write about this time? The landmarks are fuzzy, the time-frame blurs as days melt into weeks and months and nothing much changes. Progress is measured by being able to stand upright for one minute longer in a month's time, or to walk on canes another twenty feet, or to ride on the stationary bike for so many more seconds at such-and-such resistance. But the urgency to recover is no less, the desperate need to be how and who I was before a weakened knot of blood vessels bisected my life. I want clear answers, steady progress towards a concrete goal, but the will-she/won't-she slow dance of rehabilitation gives me only uncertainty.

Journal: April 27
A few days ago, one of my Studio D friends called to ask if I was going to the Canadian Women's Film Festival in Israel next month. I was embarrassed to admit that no one had told me about it, despite the fact that they're screening both *Not a Love Story* and *Speaking Our Peace*. I was especially frustrated because Michael and I are going to Israel a few weeks later — he has a conference and a month-long visiting professorship in Beer Sheva. If I had known, we might have been able to leave in time for the film festival.

Then, yesterday, as I was sitting in the front hall, waiting for the Transport Adapté to take me for my first session back at the Institut, the festival organizer called. One of the invited filmmakers had to cancel — would I like to attend? My immediate response was anger — why hadn't she invited me in the first place? Now Michael has commitments he can't rearrange in order to go two weeks earlier. She didn't seem to understand that I can't travel alone.

She told me they needed an answer right away, in order to find someone else if necessary. So, with the Transport Adapté beeping its horn in my driveway, I turned down an opportunity which likely won't recur — a coming together of three of my previous passions: women, film and Israel.

At the Institut, the halls were lined with people slumped in wheelchairs. The carpets stank of stale smoke. There was no one I wanted to see. Michel Danakas sprained his back lifting a quadriplegic patient twice his size, and is away on a one-year disability leave. Judith is on holiday. With that news, I decided not to return to the outpatient program. Why go through all the Institut hassle in order to work with strangers? I will seek out my own therapists.

I had another frustrating forty minute wait for the Transport Adapté in the smoky lobby. Finally, I made my way up the stairs to the house, miserable. Naomi was coming out on her way to work. She hugged me and I poured out my woes: I don't want to be handicapped — it's lousy and it's lasting forever. I hate the Institut and the Transport Adapté. And I can't go to the film festival because I can't travel alone! When Naomi heard the whole story she offered to quit her job a month early and go with me.

I called the festival organizer immediately, only to learn she'd offered the trip to someone else who is thinking about it overnight! I should have been more assertive in the first call. Why didn't *I* ask for some time to consider? When Michael came home, he brushed aside my self-blame and suggested Naomi and I go anyway, despite the expense. "Why do you need to be officially sponsored?" he asked. I had no answer, but in my heart I still wish I had that validation.

At my pre-trip check-up, Joe Carlton congratulated my decision to go to the festival, saying, "It's time to resume your life, and come to terms with where you are now."

I walked out of his office swallowing my tears. Was he, my would-be tennis partner, telling me it was time to give up and accept my greatly-reduced physical status?

ISRAEL

Naomi: As soon as we got to the baggage claim area in Ben Gurion airport, my mother announced, "Everyone looks like my cousin."

It's true, they did. Black kinky hair, olive skin, lots of emotions. Even the hippyish flowing clothing is the kind my mother loves. Like a family reunion only you don't know anyone.

That was the problem with Israel. Our hopes were too high and the trip was doomed from the start. This was a voyage to the homeland but my mother had been rejected

before we even arrived. Grudgingly invited, then disin-
vited, then made to pay her own way. But once we got
to Israel, Mom was a media star. Her picture was in the
major Hebrew newspaper and she was on the Israeli
equivalent of "60 Minutes." *Not a Love Story* was the
sensation of the festival, more screenings had to be scheduled, more press conferences, more discussion groups.

The festival organizers seemed to resent it. They planned
parties and "forgot" to invite us. They didn't sit with us
in the theatres. We didn't even eat together. Within a day
of our arrival, it became pretty clear that Mom and I
were on our own in Israel; no one was going to help us
out. It seemed as if her disability was a big inconvenience:
she wasn't just showing them up, she was slowing them
down. The festival was a turning-point in my mother's
recovery. It was her first big trip without Dad since her
stroke, her re-entry into the world of film. She should
have been made to feel like a hero because it was a truly
momentous and joyful occasion. Instead she was made to
feel like a drag.

Journal: May 22, 1989
We've been here one week now. It has been stressful and
not much fun so far. I keep wondering if it's our fault, our
attitude or something, but I don't think so.

I can no longer move in what used to be my world. The
organizers had promised to "accomodate" me, but instead
I'm expected to fit in and keep up. My films are scheduled
late at night when I'm tired and press conferences and social
events are held in physically inaccessible places. It's as if I've
been used for my films and my name, but made invisible as
a person. I feel the festival organizers are ashamed of me

because I no longer project the feminist ideals of strength, competence, and independence. An Amazon I'm not — I can't even fake it.

Naomi: *Not a Love Story* not only upstaged the other women's films, it upstaged my mother's other, more recent films like *Speaking Our Peace* and *Mile Zero*. The Israelis were having the porn debate with all the emotion and fervour that North Americans had ten years before. Women wept. Men screamed. The media went nuts.

Fortunately for me, I had missed the debate the first time around. I was eleven when *Not a Love Story* came out. It was gross and embarrassing; that's all I knew. I was made fun of by kids at school. "Naomi's mother makes pornos!" — a unique grade school torment. The worst part was that, according to my mother, *I* was the inspiration for *Not a Love Story*. "How does this make my daughter feel about her own little body?" says her voice-over in the porn section of the grocery store. I refused to watch when she was interviewed on TV and wanted to separate myself as much as I could from her and feminism.

Eight years later, sitting next to my mother in the front row of the Cinemateque in Jerusalem, I watched *Not a Love Story* for the first time. And I cried. I was incredibly moved and convinced by it. I bought the anti-porn argument (which I have since reconsidered) hook, line and sinker. Representation equals reality. Change the representation, you change the reality. Pornography is violence against women.

But the strangest thing was hearing my mother's narration in the first five minutes of the film. The woman next to me leaned over and asked, "Is that your mother talking?" I said "No, I think she got somebody else to read it." It wasn't until the end of the film that I realized it *was* her voice — her old voice.

Journal: May 24, 1989
Watching *Not a Love Story* after so many years, I see that it's really about voice — or lack of it. The dialogue about pornography and erotica has evolved since 1981 and become more complex, but *Not a Love Story* was part of breaking women's silence, opening our eyes and our mouths. Seeing it now in Israel, I realize the coherence of my life's work. It wasn't a series of unrelated films, but variations on a related theme: speech vs. silence, peace vs. violence, solidarity vs. isolation.

When someone in the audience asked Naomi about her own reaction to *Not a Love Story*, she said, "It hurts." One man protested, "But pornography has always been with us; it's part of human nature."

"We don't know what human nature is," Naomi answered. "That's an excuse for refusing to change."

Naomi: It was the first year of the intifadah and much as the tourism department tried to play it down, Israel was a country at war. The news was filled with reports of random bombings and shootings, and, as always, the streets were filled with eighteen-year-old boys carrying Uzis.

Our hotel was on a hill in the outskirts of Jerusalem. We couldn't go anywhere without scaling a sixty-degree slope which my mother couldn't begin to wheel by herself in her manual chair. Besides, the black metal wheel rims were too hot from the summer heatwave to even touch.

People responded to us in two ways: with total indif-
ference, as from taxi drivers who popped their trunks,
refusing to get out of their cars to help me load and
unload the wheelchair; or with totally overbearing and
intrusive "help." If we were having trouble getting up a
curb or out of a cab, passers-by would physically push me
aside and man-handle my mother, often lifting the wheelchair with her in it without asking her permission. Yes,
everyone looks like your cousin, but they also act like they
own you — as only families can.

The trip to Israel was supposed to be a show of independence for my mother and of adult responsibility for
me, and we both were failing. Without my Dad's legit-
imizing presence, it became clear that the "you can do
anything" feeling that my mother had up until our trip
was slipping away. I just couldn't give it to her. It seemed
that everything about the country — the landscape, the
climate, the people, the ground itself — was conspiring
to make disability more difficult.

Journal: May 27
I had a moment of crying in the bank today. Naomi was
upstairs getting some money changed, and I was in line to
cash a traveller's cheque. I think it was the waiting. No, it
was the aloneness in the wheelchair, and the realization of
how much I hate it. I don't want to become wheelchair-
independent — to go out among the crowds and curbs with
no one I can count on but myself. It's a hard admission: I
want to be taken care of.

Later I swam and exercised in the water — better, harder
and longer than ever before. Sometimes despair leads to

depression. Sometimes it can be motivating. People call this "courage," but it's not that. It's just the desire to heal, to get on with living as I wish to live, to see our children's lives unfold. Naomi says I'll find new energy once I settle into wherever I do land physically. She offers no promises of total recovery, just the observation that it's been a very long time, that I'm sick of being sick, and that I'm still recovering. I don't fully understand what she means but I feed off her optimism. I keep wondering if true acceptance means to stop challenging myself to do things as I used to, which was exhausting even when I was "normal," and avoid the frustrating comparisons with Before. Maybe "independence" is a misleading concept. Each of us is dependent on others. Perhaps independence is not the ultimate goal, but inter-dependence: the possibility of doing with and for each other, the ability to ask for the help that we each need.

INTERLUDE: MAKING A STINK

Journal: April 12, 1994
Every trip I take, the airline acts as if it's the very first time they've encountered an electric scooter. There's a general airline rule that wet-cell batteries must be disconnected and shipped in their own box because pressure changes can make them leak or explode. For that reason, Gladys's batteries are dry cell — a different matter altogether. On the several

occasions when the airline has insisted on removing her batteries anyway, trouble inevitably followed. One time the battery boxes were lost in transit, never making it to our destination. I was immobilized in a hotel room for six days as we called back and forth to the airport collecting excuses and lies. Ultimately we had new batteries shipped from Montreal. Another time, the person who disconnected the batteries broke the connections. Michael taped them back together, and Gladys has remained in that delicate jury-rigged state ever since.

Today I am flying home from Boston where I attended a workshop for people with disabilities and our allies led by Marsha Saxton, a long-time disability rights activist and co-editor of *With Wings: an Anthology of Literature by and about Women with Disabilities*.

At the airport I check in early, and calmly explain that dry-cell batteries do not need to be disconnected or removed. Michael has made some clear graphics which I mount on Gladys before every plane trip: "STOP. These batteries are dry cell in self-contained plastic cases."

My trip to the workshop had gone smoothly, but just now as I checked in for my return flight, an Officious Official overrode the check-in agent, snapping that the scooter would be taken now and the batteries removed. Never a greeting, never an acknowledgment that I was anything other than a hassle. I insisted on speaking to the chief baggage-handler before I would dismount. The OO angrily paged him, "to speak to a wheelchair." Ever ready to blame myself (I think it's called "internalized oppression") I checked that the OO wasn't unduly rushed (I was seventy minutes early, there were five desk employees and only two other passengers), that I was my usual cheerful-when-well-rested and well-shopped-at-Filene's-Basement self. I had no chip on my shoulder; rather, I had every expectation that my request would be met.

Eventually the Chief Honcho appeared, flanked by the OO, again no greeting. I was beginning to feel as if I had violated some international agreement.

"The batteries will have to be removed," the CH brusquely ordered. "They're wet cell."

This was going to be easy. "No," I told him, "They are dry cell, like the sign says."

"Oh, well, then it's OK." He turned and left.

I was relieved, but one of my fellow passengers was outraged. "I've never seen anything like that. They were so menacing."

He was right. Why didn't he speak up? Why didn't *I*? Why do I become passive, shamed and silent? I remembered the commitment I made at Marsha's workshop: to expect my needs to be met or to Make a Stink. OK, here goes.

As the OO withdraws, I ask his name.

"Oh! Is something wrong? I get these rules all mixed up — dry cell or wet cell. I thought this was a wet cell and I know they're a problem."

"What is your *name* please?"

"Gary."

"Yes, Gary, there is a problem." As my anger mounts, my voice shakes. "I respect airline safety regulations. I told you what kind of batteries I have, and you chose not to listen. I don't expect you to know everything about scooters — that's my job. But I do expect you to listen when I teach you. You caused me unnecessary worry. My scooter is not baggage, it is my legs. It is my mobility when I get to my destination. And you did not even apologize when you were wrong.

This is the only airline which is consistently rude and rigid and makes me feel unwelcome. I will not travel with this airline again."

Well, Gary was grovelling. He would do anything to shut me up. I was no longer a "wheelchair" but a very angry and articulate woman with a large and growing audience. I now knew his name: maybe his superiors would not appreciate what a good job he was doing.

Did I want a glass of water? Better yet, would I allow him to upgrade me to executive class? I did not accept the upgrade and said I hoped this would not happen again. I'm proud that I spoke out for myself, and for all my fellow-travellers with wheels.

MONTREAL

Journal: July 10, 1989
I've been feeling down ever since we got home. I seem to have lost that incredible sense of aliveness, of living-on-the-edge.

We were so high that first post-stroke year. The lows were correspondingly low, but it was an intense experience filled with love and discovery. But now, near the end of the second year, reality has sunk in. I'm constantly confronted by all the things I can no longer do. My progress is barely measurable. Anyone watching me walk would see struggle and pain. I lean heavily on the canes. My knees are rigidly locked, making my back hyper-extended. My right hip sinks back and my shoulders corkscrew in opposite directions. My gait is broad, with the right foot dragging and slapping down. My eyes stare at my feet. On the rare occasions when I look up and catch a glimpse of myself in a mirror or window, I look like a robot.

I can no longer regard this as a passing phase. Normal life has resumed for Michael and my other loved ones, but I'm still not normal. I swore I would never again take life for granted, but now I have whole days where I can't wait for night to come so I can collapse on my bed.

Summer dragged by. In September, Naomi and Seth left for the University of Toronto. I spent the last weeks before they went in what was to become a familiar pattern: telling myself to enjoy the time we had, and then spoiling that time by clinging. The day they left, I was determined to be brave and not make them feel bad. Seth woke early and made them both sandwiches. Later I tortured myself, thinking: that's what a Real Mom would have been doing instead of tossing through a sleepless night. The car was stuffed, mostly with Naomi's things. She'd been rummaging for weeks in our basement for objects to beautify her dorm room. I gave her a crystal to hang in her window, with a quote from the poem she had written two years before: "I give to you now / what you have given to me ... "

Seth and I had said goodbye many times over the past three years. But this was Naomi's first year away from home, and my first year with both our children gone. Our goodbye was an intense mix of exuberance and sadness. Naomi was beaming as she said, "I'm sorry." Sorry she's leaving? Sorry she's growing up? Sorry for past sins? "I'm not sorry," I told her, which was a lie. I was drowning in regrets and self-pity, remembering all the times I was unavailable to Naomi. When she was little she would sometimes call my office after school, bored and lonely, and ask me what she could do. I was often too busy to talk for long. When I had to go away for a film shoot, she would say "Don't go Mommy!"

Now it was I who needed her, and she who was busy with her life. I didn't know how to behave. I desperately wanted to ask her if I'd been a good mother to her, but I restrained myself. I wanted to be generous about letting go, but my heart had not stopped grieving. My losses were interconnected: I mourned my mother, my daughter, my future, my self.

Journal: September 27, 1989
I feel like Michael and I are at a stage in life where little will be new. We've got the mid-life, empty-nest blahs. I notice how much more we laughed with the kids around, how much intellectual stimulation their daily presence gave our lives. I've been taping interviews with friends, but I wonder if it's just an empty exercise for a book I'll never write. I find myself tuning out ideas that once absorbed me. I have subscriptions to all the same magazines, but now when they come in the mail I put them aside, unopened. It scares me. Feminism gave me a way to understand my place in the world, but I don't seem to belong there any more. I don't know where I belong.

As autumn settled in, my depression intensified. I was still too weak — and too nervous — to go out alone, and even in good weather organizing someone to go with me often seemed more trouble than it was worth. My friends were busy with their own lives and work. I remember one trip to Clement's grocery store pushed by Eileen, a young woman who'd been transcribing my journals. It was my first time there since the stroke, and I was thrilled with the smell of fresh bread, the familiar trout swimming in their murky tank, the chickens barbecuing. I felt good to be buying lunch and dinner for Michael — Meena was home with a cold and besides I wanted to wean my dependence on her. I smiled to the familiar clerks and got nothing but cold stares. The cashier, a woman I'd seen for years, didn't recognize me, so she called the manager to verify my cheque. Fair enough, I thought. The manager asked for a driver's licence. As I was fumbling for my old one (cancelled since my stroke), feeling bad for the people waiting behind, I explained to him that I'd been a customer for over ten years.

"I have to ask for this — it's a formality," he responded, looking at Eileen. I thought he must be cross-eyed — always giving the benefit of the doubt. Why else would he address Eileen when I was there talking to him, obviously competent. So I answered that I understood, and he again spoke to Eileen, unmistakably, referring to me in the third person: "She won't have to show it next time, once we know her. It's the rules." There was no next time.

Journal: October 15

In my ongoing push to resume "real life," I've been trying to add more social exercise to my rehab routine — with mixed success. I had a delicious swim at our local YMCA pool yesterday; then I fell in the shower room. It was maddening because I had asked them to get non-slip matting around the pool and in the shower. According to the director, they used to have some, but it started to stink from chlorine and they threw it out. Sure enough one of my canes slipped on the wet floor, and I did a slow-motion fall. Luckily I wasn't hurt or bruised, but every fall brings the threat of breaking a bone, creating even greater limitation. By the time I was dressed and leaving, the executive director had sent word that she will be sure mats are purchased next week. I'm optimistic they will be, if only for fear of liability, though it is hard not to hear echoes of the membership director who told Michael last month, "This is not a priority."

Last week I signed up for a course in t'ai chi for seniors. I've taken t'ai chi before, in my "old life," and liked it. I figured a seniors' class would be slow enough for me, and it might make me feel good to be taking an "almost normal" class instead of always having to go to special handicapped programs or not go at all. It might even make me feel graceful.

But when the time came, I couldn't do it. What was I thinking of? My self-image hasn't adjusted to this massive change at all. Did I imagine I could stand and sink down at my knees and shift my weight as I gracefully turned my body? I can't balance on two feet, let alone one. I spent the class listlessly doing the arm motions in my chair.

With no formal rehabilitation program, I was desperately seeking alternatives to keep up my motivation and hope. We researched nutritional supplements and added an array of vitamins and minerals, ginseng and foul-tasting Chinese herbs to my daily regime. I never knew there were so many healers around, so many varieties of touch, massage, movement and dance. I tried everything, looking for the right match of teacher and method. After many trials and false starts I met Diane Genereux, a former physio who now taught Feldenkrais, the method to which Judith Blumberger introduced me when I was still at the Institut. Twice a week Diane came to my house. One session was for hands-on floor work, in which her hands gently guided me to an awareness of how I used my body, especially where I held tension. The other session was more active, with a series of subtle movements which I visualized before performing. I learned to move with the least amount of effort. The aim of this work was not to regain lost functions but to maximize what I had through focus and awareness.

When I pushed her to tell me, Diane agreed with Michel Danakas that my walking still wasn't functional, but suggested I use one cane as a bridge to walking free. That would mean I could carry things in my other hand — a huge step forward — my first really tangible step in months. I couldn't wait to show Michael! In a burst of enthusiasm, I hid my second cane in the back of the hall closet and wore myself out (and smashed several dishes) trying to make dinner all by myself. The freedom of one cane was counterbalanced by exhaustion and muscle pain — a poor trade-off. The other cane came back out of the closet — just for longer walks, I told myself, just for awhile. But almost without noticing, I slipped back into using two canes for everything.

As Fall slid into winter, I was housebound for days at a time. Michael and I walked around the block during a brief break in the weather. It took the better part of an hour, with Michael cheering me on, but I was steady on my canes, never had to stop, and recovered after a twenty-minute lie-down. I phoned Naomi to brag about my progress.

"You can walk!" she crowed.

"It's not real walking," I corrected her immediately, my moment of triumph dashed.

I continued to attempt "real" walking, without canes. It came in unpredictable, unrepeatable spurts, and when it came there was no stopping me.

Journal: November 5

Last night I got the urge, and I walked around our house without canes. I shifted my full weight with each step, and felt the floor with my feet. Michael and I sang to give me a good rhythm. When I felt as if I was falling, instead of grabbing at the wall, I corrected myself without panicking. I was stiff-kneed, with a wide gait, but I felt confident, sure-footed and not dizzy. I screamed with joy, and so did Michael. "This means a full recovery!" he said. "It may take a few more years but nothing will stop you."

It's so mystical and absurd, this short-circuit between my brain and my muscles. But moments like this give me a sense of what's possible, and I feel like dancing all the time.

There are no journal entries for the next day, no record of the inevitable letdown, Michael's steady encouragement hiding his disappointment, my waning effort, exhaustion, despair. Again and again I celebrated my "big breakthrough" only to see it slip from my grasp the next day. Each time, Michael celebrated with me, as convinced as I that this was it.

In late November, I went for my driver's test. The examination took place at the Lethbridge Rehabilitation Centre in nearby Montreal West. It was the first time I had driven since my stroke. Once I had sat in our parked car, trying to shift from the gas to the brake, but my foot kept getting caught under the pedals. It didn't seem like I'd be safe going out on the road to practise, even with Michael (famed impatient driving instructor) beside me. But the Lethbridge Centre had cars with hand controls for disabled drivers, and brakes for the instructors. Michael had encouraged me to try for my licence in one of those. Once I learned to drive (and conquered my fear of going out alone and developed the strength to unload my wheelchair from the car and wheel myself from where I parked to where I wanted to go, or better yet learned to walk longer distances with or without canes), then I could start being truly independent.

So with no practice, in a heavy snowfall, I drove along Sherbrooke Street and didn't kill anyone. I drove with regular foot controls until fatigue set in, then with hand controls until total panic set in and I begged the instructor to take me home. But I got a licence! It was restricted to driving with an official handicapped driving instructor until I was reevaluated. But it was a start.

As I was leaving the Rehab Centre I saw someone driving up on a motorized three-wheeled vehicle. I had never seen an electric scooter before. They didn't seem to exist on the streets of Montreal. The young man astride the scooter had a jaunty look, in control of his destiny and destination. When I got home, I called the Institut and inquired. Everyone was horrified at the idea. If I had a scooter, I would no longer work at learning to walk, and besides, it would be an admission of failure. No one wanted to talk further about it.

Journal: November 26
This weekend we moved all our Vermont furnishings to an accessible cottage at Black Lake in the lower Laurentians. The morning brought ice on the lake and the chattering of red squirrels and anxious jays at the birdfeeder. I rolled out of bed excited for the first time in weeks. Or is it months? I managed to walk on one cane from the kitchen to the living room, carrying a big bunch of grapes in an inelegant but unbreakable green lettuce Tupperware. I arrived with glee to "serve" Michael, after all his unpacking and setting

up the house. A small triumph tinged with the ironic awareness of how small it was indeed, to limp across a floor with
an ugly Tupperware. My pretensions to grace and elegance
are so thwarted. I can't believe I ever felt like a dancer.

Journal: December 3
Yesterday I awoke with the first light showing Black Lake
white and frozen. I wanted to run out and play in the
snow, but instead I did my exercises by the window. All the
various paths — physio, Feldenkrais, Emilie's continuum —
are leading to the same place. I concentrate on feeling the
floor under my feet, trusting my legs to bear my weight.
I hear myself saying many times a day, "It's coming. It
will come."

As I finished my workout, Michael walked in, wearing his
corduroys and gaiters, ready for the first cross-country ski of
the year. It was as if the image bypassed my brain and went
straight to my heart. I didn't want to mar Michael's joy so I
went to the bedroom with my tears. I watched him through
the window, skiing down to the lake with Lucy ecstatically
nipping at his heels.

I feel a pressure to hide my emotions — something inside
telling me, "Control yourself for the sake of those who love
you, and whom you need to keep loving you!" But whether
I'm explicit about my feelings or not, those who love me end
up having their happiness tinged with my loss.

Today was bright, beautiful and freezing cold, and I woke
up determined to go out and enjoy it. Michael pulled me
down the hill in a plastic sled, with the snow flying in my
face. Then, on the flat lake, I was able to walk on the snow-
shoes we gave Annie years ago. I used ski poles instead of
canes. Again tears came but this time for joy.

We were in the country when Anne Usher called. "Are you watching TV? Do you know what's going on?"

It was impossible to believe. There was some man inside Montreal's Ecole Polytechnique shooting engineering students — all women. He said they were feminists taking jobs from men and he shot them. I thought that kind of thing only happened in the United States. This was Canada, Montreal, our home. I passed the Polytechnique on the way to the Institut when I was an outpatient. Where was Naomi? Was she safe in Toronto? Was she scared?

I felt so isolated. I no longer had a regular women's group, as I'd had with Studio D, with whom to strategize and scream. I wanted to go to the women's candlelight vigil but it was late on a freezing December night and no one knew whether it would be accessible. For the first time, I felt disconnected from the community of women. I had no one with whom to mourn.

WINTER

Journal: February 10, 1990

We're *en route* to Israel where Michael will be instructing teachers of family medicine as he did in Costa Rica. I began this trip feeling happy and calm, even healthy. The preparation was relaxed and the kids in good shape, clearly ready to resolve their own problems. I'm looking forward to some time alone with Michael, and perhaps finding the energy to buckle down to work on my book.

El Al sat us far from the bathroom in spite of our requests — something about security not letting them assign seats in advance. It was 11:30 at night, when I'm usually asleep, and I had to walk to the next cabin to get to the toilet. The aisles were too narrow for canes. I did fine in the forward direction, using the seat backs to hold and propel me forward, with Michael stabilizing me from behind. I was almost swinging along. But on the way back I had to face all those people, who couldn't help staring at me as — Michael still behind me — I grabbed over their heads for their seat backs. I worked hard to avoid their eyes, to look stoic and dignified. When I finally reached my seat, I tried to hide my tears from Michael but he saw them and urged me to tell him what was happening. Usually he knows without words, so if he doesn't, it's only fair that I try to explain; we are living this together. I heard myself saying all sorts of reasonable things, like the trip is forcing me to face how disabled I still am. But then I blurted out what must be the deeper truth: all those people were staring at me, pitying me, and I hate it. I hate them for being normal while I'm not.

Michael listened, heard me out, then said, "They were staring at *me*. They're jealous because you're so beautiful." It sounds ridiculous now, but it was so incredibly sweet, and I think he believes it, though of course I do not.

Journal: February 13
I'm looking at the Sinai mountains, shrouded with history, and thinking how absurdly wonderful it is that we're here for Michael to *dive* of all things — a week of pure pleasure before Beer Sheva and work. Michael is ecstatic with the Red

Sea, and I'm pleased to share it. This morning was my best snorkel ever. Michael towed me, like he used to tow Naomi before she was a big swimmer, and I lasted over half an hour. I wore a pair of clear plastic beach shoes which kept me from fearing the fire coral and sea urchins as I still don't have an accurate sense of where my body is, especially my limp legs.

I'm walking quite well in the water and I can balance with the tide. I'm generally more stable on my feet. I walk further distances with my canes over incredible obstacles — flagstone paths, stony beaches, uneven sand — right into the water.

But yesterday's boat trip was exhausting. We were both muscle-sore afterwards, me from the boat crashing against the waves in a headwind. I had my usual pre-menstrual bout of jealousy — this time over a diver-doctor from Outremont. I was sure Michael would find her attractive. She was an emergentologist, shared his passion for scuba diving, did avalanche rescue and was just back from horseback-riding Arabian stallions in Egypt! But Michael was considerably less interested than I was. I hate this in myself.

Journal: February 22
In the pattern of fear leading to determination, I worked very hard in the pool. I walked a narrow line of tiles, concentrating on placing the heel of my right foot before the ball. Then I did barre exercises at the deep end, trying to move my legs with slow control. Suddenly I glimpsed myself from outside: a crazy woman doggedly trying to force her spastic foot to respond to her will.

Until now, I have believed that I will get better with hard work and the passage of time. In the pool I suddenly wondered if I am stubbornly and stupidly fighting a losing battle, refusing to accept a reality which must seem obvious to everyone but me. I've been accused before of idealistically thinking I could change the world. But I don't want to accept being handicapped. What's the difference between acceptance and giving up?

Journal: March 12
I received a call from a member of the local chapter of the Israeli Women's Network. She asked me if, as a visiting feminist, I would speak at their next meeting on the "women's issue" of my choice.

My immediate response was no, I am no longer engaged with women's issues. I have nothing of interest to say to feminists. I don't even think of myself as a feminist any more. I've been absorbed, even obsessed, with my own body for the last two and a half years.

"That's exactly what we want to know about, but we were too shy to ask," she replied.

I was taken aback, too polite to say, "Don't you have anything better to do with your time?" In the end I agreed to go.

It was a small group gathered in someone's living room. Some of the women had already met me in other contexts, or seen Michael pushing me around at the pool. Most had seen *Not a Love Story* at the Canadian Women's Film Festival. But unlike the Israeli media who swarmed me last summer, they didn't come to talk about pornography.

I had forgotten how wonderful it is to talk intimately with a group of women! Though I barely knew them, I somehow felt safe. I read random bits from my journals — the first time I had shared them. My stories prompted theirs, and we heard each other's fears about our bodies, health, and aging. Our aloneness or our dependence. Our ability to survive. We realized we rarely talk about illness and suffering, disability and dying, though we will all confront these human realities. As we talked, I remembered how I used to insist that every issue is a women's issue. Maybe I'm still a feminist after all.

By the end of the evening I felt connected as I haven't for a long time. But I was also aware that no one else at the meeting was disabled. For all our intimacy, I was still in some way Other. I was still alone.

≈

INTERLUDE: NEW REPRODUCTIVE AND GENETIC TECHNOLOGIES

Journal: November 10, 1994
I roll into the opening session of the roundtable on New Reproductive and Genetic Technologies, co-sponsored by the Dis-Abled Women's Network of Canada and the National Action Committee on the Status of Women (NRGTs, DAWN Canada, and NAC in acronym-speak). It's an historic coming together to explore the complex and emotional questions of genetic screening and eugenic abortion as they affect women's equality and freedom of choice, particularly women with disabilities.

On the stage are four women seated at a table: DAWN's Joan Meister, who spearheaded this dialogue of mainstream feminists and women with disabilities; U.S. women's health and disability rights activist Marsha Saxton; Sunera Thobani, the chair of NAC, who will speak on the "contradictions of choice"; and a woman I have never seen before on a high bar-chair at the end of the table, her bare feet crossed on the table. Her body is armless; a black silk shirt is stitched at the armholes, and she wears a flashy vest. My eyes are fixed on her animated form as she takes notes with one foot, stopping to lift a glass of water to her mouth. After each speaker, her feet clap.

Theresia Dagener is a lawyer and radical activist in Germany, well-versed in the history and ideology of eugenics. Theresia's disability is the result of Thalidomide, the wonder drug given to pregnant women in the late 1950s and early 1960s to prevent nausea, a walking warning of the fallibility of medical science.

Her position is clear: Abortion, Yes; New Reproductive and Genetic Technologies, No. She is not in favour of *laws* against the selective abortion of disabled fetuses, but neither does she consider such abortions to be acts of feminist self-determination.

"Most people, feminists included," she says, "just cannot imagine disability as a neutral condition, which is not necessarily linked with suffering or with happiness." Choosing to abort a disabled fetus is based on prejudice, the same as choosing to abort because the fetus is female. The problem is the lack of social support for people with disabilities and their families. The solution is to change society, not to eliminate people with disabilities. Disability is a part of human life; whether from illness, accidents, aging, environmental causes or genetic differences.

I can't sleep after the conference opening. My head is spinning with all I've learned. Multinational pharmaceutical companies, manufacturers of related equipment, and university medical research establishments all have huge financial investments in genetic technology. Most of us have been convinced that this technology will eliminate suffering and reduce the burden on families and society. "Science" will soon be able to create life without woman or man, and to shape that life to pre-conceived specifications of perfection. Eliminating everything undesirable, abnormal, *interesting*.

In the state between sleep and wakefulness, I find myself obsessing on Theresia — straining to remember exactly how she looked: What colour were her eyes? Did she have empty sleeves or had she cut them off? Did she take notes and adjust the mike with the same foot?

What an effect she had on me. Is this what we mean by the "Power of Difference"?

I have a vision of Theresia, a torso on a rearing white horse, leading the troops like Joan of Arc. To where, against whom? She is joined in my vision by Marsha, who was born with spina bifida, a condition for which there are now pre-natal tests; many pregnant women automatically abort. Other DAWN women are in this army (our people), looking like all forms of fetus, with missing or undeveloped limbs, facial reconstruction for "birth defects." And I am there too, with my "congenital malformation" that cost the medical system so much to fix. "We are the living fetuses," I think.

When I awake, my "censor" finds my dream melodramatic and grandiose. But I want to trust this vision of leadership by women who know in our own bodies the shortsightedness of technology, the arrogance of eugenic ideals of perfection, the hurtfulness of discrimination, the strength of survival. People with disabilities have unique perspectives on the meaning of human life.

Afterward:

What a smart move that the organizers of this roundtable did
not invite the press. It seemed to me a wasted opportunity at
first, but there's no way that we would have been so honest
with each other. Marsha said that women have been forced
to "dehumanize the fetus" to protect our right to choose
abortion. The women at the roundtable were pro-choice, but
their views are too complex for sound bites and polarized
slogans to convey. We discovered that many women were still
grieving losses they had not allowed themselves to feel. This
in a room of nearly one hundred "hard-boiled" feminists.
Sssshhh. Don't let it get out of here. It's too dangerous. Two
days ago a physician was shot fifteen minutes from where
we are assembled because he provided terminations of preg-
nancies, among other medical services. Is it any wonder we're
afraid to speak our confusion? Our words can be turned
against us.

I was proud of the honesty we achieved. Women who knew
little of feminism, some with intellectual disabilities, walked
up to the microphone to object when the dialogue grew
abstract and presumed a common understanding that was
absent. They refused to vote on our statement until it was
rewritten in plain language. And the non-disabled feminists
were brave enough to admit their ignorance and awkwardness
around women with disabilities, and to ask our help and
patience. It took faith and trust which was hard won by
each of us.

   And it really did happen even though it wasn't on the news.

COMING OUT

≈

Journal: June 19, 1990
Nelson Mandela spoke in Montreal today. After my apoliti-
cal doldrums of last winter, I surprised myself with my eager-
ness to go hear him. It's his first time in Canada since his
long imprisonment and I wanted to mark this event with my
community. Anne Usher said she'd go with me, but was concerned about wheelchair access. So I began a day of inquiry. I
ended up talking to someone at City Hall who was cordial,
but obviously had never considered the question. They would
research it and call back.

Hours later came a call from a regretful City Hall staffer:
"I am very sorry but we are not able to make special arrangements for wheelchairs. Everyone will be standing, with all the
media in the front. There will be no one to help you. All the
streets will be closed. You have to take public transit, no
cars or taxis. (*"But the metro is totally inaccessible,"* I say to
myself.)

"Mandela is next to the Pope's visit in terms of security,"
the staffer continues. (*So God forbid someone with crutches
wants to see the Pope,"* I smart-ass silently.)

"We are sorry to say it, but perhaps the best thing would
be for you to watch on TV. Otherwise, come with at least two
friends, if they are healthy, (*could I have heard right?*) and
arrive by 4:15. The streets are cobble-stoned, so it will be

difficult. And leaving will be the same problem as getting there
— it will take at least an hour for the crowd to disperse."

I hung up in a wave of disappointment. I told myself to
stop this stupid self-pity. How could I be angry? It was
Nelson Mandala, after all. Security had to take priority over
handicapped access. It wasn't the end of the world to miss a
few things, especially when I could see them on TV.

In June, an International Summit on Women and Power, was
held at the Palais de Congrès. It was a high-priced event with
Big Names (I forget which ones) and a hodge-podge of workshops. I've never liked formal congresses at the best of times,
but Naomi encouraged me to go to at least one workshop, and
with my experience at the Israeli Women's Network in mind, I
picked one called "Women and Disabilities." I told myself that
if I was going to write a book about my stroke, hearing other
disabled women was necessary research.

The workshop was completely wheelchair accessible — of
course. Of the four panelists who spoke, three used wheelchairs. I left mine in the hallway outside and on my canes
found a seat in the audience. The first panelist, Anne-Marie
Alonzo, a prize-winning poet who is quadriplegic, read a poem
called "*Merci*," in which she listed the myriad of small requests
she is forced to recite all the time, and the many accompany-
ing "*merci*'s." I heard laughter of recognition ripple throughout the audience, and as I looked around, noticed more than a
few wheelchairs parked at the back, the women in them grinning at each other.

But at the end of her reading, Anne-Marie Alonzo told us
that she was insulted that she was invited to speak at the
Women and Disabilities workshop rather than Women and
Writing which, as a poet, is her primary identity.

"Of course!" I thought to myself. "What a put-down for such a good poet to be invited to read just because she's disabled."

"But," I answered back, "if she had been at the Women and Writing workshop, I would have missed her poem."

When I set about to contact the DisAbled Women's Network (DAWN) that summer, I was still pretending that it was "research" for my book. But not too far below the surface, I knew I was desperate to meet other women with disabilities, to see how they coped, what they thought, how their lives with disability fit with their feminism.

DAWN Canada is a grassroots, self-help group formed to make the disability movement more sensitive to women and the women's movement more inclusive of disabled women. I'd first heard of them when they approached Studio D to make our screenings more accessible. We graciously acknowledged their criticism, and responded when it was convenient, choosing the occasional wheelchair-accessible venue, and enjoying the aesthetics of American Sign Language at our movies; a low-cost way for us non-disabled feminists to feel righteous. But sometimes their demands seemed excessive, even strident, in view of all the other urgent items on our feminist agenda, the ones which seemed to affect *most* of us, rather than just a handful of unfortunate women.

Now I was embarrassed to remember my attitude. Only a year and a half earlier, fresh out of hospital and using a wheelchair myself, I had chosen a theatre with inaccessible toilets to première *Mile Zero*. The ensuing months of curbs and stairs had shifted my priorities without my even noticing.

There was no listing for DAWN in the Montreal directory. I tried to reach something listed as the Handicapped Information and Referral Service and eventually talked to a person who informed me that the service no longer existed due to lack of funds. It was a harsh introduction to the economics of disability. I finally found the number of DAWN's national office — which turned out to be the kitchen table of the current Chair. She gave me a Montreal contact number and a meeting was set up at the local YWCA.

I almost didn't go. I felt tentative, apologetic about my status as a formerly "able-bodied" woman. I felt illegitimate because I was not as severely disabled as some other people. I felt guilty about the privileges of class, career and family which made my experience so much easier than that of many others. I was a newcomer to the disability movement, while many women had already been working hard on my behalf; I had not paid my dues. (Doesn't this litany sound just like a woman?)

But my sister Razelle, who was visiting at the time, insisted I go. It would be good for me, she said. She would go with me. So, hiding behind my sister and my tape recorder, I went to my first meeting of disabled feminists.

Like the Israeli Women's Network gathering, it was a small group of women, but this time I wasn't the only person who came in a wheelchair. We were a motley — some might say wretched — bunch who seemed to have little in common except our diverse disabilities, which turned out to be quite enough. I was not Other because here everyone was Other.

It was like the early days of consciousness-raising in the Women's Movement: those "clicks" of recognition, seeing yet again that the personal is political because disability, like gender, race, age and sexuality is a social as well as biological construct. We shared painful and funny experiences, swapping practical tips about how to deal with local bureaucracies and which brand of tampons were least uncomfortable for constant sitting.

I learned that the three years it had taken me to begin to search out other people with disabilities was quite typical. Perhaps it's the time required to go through the various stages of loss. It may also be the time it takes to explore and ultimately exhaust the medical routes to rehabilitation. When I ventured hesitantly that perhaps I wasn't disabled enough, they all broke out laughing. "Almost everyone thinks they're not the real thing, because there's always someone else who's in even worse shape."

The biggest lesson, and most chastening, was to make this connection with women who had not been part of my world before — women of different classes, women with less education, women with unusual physical "abnormalities" from whom I once would have averted my eyes in polite embarrassment. Most of the women were unemployed and poor. DAWN's research shows that 74% of women with disabilities are unemployed; 58% of women with disabilities live on less than $10,000 a year; and 23% of those women live on less than $5,000. Most of the women here were single and living with their parents.

One young woman with intellectual and emotional disabilities told us about having been abused by family members and caregivers. Women and children with disabilities are twice as vulnerable to violence as their non-disabled counterparts, yet very few rape crisis centres and shelters are accessible. Another woman told of her unsuccessful struggle to keep her children after she became physically disabled; their alcoholic father was considered a better parent.

I discovered that DAWN was not only a support group but part of a growing disability rights movement. People with disabilities were joining together to demand access to the same rights as other people.

The barriers that had kept me so firmly isolated from the other *bénéficiaires* at the Institut no longer seemed so insurmountable. What was the difference? Perhaps it was that we all identified as feminists. And maybe I no longer had to fight so hard against identifying myself as disabled.

Journal: June 28, 1990
It was with mixed feelings that I passed my driving test yesterday. I took the test without the manual controls, so my licence will be a regular one, not one that restricts me to an adapted car. I feel as if I conned the OT into passing me without the restriction. I can't picture myself driving. But Michael is concerned that we find some way to increase my autonomy before we leave for his sabbatical in September. We will be going from city to city as he studies qualitative research techniques and scouts out job possibilities, and I don't want to be stranded when he is busy.

I can't believe I didn't get a scooter for three years. It was Michael who pushed me to investigate those weird three-wheeled things I had seen at the rehab centre after my first driving test. We had not seen one since, probably because they're not paid for by Quebec provincial health insurance.

I had bought the argument that a motorized vehicle would be "giving up," something I would never do. Michael persisted. He found a scooter distributor in one of the shopping malls. I resisted. He insisted. I tried one and it felt unstable. I was scared of its powerful movement and unaccustomed speed. I felt like I was careening down the sidewalk on a motorcycle, when in actuality its top pace was a Lucy-trot. It felt so unprotected compared to an automobile, so vulnerable. "But it's not meant for dodging through traffic, only for sidewalks," the sales people argued.

Michael was sold; in fact, he was desperate. He saw its potential when I could see only its finality. He dubbed it my "Freedom Machine." I called it "the Machine." I would later call her Gladys, after a suffragette's first bicycle, which she learned to ride at age fifty-three, but it took almost a year to achieve that level of intimacy, or even friendship.

My manual wheelchair had a sling-back and seat made of flexible nylon, which provided no support and no leverage for wheeling myself. I sat low and slumped, a strained position for my back and neck. And I slumped even more when someone pushed me. I hated nagging about where I was placed: move me a little closer, a little further away, I'm blocking that entrance, I'M IN THE WAY.

The scooter on the other hand was *sportif*. My self-image changed. I sat straight and high. Most important, I determined exactly where I wanted to be and when. True, it was bulky and took more space, and I bumped into walls and sometimes even people, especially when going in reverse. (Why did it take four years for us to figure out I could use a bicycle mirror?)

Michael purchased a winch-type lift which would raise and lower the 200-pound scooter from the rear of our mini-van. The Machine, unlike the folding manual chair, could only go where there were no curbs, throwing me, yet again, up against the barriers of an inaccessible world.

When I first tried to drive it, I was frightened of the smallest grade and of cars darting out of driveways, and made Michael walk beside me. It was months before I would cross a street alone; curb-cuts seemed steep and bumpy, and I worried that traffic couldn't see me because I was lower than cars. But my horizon was expanded far beyond what my limited strength for wheeling a manual chair had allowed. I could select my own clothing in department stores and roam the aisles of supermarkets, ferrying items from my basket to Michael's shopping cart. I could visit friends who lived within scooting range.

Best of all, I could just take a walk (a scoot?) with Lucy and enjoy being alone.

Journal: September 27, 1990
I was determined to use my new scooter as a convenience, but not as a substitute for rehab. We decided I should get a full reassessment before we leave on sabbatical, so I called the Institut and discovered Michel Danakas was back from his sick leave and keen to work with me again.

After an hour of tests, Michel asked how much further I thought I would go. I responded that I've learned not to look towards an end-point but to just notice the ongoing progress and accept each step forward as it comes. Once rhetoric, this is now truth, with momentary lapses and grief about loss.

I asked Michel to tell me how far *he* thought I would go. At first he tried to avoid my question. I persisted. I think he sensed that I was ready to hear what he thinks.

"What is it you really want to know?" he asked.

"Do you think I'll walk without canes?"

"No, at this point I'd have to say I can't see it."

It was so direct and bare — the first time I heard it. Or the first time I let myself hear it so clearly? I teared up, but I didn't feel devastated. I was sad but not surprised. I heard myself saying I could live with that, canes aren't so bad, I have a pretty good life.

Journal: October 4
I woke up today   the morning of our departure for
Boston, first stop on Michael's sabbatical — knowing that I
won't ever walk unsupported. It doesn't feel heavy, though
my voice choked when I tried to tell Michael. I have a big
investment in positive thinking and imagining. But why do
I still think of walking as the ultimate success? Walking is
convenient, not essential. Now it seems appropriate to get
on with my life. I don't want to make a career of rehabilitation. I won't stop trying; I think I can become more stable
and comfortable. I have to figure out some weight-bearing
exercises to combat the increased threat of osteoporosis
that faces menopausal women who use wheelchairs. I'm
looking forward to meeting more people with disabilities:
learning how they live their lives, and finding out what other
devices are available like my nerve-racking but liberating
new scooter.

It took us all day to make the five-hour trip to Boston,
with frequent stops for peeing, rest and exercise. I had one
bad moment in the car. All of a sudden my foot wouldn't
move at all — oh no! that familiar feeling, stuck in paralysis.
I looked before I panicked, and saw I was indeed stuck —
with chewing gum on my sneaker.

Journal: October 10
Our first weekend in Boston. Naomi came from Toronto, and
we decided to do the tourist thing, tooling around Boston
Common. Michael and Naomi were on foot, I was on my
new scooter. I was amazed to see so many wheelchairs and
other vehicles — including what I've since learned are called
"sip and puff" chairs which are controlled by breath, and

special rigs for disabled children. "What an accessible city!" I sang happily.

Then we came upon a series of information tables — flyers, petitions, the familiar signs of a demonstration. The first table was an organization working to defeat a proposition in the forthcoming election which would make profound funding cutbacks for personal attendant care and sign language interpretation. The next table was for the Boston Self-Help Center, run by people with disabilities, who counsel each other and figure out what they need to live independently. How different from the demeaning charity stereotypes we're used to! Someone approached us with pins for sale: "Piss on Pity," "Nursing Homes Kill," "Label Cans, Not People" and "Disabled Dykes Do it with a Difference."

We had stumbled (wheeled?) into Boston's first annual Disability Pride Day! This was no casual coincidence of wheelchairs — this was a movement. Disability groups of all kinds were here, in coalition with trade unions, AIDS groups, and an assortment of progressive organizations. I was overcome, my belief in serendipity confirmed. Naomi grabbed Michael's camera and a notebook and was off to cover this event for her university newspaper.

Michael stuck with me, as I tried to steer my scooter towards the stage where the rally was beginning — over uneven terrain and around crowds of people, few of whom could move away from a collision course any faster than I could.

A gutsy and nervous young woman with the thick drawl of cerebral palsy was emcee. Not only was her voice different, but there was a whole new language being spoken here. I felt like a privileged eavesdropper at first, but at the same time she was speaking for me and about me.

She cued us for a chant: "DISABLED AND..." The crowd responded: "PROUD!" My throat jammed on the word mid chant. Is this honest? Who am I trying to fool? It's one thing to accept, but another to be proud. Proud of what? Of something I had nothing to do with? I'm proud of surviving and adapting maybe, but am I proud of being disabled? But it felt good to be shouting with hundreds of other bodies, looking happy in spite of — because of? — their deformities.

Or is the word "differences"? And are they "ours"?

That same evening, full of my new disability pride, Naomi, Michael, and I went to an old church for an event called I AM YOUR SISTER, an international, interracial conference honouring the African-American lesbian poet and writer Audre Lorde. I had filmed Audre reading her powerful essay, "The Uses of the Erotic," for *Not a Love Story*.

Women and men brought original writing, dance and art to express their own truths as Audre Lorde has inspired them to do. They talked about race, sexuality, poverty and violence. Audre's own most recent work is about her battle with breast cancer, now metastasized to her liver. An "Amazon warrior," she is living long beyond medical predictions.

Amidst the poetry and song, Marsha Saxton was introduced. She stood up and walked to the foot of the stage, her leg braces just visible below her skirt. But instead of mounting the stairs, she sat down and spoke to us from the first step. Her voice was gentle and totally lacking in blame. "In solidarity with the women who can't climb these stairs," she said, "I will read from here. This auditorium was built by a society that doesn't expect people with disabilities to speak. We are changing that."

INTERLUDE: THE DANCER INSIDE

Journal: Vancouver, April, 1992
Independence '92, an historic moment in the disability
community and, for me, my first professional work since
Mile Zero, four years ago. I had hoped the media would be
flooded with news of this, the first international conference
on disability, with over two thousand delegates from almost
one hundred countries. Instead, I found myself the only
member of the Canadian national media present. I had convinced CBC radio to send me as a participant/documentarist. I
felt very competent astride Gladys, my tape recorder in her
basket, earphones on my head and wires hanging off of me,
but also pretty nervous. I'd never worked in radio before. I
was unsure of the equipment, my capability, my stamina. The
first night, exhausted from the trip, I lost my balance and fell
in my hotel room, my worst fall in months. I lay on the floor
crying into my tape recorder about what a mistake this all
was. Why hadn't I asked Terre or Dorothy to co-direct? But
in the morning I knew why.

I had never seen anything like it — nobody had, because
nothing like it ever happened before. It was our world, for
the next few days. We were a people, a nation, a tribe: with
our own culture, history, heroes; our own languages; our
own irreverent, rude humour, our own poets and artists. My
eyes feasted on the images; so many sizes and shapes and
kinds — gridlocks of wheelchairs, knocking into each other

like bumper cars; wild arms waving for signing, guide dogs leading chains of people, one arm on the shoulder in front of them like a train. I was wide-eyed in my ignorance as I was introduced to people whose disabilities were invisible or hidden — like epilepsy, learning disabilities, environmental sensitivities. We widened the circle to include people with chronic pain and illnesses like AIDS, and people who called themselves "psychiatric survivors" — contesting traditional definitions of mental illness. I discovered that our disability rights movement is international, its goals and priorities differing from culture to culture. I felt that we were making a revolution, creating a world in which disability is not a problem but part of the solution.

I was overwhelmed by the resourcefulness and creativity of the people I met. Here were rolling models galore. It was a supermarket of conveyances — from the fanciest motorized chairs to a legless Russian navigating a wheeled board with his hands on the floor at breakneck speed. So many variations on the theme of disability, people so different from me and people so like me. Where was my camera!

Why was this the first time I had seen someone in a wheel-chair nursing a baby? Why weren't there pictures of us every-where? Our visual absence breeds fear, breeds shame.

For many years I made films in which people who were invisible or misrepresented in our culture could see them-selves. *Not a Love Story* charted the ways sexist pornogra-phy teaches us to hate our women's bodies. Now I was recognizing the ways in which society's ignorance and dis-torted images of disability have taught us people with disabilities to hate our bodies. This crowd of exuberant freaks taught me something different: something like pride.

The climax of the conference for me was a performance by three Brazilian dancers: a young girl, about ten, in a silver wheelchair; a thin, muscular woman in a wheelchair with day-glo yellow wheels; and a non-disabled woman with a mane of curly black hair. One dancer climbed under and over the chairs while another pivoted around her, pulling herself into the air, borrowing balance from the third and then tipping the silver chair to spill them all to the ground where they mingled arms, legs, torsos, not fighting gravity but dancing with it. There was nothing odd-looking about it. One woman used her legs, the other two couldn't — what could be more natural? They danced, powerfully, sensuously. We all have a primal instinct and desire to communicate, even when many of our abilities are taken away from us. Maybe when the clutter of life is gone, we're free to discover its essence.

Afterwards I interviewed the Brazilian women and then I shyly asked if I could dance with them myself. I put my canes aside. I was leaning on Rosangela, the non-disabled dancer, with every part of my body. She was giving me cues, whispering in my ear in her sultry voice: "Relax your head, lend me your arms, lean on me, trust my body, my legs will be your legs."

I let go and trusted. We moved fast and wild. I heard myself screaming with joy. I had no idea what it looked like nor did I care. The dancer inside me was out.

≈

Epilogue

Journal: June 10, 1996

I am writing at my "outdoor office" again, in the luxurious
sunshine of June. Endings are so hard. I feel like I've been
living with this book forever — so much has changed since
we started the first draft more than two years ago. Lucy no
longer lies patiently by my paisley scooter, dreaming dog
dreams. She is dead, and the original Gladys is retired to
the country.

The book ends with Independence '92 in Vancouver. I fell
in love with the city and returned to Montreal full of its
praises. But my compelling need for access and a temperate
climate didn't immediately coincide with Michael's equally
valid need for professional fulfillment. We fretted over unsat-
isfactory compromises; I even spent our twenty-fifth wedding
anniversary solemnly contemplating the possibility of living
in separate cities, soundly rejected by Michael as no solution
at all. But a year later, Michael found a challenging position
in Vancouver as Head of Family Practice at the B.C. Women's
and B.C. Children's Hospitals.

Vancouver is one of the world's most accessible cities. It's
not perfect, of course, but thanks to years of work by a well-
organized disability movement, I am free to live as I want: I
can scoot along the many bicycle paths and depend on finding

curb-cuts in the streets and ramps for most buildings. I still don't drive, but many buses are lift-equipped, and there is also a superb parallel transportation system known as HANDI-DART, run by its users, a Board of people with disabilities. And our municipalities are required to supply a certain number of subsidized ramped taxi-cabs — for the ultimate in spontaneity.

The result is that I have a community of other people with disabilities: strangers in wheelchairs and scooters to beep to, close friends with whom to share my fears and triumphs, and organizations like the B.C. Coalition of People with Disabilities and DAWN Canada with whom to think through our issues and advocate for our equality and dignity. The heady feelings I had at Independence '92 have given way to a more realistic sense of the work ahead of us to build a strong human rights movement; this too will be a long haul.

The stroke has forced me to transform my life, to abandon the clock and calendar and to heed my body's requirements. I've learned to be more patient, as have those around me. I have to ration my limited energy and choose carefully whom I see and what I do. Every day I swim, exercise and nap. Every week I get body work — massage or sometimes chiro-practic or acupuncture — to maximize fluidity and minimize pain. Once prescriptive, these rituals have become part of my new life, a life which seems to me balanced and healthy.

I no longer consider myself in "rehabilitation," but I feel as if I am still progressing after nine years! The changes are subtle; maybe only I can see them. After several years of lessons in the Alexander Technique, I can stand comfortably — and even dance — for longer periods of time. I can roll to Granville Market and buy farm-fresh vegetables and fish for Michael and me to make for dinner.

Seth has joined us in Vancouver, where he has completed his Master's degree in political science and is continuing his social activism. Michael's parents, Annie and Philip, immigrated to Canada to spend their eighth decade close to family, and are now living a short ferry ride away in a warm rural community on the Sunshine Coast. Philip recently had severe heart and lung illness, and we all took turns sitting with him day and night for many weeks so he would not be alone in the ICU. He is now out of hospital and scooting to the village post office and general store on Gladys I.

Naomi is thriving in Toronto, where she is working as a newspaper columnist and magazine writer. We manage to stay close to each other's lives through outrageous phone bills, now e-mail, and frequent flyer points — as we do with other friends and family who are now far away.

And — happy news — I am raising a new puppy, a calm golden retriever we named Louie. I dream of training him to be a balance dog when he's full-grown, using a stiff harness to support me so I can sometimes walk with one cane.

Many people ask if I think about making films again. One of the great gifts of the stroke has been to discover that I can live well without the role or title of filmmaker. I am happy to be identified as unlabelled Bonnie Sherr Klein, institution-free. I still have the desire to share what I am learning — maybe more than ever. I don't want to close any doors, but I want to open some of the new doors to which I now have access. Making radio documentaries for the CBC turned out to be a perfect adaptation to my new limitations. And writing this book has been even more stimulating and pleasureful.

Before my stroke, I had a mistaken notion that feminism meant "independence"; the unspoken corollary was that disability (and aging) meant shameful dependence on others.

What I've learned finally is that in asking for help I offer other people an opportunity for intimacy and collaboration. Whether I'm asking for me personally or for disabled people generally, I give them the opportunity to be their most human. In Judaism, we call this gift a mitzvah.

I had the rare chance to be present at my own eulogy, proud and pleased with my old life, and then to start again, inventing a new life, even embracing the unknown.

Who would have dreamed that my stroke would have brought me to this moment, this place, this parkbench? Gladys II is parked next to me, still factory-bright. Michael suggests we paint her with spits of flame like a motorcycle. But Louie is restless now; he wants to roll in the grass and play catch in the nearby park. And so do I.

ACKNOWLEDGMENTS

I am deeply grateful to the many friends and relatives who played a role in my survival and recovery — only some of whom are mentioned in this book. You will never be forgotten.

Muriel Duckworth and Judy Steed first suggested I write a book. Many individuals encouraged and supported the idea, especially Leah Appet, Jeff Borkan, Leon Bibb, June Callwood, Sandra Campbell, Josh Freed, Ruth Hundert, Jackie Kaiser at Penguin Books, Gabor Kalman, Barbara Kay, Sheila Kitzinger, Abby Lippman, Barbara Pulling, Shirley Turcotte, Patrick Watson, Anne Wheeler and Merrily Weisbord.

The Canada Council Explorations Program, now regrettably defunct, funded the transcription of my journals and tapes. The transcribers were Nora Allyne, Lauren Banerd, Pat Billing, Gigi Grein, Kathleen Kelly, Eileen Lavery and Irit Shimrat.

Susan Furze, an invaluable personal assistant during that crucial first year in Vancouver, organized my office and computer system.

Several brave souls tried to teach me computer skills: Andy Orkin, Bill Lake and especially Lani Levine, who insists that I am "not stupid, just slow," and promises to teach me how to transfer files without taxicabs.

My daughter Naomi Klein accompanied me back to the Jewish General Hospital and Institut de Réadaptation de Montréal to interview staff, read and indexed the transcripts of my journals, and helped me to see the book not as a dwelling on the painful past but a bridge to my future.

My agent, Denise Bukowski, has been indefatigable. Janet Turnbull Irving offered generous advice.

Knopf publisher Louise Dennys, who believed in the book before I'd written a word, supported me with patience and edited with brilliance and tact; Bernice Eisenstein thinned the ponderous first draft; and Diane Martin clarified the manuscript with loving care and brought it to its form as a book.

People in the disability rights and writing community became my mentors and friends, and informed my disability consciousness: Marsha Saxton, who helped me understand both disability oppression and liberation; Nancy Mairs, who writes so personally and truthfully about all the bad stuff as well as the blessings of being disabled; Jean Stewart, who offered valuable guidelines after reading a very early stage of this manuscript; Judy Heumann, a leader in the international disability rights movement, now U.S. Assistant Secretary of Education; Ed Roberts, a gutsy pioneer in the independent living movement, and Irving Kenneth Zola, an original thinker and leader in the disability studies and self-help movements, both deceased; Susan Harkins, my "stroke sister," who is now surviving an even crueller stroke; Joan Meister, who urged us to move to Vancouver, and Carol Herbert, who helped make it happen; and Maxine Tynes, poet, who confirmed the need to tell our stories at a Women In View's workshop, "The Writer as Social Activist."

For sharing their first-hand knowledge of disability, I

thank: Sally Aitken, Gerald Batista, Margaret Birrell, Mary Lou Breslin, Diane Dolan, Ellen Frank, Susan Griffin, Jan Hamilton, Ronnie Wenker Konner, Diane Lipton Armstrong, Bill Livant, Margot Massie, Shirley Masuda, Pauline Rankin, Connie Rockwood, Susan Wendell, Ellen Wiebe, Mary Williams, and the many people who participated in Marsha Saxton's co-counselling workshops for people with disabilities and allies.

For reading the manuscript at various stages: Ruth Nemzoff Berman, Sherry Bie, Dr. Betty Callum, Diane Carrière, Ellen Frank, Razelle Frankl, Jan Hamilton, Dorothy Todd Hénaut, Anne Henderson, Dr. Carol Herbert, Signe Johansson, Sidonie Kerr, Mark Limont, Della McCreary, Joan Meister, Gaby Minnes, Terre Nash, Eileen O'Brien, Gerry Rogers, Marsha Saxton, Kathleen Shannon, Dr. Ellen Wiebe, Norma Zack, Lillian Zimmerman, and all my family.

For the Hasidic story, Reb Hillel Goelman and Leonard Angel.

Thanks to the Canadian Association of Occupational Therapists for inviting me to be keynote speaker at their annual conference; and to Tim Readman, Sandra Bressler, and especially Dr. Helene Polatajko for our Crawford Lectureship dialogue about synergistic therapist-client relationships.

CBC radio colleagues: Nancy Watson, Joe Moulins, Peter Leo, Shelley Pomerantz, David Gutnick, Peter Gzowski, Stuart McLean and especially Alex Frame, who had the vision and provided the support; hurrah for public broadcasting!

Robin Morgan at Ms. magazine, for commissioning my first article, "We Are Who you Are: Feminism and Disability"; Judy Razminsky for editing it; and Shirley Masuda for the title.

My co-counsellors Claire Kujundzik, Bill Horne, and especially Elizabeth Shefrin, with whom I retrieved some important memories.

My son Seth Klein and his "farm" friends.

For holding body and soul together: massage therapists Coleen Quinn, Vicki Hall, Mary Boulding, Kendall Dixon; cranial therapist Patricia Pucher; Alexander teachers Lyn Charlsen, Gabriella Minnes Brandes; chiropractors Jean Chevrefils and Aaron Hoy; and family physician Dr. Joy Russell.

People who loaned us their homes as writing retreats and nurtured us: Lanie Melamed, Rob Melamed, Rhema Cossover, Isadora's Restaurant, Cora Domingo, and especially Annie and Philip Klein.

Sun-Life for excellent service with my disability insurance.

Persimmon would like to thank Della McCreary for listening to each revision of every chapter, hot off the computer. Her complex perspectives on disability combined with her love of words made for invaluable feedback.

Persimmon would also like to thank Bonnie Sherr Klein for more than is possible to list here, but most especially for the irrepressible exuberance she brought to even the most picky parts of this process.

RECOMMENDED READING

The following is a list of books on illness or disability — both fiction and non-fiction, personal and general — that I found useful, illuminating or inspiring.

Allende, Isabel. Peder, Margaret S. trans. *Paula*. New York: HarperCollins, 1995.

Asch, Adrienne and Michelle Fine. *Women With Disabilities: Essays in Psychology, Politics, and Policy*. Philadelphia: Temple University Press, 1988.

Blackbridge, Persimmon. *Sunnybrook: A True Story with Lies*. Vancouver: Press Gang Publishers, 1996.

Blackbridge, Persimmon, and Sheila Gilhooly. *Still Sane*. Vancouver: Press Gang Publishers, 1985.

Borysenko, Joan. *Minding the Body, Mending the Mind*. New York: Bantam Books, 1988.

Brightman, Alan J., ed. *Ordinary Moments: The Disabled Experience*. Baltimore: University Park Press, 1984.

Brown, Sharon. *Some Become Flowers: Living with Dying at Home*. Bridgeport, CT: Harbour Publishing, 1993.

Brown, Susan E., Debra Connors, and Nancy Stern, eds. *With the Power of Each Breath: A Disabled Woman's Anthology*. Pittsburgh: Cleis Press, 1985.

Butler, Sandra, and Barbara Rosenblum. *Cancer In Two Voices*. San Francisco: Spinster Books, 1991,

Callahan, John. *Don't Worry, He Won't Get Far on Foot*. New York: Vintage Books, 1989.

Callwood, June. *Twelve Weeks in Spring*. Toronto: Lester & Orpen Dennys, 1986.

Cousins, Norman. *Anatomy of an Illness As Perceived by the Patient: Reflections on Healing and Regeneration*. New York: W. W. Norton & Co, Inc., 1979.

———. *Head First: The Biology of Hope and the Healing Power of the Human Spirit*. New York: Viking Penguin Books, 1989.

Driedger, Diane. *The Last Civil Rights Movement: Disabled Peoples' International*. New York: St. Martin's Press, 1989.

Finger, Anne. *Past Due: A Story of Disability, Pregnancy, and Birth*. Seattle: Seal Press, 1990.

Frank, Arthur W. *At the Will of the Body: Reflections on Illness*. Boston: Houghton, Mifflin, 1991.

———. *The Wounded Storyteller: Body, Illness, and Ethics*. Chicago: University of Chicago Press, 1995.

Frankel, Viktor. *Man's Search for Meaning*. New York: Pocket Books, 1985.

Goffman, Erving. *Stigma: Notes on the Management of Spoiled Identity*. New York: Simon & Schuster, 1963.

Hannaford, Susan. *Living Outside Inside*. Berkeley: Canterbury Press, 1985.

Hansen, Rick, and Jim Taylor. *Rick Hansen: Man in Motion*. Vancouver: Douglas & McIntyre, 1987.

Heilbrun, Carolyn G. *Writing a Woman's Life*. New York: W.W. Norton & Co., Inc., 1988.

Heymann, Jody, M.D. *Equal Partners: A Physician's Call For a New Spirit of Medicine*. New York: Little Brown & Co., 1995.

Hillyer, Barbara. *Feminism & Disability*. Norman, Oklahoma: University of Oklahoma Press, 1993.

Hockenberry, John. *Moving Violations: War Zones, Wheelchairs and Declarations of Independence*. New York: Hyperion, 1995.

Hull, John M. *Touching the Rock: An Experience of Blindness*. New York: Pantheon Books, 1990.

Keith, Lois, ed. *What Happened to You? Writing by Disabled Women*. New York and London: The New Press, 1996.

Kleinman, Arthur. *The Illness Narratives*. New York: Basic Books, 1988.

Krotoski, Danuta M., Margaret A. Nosek and Margaret A. Turk, eds. *Women with Physical Disabilities: Achieving Health and Well-Being*. Baltimore: Paul H. Brookes Publishing Co., 1996.

Lear, Martha Weinman. *Heartsounds: The Story of a Love and Loss*. New York: Simon & Schuster, 1980.

Levine, Stephen. *Healing Into Life and Death*. New York: Anchor Press, Doubleday, 1987.

———. *Who Dies?* New York: Anchor Books, 1982.

Lorde, Audre. *The Cancer Journals*, 2nd ed. San Francisco: Aunt Lute Books, 1987.

Lorde, Audre. *A Burst of Light*. Ithaca, New York: Firebrand Books, 1988.

Mairs, Nancy. *Carnal Acts*. New York: HarperCollins, 1990.

———. *Plaintext: Deciphering a Woman's Life*. Tucson: University of Arizona Press, 1986.

———. *Remembering the Bone House: An Erotics of Place and Space*. New York: Harper & Row, 1988.

————. *Voice Lessons: On Becoming a (Woman) Writer.*
Boston: Beacon Press, 1994.

————. *Waist-High in the World: A Life Among the
Nondisabled.* Boston: Beacon Press, 1997.

MacPhee, Rosalind. *Picasso's Woman: A Breast Cancer Story.*
Vancouver: Douglas & McIntyre, 1994.

Matthews, Gwyneth Ferguson. *Voices from the Shadows.*
Toronto: Women's Educational Press, 1983. (A collection
of interviews.)

Morris, Jenny. *Pride Against Prejudice: Transforming
Attitudes Toward Disability.* Philadelphia: New Society
Pubs., 1993.

Morris, Jenny, ed. *Able Lives: Women's Experience of
Paralysis.* London: The Women's Press, 1989.

Murphy, Robert F. *The Body Silent.* New York: Henry Holt
& Co., 1987.

Panzarino, Connie, *The Me in the Mirror.* Seattle: Seal Press,
1994.

Prescott, Ellen. *Mondays Are Yellow, Sundays Are Grey*
Vancouver: Douglas & McIntyre, 1994.

Rousso, Harilyn. *Disabled, Female and Proud! Stories of Ten
Women with Disabilities.* Boston: Exceptional Parent
Press, 1988.

Sacks, Oliver. *The Man Who Mistook His Wife for a Hat.*
New York: HarperCollins, 1987.

————. *A Leg to Stand On.* New York: HarperCollins, 1994.

————. *An Anthropologist on Mars: Seven Paradoxical
Tales.*Toronto: Alfred A. Knopf Canada, 1995.

Sarton, May. *After the Stroke: A Journal.* New York: W.W.
Norton & Co. Inc., 1988.

Saxton, Marsha and Florence Howe, eds. *With Wings: An
Anthology of Literature By and About Women With*

Disabilities. New York: Feminist Press at the City University, 1988.

Schrieber, LeAnne. *Midstream*. New York: Viking Penguin, 1990.

Shapiro, Joseph P. *No Pity: People with Disabilities Forging a New Civil Rights Movement*. New York: Times Books, 1993.

Shaw, Barrett, ed. *The Ragged Edge: The Disability Experience From the Pages of the First Fifteen Years of* The Disability Rag. Advocado Press, 1994. (P.O. Box 145, Louisville, KY 40201-0145).

Sontag, Susan. *Illness as Metaphor*. New York: St. Martin's Press, 1989.

Stewart, Houston, Beth Percival, Elizabeth R. Epperly, eds. *The More We Get Together*. Charlottetown, PEI: Gynergy Books, 1992. (Proceedings of the Canadian Research Institute for the Advancement of Women Annual Conference on Women and Dis/Ability.)

Stewart, Jean. *The Body's Memory*. New York: St. Martin's Press, 1989.

Weintraub, Rabbi Simkha Y., ed. *Healing of Soul, Healing of Body*. Woodstock, VT: Jewish Lights Publishing, 1994.

Wendell, Susan. *The Rejected Body: Feminist Philosophical Reflections on Disability*. New York: Routledge, 1996.

Williams, Donna. *Nobody Nowhere: The Extraordinary Autobiography of an Autistic*. Toronto: Doubleday, 1992.

Zola, Irving Kenneth. *Missing Pieces: A Chronicle of Living with a Disability*. Philadelphia: Temple University Press, 1982.

Zola, Irving Kenneth, ed., *Ordinary Lives: A Collection of Voices of Disability and Disease*. Cambridge/Watertown, Mass.: Apple-wood Books, 1982.

BIOGRAPHY

Bonnie Sherr Klein was the subject of her own award-winning CBC radio series, "Bonnie & Gladys," in which she explored being a person with a disability. She gets around with two canes or on Gladys (her motorized scooter). As passionate an activist as ever, she now counsels and speaks about health care, rehabilitation and disability rights. She lives in Vancouver and on the Sunshine Coast.

Persimmon Blackbridge, with whom Bonnie Klein collaborated in the writing of *Slow Dance,* is a visual artist and writer whose new novel, *Prozac Highway,* is forthcoming in the fall of 1997.